The Most Dangerous Area in the World

The Most Dangerous Area in the World ⭐ John F. Kennedy Confronts Communist Revolution in Latin America ⭐ by Stephen G. Rabe

The University of North Carolina Press

Chapel Hill and London

© 1999
The University of North Carolina Press
All rights reserved
Set in Janson type
by Tseng Information Systems, Inc.
Manufactured in the United States of America
The paper in this book meets the guidelines for
permanence and durability of the Committee on
Production Guidelines for Book Longevity of the
Council on Library Resources.
Library of Congress Cataloging-in-Publication Data
Rabe, Stephen G.
The most dangerous area in the world : John F. Kennedy confronts
Communist revolution in Latin America / by Stephen G. Rabe.
  p. cm.
Includes bibliographical references (p.   ) and index.
ISBN 0-8078-2461-5 (cloth: alk. paper). —
ISBN 0-8078-4764-x (pbk. : alk. paper)
1. Latin America—Foreign relations—United States. 2. United
States—Foreign relations—Latin America. 3. United States—Foreign
relations—1961-1963. 4. Kennedy, John F. (John Fitzgerald), 1917-
1963. 5. Communism—Latin America—History. 6. Counter-
insurgency—Latin America—History. 7. Alliance for Progress.
I. Title.
F1418.M24 1999
327.7308—dc21   98-23112
                CIP

Portions of this work appeared earlier, in somewhat different form, in
"Controlling Revolutions: Latin America, the Alliance for Progress, and
Cold War Anti-Communism," in *Kennedy's Quest for Victory: American
Foreign Policy, 1961-1963*, edited by Thomas G. Patterson, copyright ©
Oxford University Press, Inc., used by permission of Oxford University
Press, Inc., and in "John F. Kennedy and Constitutionalism, Democracy,
and Human Rights in Latin America: Promise and Performance," *New
England Journal of History* 52 (Fall 1995), used with permission of the
journal.

03 02 01 00 99   5 4 3 2 1

TO THOMAS G. PATERSON,

friend, advisor, and inspiration

to historians of U.S. foreign relations

Contents

Acknowledgments

In investigating and writing this book, I incurred many scholarly debts. I thank the archivists at the Roosevelt, Eisenhower, Kennedy, and Johnson presidential libraries for their assistance. I am also grateful for the help I received from staffs who guided me through manuscript collections at the University of Arkansas, the University of Oregon, and the University of Texas at Austin. Without financial aid, it would have been impossible to visit these institutions. The Lyndon Baines Johnson Foundation has generously supported my research over the past twenty years. I was able to devote a full year to writing with a Special Faculty Development Grant from the University of Texas at Dallas. I salute Provost and Academic Vice President B. Hobson Wildenthal and Dean Michael Simpson for developing this generous program. I also thank Dean Dennis Kratz for his support. Small portions of this work first appeared in *Kennedy's Quest for Victory* (1989), edited by Thomas G. Paterson. Oxford University Press kindly granted me permission to use this material. Finally, I would like to thank Professor Elizabeth Cobbs Hoffman of the University of San Diego and Professor Mark Gilderhus of Texas Christian University for their scholarly advice.

Stephen G. Rabe
Dallas, Texas
17 March 1998

The Most Dangerous Area in the World

⭐ Introduction

President John Fitzgerald Kennedy (1961–63) continues to be a beloved figure both in Latin America and in the United States. For me, a memorable example of the president's standing with Latin Americans came in August 1993, when I was sitting in an outdoor restaurant in a San José neighborhood not normally frequented by tourists. A middle-aged Costa Rican man, who was clearing the tables, hesitantly approached me. Perhaps he had overheard me reviewing some terms in Spanish with my eleven-year-old daughter. After a few Spanish-language pleasantries, he came directly to his subject. What he wanted to tell this U.S. visitor was that thirty years ago he had been in the streets with tens of thousands of his countrymen to welcome President Kennedy. As he recalled, it had been *un gran día* for Costa Rica. It was a fine day for the president also. So tumultuous was the welcome, so vibrant were the shouts of "Viva Kennedy" that Kennedy wistfully remarked to his aides that he wanted to move the Costa Rican crowd to Ohio for the 1964 election so "I might carry the damn state."[1]

My Costa Rican friend's attachment to the memory of President Kennedy is commonplace throughout Latin America. His visits to Venezuela, Colombia, and Mexico evoked wild enthusiasm. Half of Bogotá's population waved to the president's motorcade. His picture, right next to those of Jesus Christ and the pope, adorned the walls of the humble homes of urban shantytown dwellers and rural *campesinos*. In no other region of the world was his death felt more profoundly. Latin Americans stood in line for hours to sign condolence books at U.S. embassies. The U.S. ambassador to Argentina, who arrived in Buenos Aires in 1964, wrote that "in my four years in Argentina, I was asked at least once a month to participate in the dedication of a Kennedy school, road or bridge."[2]

Kennedy's personal qualities partially account for his enduring popularity in Latin America. He was young, vigorous, handsome, and a Roman Catholic. Accompanying him was his accomplished and elegant wife, Jacqueline Bouvier Kennedy, who spoke fluent Spanish. But Latin Americans responded to more than just the Kennedy charisma. The president cared about the poor of Latin America and vowed to fulfill their yearnings for economic progress, social change, and democracy. In a stirring address on 13 March 1961, which was broadcast throughout the hemisphere, the new leader pledged that the United States would join in a "vast cooperative effort, unparalleled in magnitude and nobility of purpose, to satisfy the basic needs of Latin American people for homes, work and land, health and schools—*techo, trabajo y tierra, salud y escuela.*"[3] Dubbed the Alliance for Progress—Alianza para el Progreso—the new program ostensibly represented a Marshall Plan for Latin America.

The president and his advisors subsequently provided substance to the soaring rhetoric. At an inter-American conference held in August 1961 at Punta del Este, a seaside resort in Uruguay, Secretary of the Treasury C. Douglas Dillon assured Latin American delegates that they could count on receiving $20 billion in public and private capital over the next ten years. With this influx of foreign money combined with an additional $80 billion from internal investment, Latin American nations could expect to achieve a real economic growth rate of 2.5 percent a year, approximately double the rate of economic growth in the late 1950s.[4] Other administration officials surpassed Dillon's optimism. Adolf A. Berle Jr., an architect of the Alliance, confidently prophesied that the United States would raise the living standard of every Latin American by at least 50 percent.[5]

The Alliance for Progress failed, however, to achieve its goal of building democratic, prosperous, socially just societies. During the 1960s, extraconstitutional changes of government constantly rocked Latin America. During the Kennedy years alone, military men overthrew six popularly elected Latin American presidents. Latin American economies performed poorly, registering an unimpressive average annual growth rate of about 2 percent. Most of the economic growth took place at the very end of the decade. The number of unemployed Latin Americans actually rose from 18 million to 25 million, and agricultural production per person declined. The Alliance for Progress also made imperceptible progress in achieving its objectives of adding five years to life expectancy, halving the infant mortality rate, eliminating adult illiteracy, and providing access to six years of primary education for every school-age child. At the end of the decade, more than one-half of the population of the region continued to live on an annual per capita income of $120.[6] Whatever the sources of failure, Latin Americans do not blame President Kennedy. As one historian noted, frozen in the memory of millions of Latin Americans was the image of "a young, heroic, idealistic leader who understood them and had dedicated himself to helping them solve their problems."[7]

President Kennedy's commitment to bold, ambitious change left a lasting impression on not only Latin Americans but also his fellow citizens. In 1996 a *New York Times*/CBS News public-opinion poll found that if U.S. voters could pick any former president to govern the country, they would choose Kennedy. The Massachusetts Democrat easily outpolled Franklin Delano Roosevelt, surely the most influential U.S. political leader of the twentieth century. The poll's respondents even preferred Kennedy over the featured players on Mount Rushmore—George Washington, Thomas Jefferson, Abraham Lincoln, and Theodore Roosevelt. When asked to explain their choice, the respondents cited Kennedy's quality of leadership.[8]

Not all scholars share this wild enthusiasm for Kennedy. In professional surveys, U.S. historians have rated him as an "above average" or "average (high)" president, which are respectable rankings in view of his brief tenure in office. Of course, Kennedy finished far behind Franklin Roosevelt and the Mount Rushmore crowd.[9] Those historians who participated in the survey might have pointed out that Kennedy could not persuade the U.S. Congress to enact his domestic agenda. Of the twenty-three bills he submitted to Congress early in his administration, only seven were enacted into law. Programs such as a tax cut to stimulate the economy and federal aid to education would not receive congressional backing until President Lyndon Baines Johnson had the opportunity to employ his remarkable legislative skills. President Kennedy also only belatedly embraced the central moral issue of his time, the movement for civil rights for African Americans. He waited until 1962 to sign an executive order banning discrimination in public housing, and he nominated proponents of segregation to serve as judges in the federal courts. Kennedy eventually responded to the movement for social justice led by Dr. Martin Luther King Jr. and his followers. In mid-1963, he submitted a comprehensive civil rights bill to Congress, and he began to speak eloquently about the need for simple justice in the nation's life.

Scholarly analyses of Kennedy's foreign policies are similarly mixed. The president's initial biographers helped sustain popular affection for the fallen leader. Presidential aides Roger Hilsman, Arthur M. Schlesinger Jr., Theodore C. Sorensen, and the president's brother, Attorney General Robert F. Kennedy, testified to Kennedy's prowess as a world statesmen. Through a rare combination of restraint of manner and toughness of purpose, he had, in Schlesinger's words, created "a new hope for peace on earth." In particular, these accounts point to Kennedy's adept management of the Cuban Missile Crisis. With courage and skill, he forced the Soviet Union to remove their nuclear-tipped missiles from Cuba. But in the aftermath of this diplomatic triumph, he eschewed confrontation and wisely persuaded Soviet premier Nikita Khrushchev to agree to the Nuclear Test Ban Treaty (1963).[10] Far more critical accounts of the Kennedy presidency began to appear by the early 1970s, however. Distraught over the war in Vietnam, journalists like David Halberstam charged that Kennedy and his advisors bore significant responsibility for the debacle.[11] Other analysts launched frontal assaults on the president's foreign policy, charging that his Cold War rhetoric was needlessly provocative. They also denied that the Cuban Missile Crisis was an example of superb crisis management. As Richard J. Walton argued, Kennedy acted like John Foster Dulles, the epitome of the moralistic Cold Warrior. The president had embarked "on an anti-communist crusade much more dangerous than any policy [President Dwight D.] Eisenhower ever permitted."[12] Some scholars have tried to split the difference between the two schools of interpretation. Historian Robert A. Divine conceded that Kennedy accepted "the Cold War shibboleths" of Dulles, believing that "only a tough determined American response, grounded in military superiority, could ensure the nation's survival." But the harrowing experience of the missile crisis sobered the president. As revealed in his conciliatory speech at American University in June 1963, Kennedy displayed during his last year in office a "far more mature concern for the ultimate questions of war and peace in the nuclear age."[13]

During the 1980s and 1990s, scholars have begun to produce studies grounded in the documentary record, although they have been hampered by the painfully slow release of records. Predictably, they have focused on the Kennedy-era flashpoints: Berlin, Cuba, and Vietnam. They also have attended major conferences, which have included participants from Cuba, the Soviet Union, and the United States, and have explored the hidden history of the missile crisis. In historiographer Burton I. Kaufman's judgment, interpretations of U.S. foreign policy have emerged that "are more complex and more ambiguous than either the Kennedy apologists or the early revisionists have allowed." Historians continue to ask hard questions but "have become increasingly subtle and sophisticated in their arguments," placing Kennedy within the context of Cold War history.[14] Thomas G. Paterson, editor of a collection of essays on Kennedy's foreign policy, summarized the interpretations of his authors when he noted that, despite his reputation for bold, innovative reasoning, "Kennedy remained attached to the core of Cold War thinking." Like other twentieth-century U.S. leaders, he "revealed himself as an American traditionalist extending America's considerable global power."[15] James Giglio, in his balanced survey of the administration, agrees that Kennedy was far more traditional than his rhetoric suggested. He spoke about being sensitive to Third World nationalism but showed little patience with those African and Asian leaders who criticized U.S. policies. Nonetheless, Giglio suggests that Kennedy merits his above-average presidential rating. With programs like the Peace Corps, he improved the U.S. image in the Third World, and he successfully helped resolve crises in Laos and the former Belgian Congo.[16]

Analyses of the Alliance for Progress have followed a path similar to general interpretations of Kennedy's foreign policies. Schlesinger, who helped design the Alliance, set the initial tone in his loving biography by lavishly praising the president for reversing the Eisenhower administration's policies. Eisenhower denied economic aid to Latin America and coddled dictators, whereas Kennedy uplifted the Latin American poor and championed decent democrats like the Venezuelan leader Rómulo Betancourt.[17] Sorensen similarly applauded his boss's efforts, although he conceded that "reality did not match the rhetoric which flowed about the Alliance on both sides of the Rio Grande."[18] When it became apparent at the end of the decade that the Alliance had failed, Schlesinger blamed the Johnson administration for abandoning the Alliance's reformist goals. As Schlesinger saw it, "The Alliance was never really tried. It lasted about a thousand days, not a sufficient test, and thereafter only the name remained." Schlesinger has subsequently admitted, however, that the Alliance was plagued by bureaucratic torpor and that the president and his brother unwisely listened to national security officials who wanted to combat Latin American radicals with counterinsurgency programs. Counterinsurgency doctrine, "a ghastly illusion," distorted and perverted the Alliance's reformist goals.[19] But in March 1986, at a conference marking the twenty-fifth anniversary of the president's Alliance speech, Kennedy administration officials again paid homage their leader's idealism and claimed that, whatever its immediate shortcomings, the Alliance had constructed the foundation for long-term economic development in Latin America.[20]

Critical accounts of the Alliance emerged in the 1970s, although Simon Hanson, the editor of *Inter-American Economic Affairs*, had carped during the 1960s that the architects of the Alliance knew little about

Latin America and that they foolishly ignored the ideas of private U.S. foreign investors.[21] In *The Alliance That Lost Its Way* (1970), journalists Jerome Levinson and Juan de Onís thoroughly documented the Alliance's dismal economic statistics. The best that could be said was that "in financial terms, the Alliance for Progress has done more to avert, or at least to postpone, economic disaster than to stimulate economic development."[22] Why the Alliance failed to meet its qualitative and quantitative goals became the subject of debate. Some focused on the daunting nature of Latin America's problems and concluded that the task had been too formidable for the United States.[23] Ambassador to Brazil Lincoln Gordon, who served under both Presidents Kennedy and Johnson, dismissed Schlesinger's charge that Johnson had undermined the Alliance, acidly labeling such assertions as "Camelot myth making." Gordon argued that the Alliance began to show results in the late 1960s, with a modest gain in the economic growth rate in 1968. He shifted blame to the Richard M. Nixon administration, accusing it of ignoring Latin America.[24] Abraham Lowenthal, adopting the "bureaucratic politics" model developed by political scientists, theorized that the president and his White House advisors had designed an ambitious plan that would foster a thoroughgoing reform of Latin American societies. But Department of State bureaucrats, who preferred stability over change, gained control over the implementation of the Alliance and reached accommodations with both the ruling elites of Latin America and U.S. multinational business interests.[25] Other scholars, such as Federico G. Gil, Joseph S. Tulchin, and William O. Walker III, have questioned whether the Alliance represented a watershed in the history of inter-American relations. In their essays, they have stressed continuities, noting points of contact between the Alliance and traditional U.S. approaches to Latin America during the twentieth century.[26]

Whatever their methods, scholars have faced difficulties in writing about the foreign policies of John F. Kennedy. Important White House and State Department records remained closed, and, unlike the Eisenhower and Johnson presidential libraries, the Kennedy Library did not successfully expedite the declassification process. Moreover, scholars have not enjoyed equal access to the records of the Kennedy family. For example, Arthur Schlesinger gained special permission to use the papers of Robert Kennedy.[27] But in the second half of the 1990s, scholars began to encounter fewer roadblocks in their attempts to construct the historical record. For historians of U.S. foreign relations, a central source has long been the U.S. State Department's *Foreign Relations of the United*

States (*FRUS*) series. In 1991 President George W. Bush signed into law a congressional mandate that the *FRUS* volumes should be published no more than thirty years after the events they document. Although the Historical Office of the State Department has been unable to adhere to the thirty-year rule, it has been releasing numerous Kennedy-era volumes, including those covering U.S. relations with Latin America. President William Jefferson Clinton has also issued an executive order easing the declassification process, although agencies such as the Central Intelligence Agency (CIA) have not always readily conformed to the spirit of the new order.[28] The CIA allegedly burned records of Cold War interventions, including records of its covert intervention between 1961 and 1964 in the South American country of British Guiana (Guyana).[29] Nevertheless, historians now have available an abundant quantity of official records and can confidently proceed to an intensive examination of the foreign policy record of the Kennedy administration.

What follows is an examination of the Latin American policies of the Kennedy administration, with a special emphasis on its regional reform program, the Alliance for Progress. The study will examine change and continuity questions, the traditional subjects of historical inquiry. Was the Alliance period a unique event in the history of inter-American relations or was it just another Cold War weapon of the United States? How similar were the liberal plans to redesign the social structure of Latin America to the interventionist schemes promoted by progressive presidents like Theodore Roosevelt and Woodrow Wilson? Put another way, was the Alliance part of the customary U.S. search for hegemony in the Western Hemisphere? The answers to these questions can perhaps explain why President Kennedy repeatedly referred to Latin America as the "most critical area" and "the most dangerous area in the world."

Because the Alliance failed to achieve its enumerated goals, historians must also ask what happened to the substantial U.S. foreign aid and who bears responsibility for failure. Did either the Johnson or Nixon administrations destroy the Alliance, as Kennedy's partisans have alleged? Or can failure be simply ascribed to the tenacious resistance to change that has long characterized elite rule in Latin America? Questions of responsibility involve issues concerning the executive abilities of President Kennedy. Did he make the critical decisions in the area of Latin American policy or did he focus his attention on other areas of the world? Was he able to motivate the various governmental departments—the Department of Defense, the Agency for International Development, the CIA—to carry out his idealistic policies? What was the depth of the president's commitment to reform? How did he balance his clarion call for change in Latin America with his Cold War concerns for stability and anticommunism? Why did he send both Peace Corps volunteers and U.S. military and police advisors to Latin America?

This study will address such issues by analyzing not only the Kennedy administration's regional policies but also its bilateral initiatives. Insights into the essence of the Alliance for Progress can be gained by comparing the administration's warm support for Betancourt's Venezuela with its disdain for Brazil's president, João Goulart. Scholars similarly need to ask why the administration denounced the Peruvian military's overthrow of a constitutional government and overlooked the Argentine military's removal of a popularly elected president. The administration's inconsistent policies toward authoritarians—the Trujillo family of the Dominican Republic, the Somozas of Nicaragua, François Duvalier of Haiti, and Miguel Ydígoras Fuentes of Guatemala—also bear examination.

What is not a central feature of this study, however, is U.S. policy toward Fidel Castro's Cuba. President Eisenhower broke diplomatic relations with Cuba on 3 January 1961, some two weeks before Kennedy took office. Thereafter, Kennedy intensified his predecessor's war against the Cuban. The Bay of Pigs invasion, Operation Mongoose, and the Cuban Missile Crisis, the key episodes in the U.S. confrontation with Cuba, all merit separate studies. Although Castro and the Cuban Revolution are not the subjects of this study, they were the objects of U.S. policy toward Latin America. The architects of the Alliance tried to immunize Latin American societies against radicalism. President Kennedy measured Latin American leaders by their position on Castro, and U.S. diplomats repeatedly lobbied Latin American governments to sponsor anti-Castro resolutions in international forums. Indeed, Kennedy administration officials rarely spoke about the Alliance for Progress without simultaneously expressing their fear and loathing of the Cuban Revolution, Castro's conversion to Marxism-Leninism, and his turn toward the Soviet Union.

With the newly available primary sources, scholars now have the opportunity to offer a sober analysis of U.S. foreign policy during the Kennedy years. They also can now test the quality of President Kennedy's leadership and assess whether the abiding respect and love that the people of the Americas hold for him can be sustained by the historical record.

1 ★ Origins

Within two months after assuming office, President John F. Kennedy pledged that the United States would transform Latin America into a vibrant, progressive area of the world. The president and his advisors responded rapidly because of what they perceived as both an ominous socioeconomic crisis and a deep yearning for change in Latin America. They also acted confidently, certain they knew how to "modernize" societies and build sturdy, self-reliant democracies. But their confidence was mixed with alarm. They feared that the region was "ripe for revolution" and that Latin Americans might embrace communism and the Soviet Union. The security of the United States depended on winning the Cold War in Latin America.

★ President Kennedy presented his reform program for Latin America in an impressive and unusual White House ceremony. The new president and his wife, Jacqueline Bouvier Kennedy, hosted an elegant reception in the Red, Blue, and Green Rooms for 250 people, including the diplomatic corps of the Latin American republics, U.S. congressional leaders, and their spouses. At the appointed time, the guests then moved to the East Room, where they seated themselves on gilt-edged chairs arranged in semicircles on both sides of the rostrum. The president soon addressed them. The speech, which lasted only twenty minutes, was simultaneously broadcast by the Voice of America in English, Spanish, French, and Portuguese, the languages of the Western Hemisphere. Kennedy thrilled his attentive audience, telling the Latin Americans what they had been waiting for nearly two decades to hear. The United States would underwrite the region's social and economic transformation. To be known as the Alliance for Progress—Alianza para el Progreso—the new program would be a Marshall Plan for Latin America.

In his stirring speech of 13 March 1961, the president outlined a ten-point program to transform the Americas during the 1960s—"the decade of development." The United States agreed to support long-range economic planning, economic integration and common markets, and solutions to commodity market problems. Scientific and technical co-operation would be expanded and cultural relations strengthened. The United States also intended to rush emergency shipments of food to Latin America and cooperate with Latin Americans to curb unproductive military spending. As a down payment to his good intentions, the president promised to ask Congress immediately to appropriate $500 million to begin a campaign to eradicate illiteracy, hunger, and disease in the hemisphere. But the Alliance for Progress, the president vowed, meant more than economic aid. Political freedom and social reform must accompany material progress. Archaic tax and land-tenure structures had to be dismantled and self-serving tyrants cast aside. North and South Americans had "to demonstrate to the entire world that man's unsatisfied aspiration for economic progress and social justice can best be achieved by free men working within a framework of democratic institutions." [1]

The Kennedy administration soon turned these promises into results. It quickly secured from Congress the requested $500 million to initiate the war against poverty in Latin America and an additional $100 million to help Chile recover from a recent destructive earthquake. It established a Seasonal Marketing Fund for the purpose of stabilizing the price of coffee, Latin America's chief export; in addition, the United States joined an international study group to find permanent solutions to the world oversupply of coffee.[2] And the administration hastily assembled economic rescue packages for hard-pressed nations such as Bolivia, sending it $50 million in loans and grants.[3] U.S. officials also began intensive preparations for the inter-American economic conference, to be held in August 1961, that would write the charter for the Alliance for Progress.

✦   The Kennedy administration decided to embark on a campaign to underwrite change and development in Latin America because U.S. officials feared that the region seemed vulnerable to radical social revolution. In the late 1950s, a series of crises had rocked inter-American relations. In mid-1958, angry South Americans hounded Vice President Richard M. Nixon during his tour of the continent, and in Caracas, a howling mob tried to assault the vice president. These protesters claimed that the United States had supported military tyrants like Marcos Pérez Jiménez (1952–58) of Venezuela and ignored Latin America's pressing socioeconomic needs. The next year, violent anti-U.S. demonstrations erupted in Panama. Guerrillas, who espoused a variety of leftist doctrines, also began to operate in the mountains of Colombia and Venezuela. And, in what would prove to be the most momentous of changes, Fidel Castro overthrew the pro-American dictator of Cuba, Fulgencio Batista, and turned the Cuban Revolution into a bitterly anti-American movement.

The turmoil in Latin America unsettled the Dwight D. Eisenhower administration. In the aftermath of the Nixon trip and Castro's triumph, administration officials concluded that Latin America had become a critical Cold War battleground. They also privately admitted that Latin Americans had reason to object to U.S. policies. The administration had proffered medals and military support to unsavory dictators like Batista, Pérez Jiménez, and Peru's Manuel Odría because they professed to be Cold War allies of the United States. Calculating also that dictators could keep their countries secure, stable, and resistant to internal subversion, the administration had largely ignored Latin America when it came to parceling out foreign economic assistance. Between 1945 and 1960, the small European countries of Belgium, Luxembourg, and the Netherlands had received more foreign aid from the United States than had Latin America. The United States had even favored Communist Yugoslavia over its southern neighbors. But the dictators could no longer be counted on to follow dutifully the U.S. lead on the international stage and muzzle dissent at home. Between 1956 and 1960, ten military dictators fell from power. The United States, according to national security officers, now had to forgo "the easy luxury of being simply anti-Communist" and respond "dynamically and creatively to our age of revolution."[4]

The Eisenhower administration offered a series of new policies to control the revolutionary ferment and "to align and keep Latin America on our side." Between 1958 and January 1961, President Eisenhower established a regional lending agency, the Inter-American Development Bank, and asked Congress to authorize funds for a Social Progress Trust Fund to alleviate poverty and ignorance in Latin America. The administration conspicuously began to spurn dictators, breaking relations in August 1960, for example, with Rafael Trujillo of the Dominican Republic, and to support reformers like Arturo Frondizi of Argentina and Rómulo Betancourt of Venezuela who favored, in the words of the National Security Council (NSC), "rising living standards and a more equitable distribution of national income within the general framework of a free enterprise system and through peaceful means rather than violent." The administration also made a series of confidential decisions about the region. The CIA tried to accelerate the pace of social re-form in Latin America by funding schools of democracy for politicians and labor leaders. The CIA used private foundations, newspaper guilds, and U.S. labor unions as both conduits and covers. The administra-tion also began to reassess its military aid program. During the 1950s, it had transferred approximately $400 million in military aid to Latin America, ostensibly to help the region resist an external attack by the Soviet Union. In light of Castro's successful guerrilla campaign, the NSC now wanted Latin American military units to attain "a reasonable mili-tary capability to maintain internal security against civil disturbances or insurrections." U.S. officials began talking about teaching counter-insurgency and riot control techniques at its inter-American military schools in Panama. Finally, in March 1960, Eisenhower authorized the CIA to develop a plan to overthrow Castro. The plan contemplated an invasion of the island by U.S.-backed Cuban exiles.[5]

✦   The new Kennedy administration swiftly built upon its prede-cessor's initiatives, although neither Kennedy nor his closest advisors had given extensive thought to the region prior to January 1961. As a young man, Kennedy had visited Argentina. During the 1950s, he vacationed in Cuba with his congressional friend, George Smathers of Florida, and he took his new wife to Acapulco, Mexico. Unlike his wife, Kennedy did not speak Spanish and struggled with the pronunciation of Spanish-language words he inserted in his speeches on inter-American affairs. During his twelve years in Congress, the Massachusetts Demo-crat did not focus on Latin American issues. In the aftermath of the Nixon trip, the Senate Foreign Relations Committee held extensive hearings in public and in executive sessions on the U.S. role in Latin America. Senator Kennedy listened while colleagues such as J. William Fulbright (D.-Ark.), Wayne Morse (D.-Ore.), and Hubert Humphrey (D.-Minn.) assailed the Eisenhower administration for the disarray in inter-American relations. Kennedy objected, however, when Humphrey and Senator Albert Gore (D.-Tenn.) proposed eliminating military aid to Latin America as a way of avoiding the "embarrassing predicaments" of seeming to support dictators like the Dominican's Republic's Tru-jillo. Kennedy agreed that military aid would have no practical value in a war against the Soviets and was "down the drain in a military sense." Nonetheless, he argued that military aid was a politically useful tool to maintain influence with the Latin American military.[6] On 15 December 1958, shortly after his smashing reelection to the U.S. Senate, Kennedy gave his first major address on inter-American affairs at a Democratic Party dinner in San Juan, Puerto Rico. The senator admitted to his audience that he did not have a new program for Latin America and supported Eisenhower's post-Nixon trip initiatives like the Inter-American Development Bank. But with Castro's bearded guerrillas bearing down on Batista's forces, he blamed the administration for the turmoil in Cuba. U.S. policy, Kennedy charged, had been "weighted in favor of an oppressive regime whose persecutions and brutalities far exceeded the retributions of the Castro regime." He added that, although he was disturbed by Castro's brutality toward his opponents, the Cuban's actions were "not untypical of revolutions." Kennedy would later add to his San Juan speech, which was published in his campaign book, *The Strategy of Peace* (1960), that Castro might "have taken a more rational course after his victory had the United States Government not backed the dictator so long and so uncritically."[7]

Although he had not carefully considered U.S. relations with Latin America, Kennedy had taken stands during his congressional career that appealed to Asians, Africans, and Latin Americans—the people of the developing world. In July 1957, Kennedy gained national and international attention by denouncing France on the Senate floor for its suppression of Algerian independence. He identified nationalism as "the most powerful force" in the world and Soviet and Western imperialists as the enemies of freedom. He reasoned that "the single most important test of American foreign policy today is how we meet the challenge of imperialism." The senator also argued that the United States needed to finance economic development in poor regions and introduced legislation in 1958–59 to give special assistance to India.[8] Although sympathetic to nationalist movements, Kennedy set limits on their direction. As he told his fellow Democrats in San Juan, he supported the doctrine of nonintervention, the guiding principle of inter-American relations since the Franklin Roosevelt era and the centerpiece of the charter of the Organization of American States (OAS). But there would be "little question that should any Latin country be driven by repression into the arms of the Communists, our attitude on non-intervention would change overnight."[9]

The mounting hostility between the United States and Castro's Cuba insured that inter-American relations would be an issue during the 1960 presidential campaign. Soviet Vice-Premier Anastas Mikoyan's commercial mission to Havana in February 1960 and the growing political and economic ties between Cuba and the Soviet Union gave Democrats the opportunity to return the China favor of the 1950 and 1952 campaigns and blame Republicans for "losing" a country. Kennedy abandoned the sympathetic appraisal of Castro's actions that he had offered in *The Strategy for Peace*. He told a crowd in Nashville that Eisenhower and Nixon had "permitted a Communist satellite ninety miles off the coast of Florida, eight minutes by jet." Cuba imperiled not only the United States but also Latin America. Kennedy warned supporters in Cincinnati that Cuba could serve as "a base from which to carry Communist infiltration and subversion throughout the Americas." In late October, the Democratic candidate even suggested in a press release that the United States should strengthen groups in the United States and in Cuba "who offer eventual hope for overthrowing Cuba." Kennedy quickly backed away from the suggestion when Nixon accused him of violating the OAS's nonintervention principle. But Kennedy generally stuck with his apocalyptic language. In Salt Lake City, he portrayed the Cold War to a gathering of Mormons as "a struggle for supremacy between two conflicting ideologies: Freedom under God versus ruthless, godless tyranny." [10]

Although he depicted Castro's Cuba as a regional threat, Kennedy infrequently addressed Latin American issues during the presidential campaign. By comparison, he mentioned Africa over 500 times. In mid-1960, he enlisted the help of Adolf A. Berle Jr. A campaign aide, Archibald Cox, explained to Berle that Latin America "was a region to which Kennedy had not given much thought." [11] Berle, one of Roosevelt's "brain trusters," had served as ambassador to Brazil and had been a persistent liberal critic of Eisenhower's Latin American policies. During the 1950s, he had befriended Latin American democrats like Betancourt and José Figueres of Costa Rica. He assisted Kennedy by publishing a scathing attack on the Eisenhower administration in the influential journal, *Foreign Affairs*, alleging that the State Department had been friendly, "sometimes intimate," with dictators. [12] Berle's ideas also appeared in Kennedy's major statement on Latin America, a speech in Tampa, which was not actually delivered, on 18 October 1960. The statement presented a twelve-point program for Latin America, with Kennedy pledging to support democracy and economic development. The blueprint did not, however, make any concrete financial promises. The speech had strong partisan overtones, calling Eisenhower's military aid to Latin America "a disaster." Like other campaign press releases, the statement also invoked a sense of impending doom, alleging that "time was running out for the United States in Latin America" and that "although the cold war will not be won in Latin America—it may well be lost there."[13] At the suggestion of campaign aide Richard N. Goodwin, the "Alianza para Progreso" phrase first appeared. The phrase, which lacked the definite article "el," was grammatically incorrect and was initially translated as both "Alliance in Progress" and "Alliance for Progress."

In his Tampa statement, Kennedy had argued that ultimately the president had to provide direction and guidance to Latin American policies. Throughout the campaign, he called for presidential initiative and leadership in foreign affairs, "if we are to rebuild our prestige in the eyes of the world." He believed that Eisenhower had forfeited too much power to his staff and spent excessive time meeting with the NSC, pondering policy options. He wanted a foreign policy team that acted boldly and decisively. In fact, Kennedy established a distinctive management style as president. He disliked formal, regular meetings, preferring small, ad hoc discussions. Unlike President Eisenhower, Kennedy did not attempt to reach consensus through formal, approved policy papers, and he frequently did not require aides to record his discussions with his advisors. He used NSC meetings to inform subordinates and ratify decisions previously made. Both by design and by happenstance, he controlled policy. As one historian has asserted, "No president kept a tighter rein on foreign policy." The editors of his foreign policy papers agreed that "President Kennedy, with advice from his key advisors, made the major foreign policy decisions during his presidency."[14]

Kennedy also had promised in his Tampa statement that his secretary of state would work with him in making Latin American policy. But his relationship with Secretary of State Dean Rusk was cool and distant, and in private the president belittled him and his agency for being indecisive and unresponsive. For his part, Rusk evinced little interest in the region, stirring himself only when the issue involved Castro and communism. One subordinate lamented that Rusk gave as much time to Western New Guinea as he did to Latin America.[15] Under Secretary of State Chester B. Bowles followed development issues and, unlike most administration officials, opposed military aid to Latin America and defended the nonintervention principle. But in November 1961, the president replaced Bowles with George W. Ball. Kennedy's advisors, especially Attorney General Robert Kennedy, felt Bowles had been disloyal after the Bay of Pigs debacle.[16] Bowles's successor focused on North Atlantic affairs. At the assistant secretary level, Kennedy went through three officers—Thomas C. Mann, Wimberly De R. Coerr, and Robert F.

Woodward—before appointing Edwin McCammon Martin in March 1962. Martin, who had served in the economic section of the State Department, spoke no Spanish and had little experience in inter-American affairs. Although a competent administrator, he questioned the abilities of Latin Americans, alleging that they lacked a sense of personal responsibility and lived in "immature and inexperienced societies, seriously short of political and other skills." [17] Teodoro Moscoso, who served as coordinator of the Alliance for Progress, proved to be an eloquent visionary and an ineffective administrator. Frustrated with the State Department, the president repeatedly took up Adolf Berle's idea of naming a distinguished political figure to a special position of under secretary of state for Latin American affairs. But Rusk always resisted, pointing out that other regions of the world would demand equal treatment.[18]

Kennedy understandably looked to his cabinet and White House staff for help on Latin America. Secretary of the Treasury C. Douglas Dillon had some experience in inter-American affairs, having led the movement within the Eisenhower administration to respond to Latin America's economic plight. As under secretary of state in 1960, Dillon had also coordinated that administration's campaigns against Castro and Trujillo. Dillon presented the Alliance for Progress package to Latin Americans in August 1961 but thereafter limited his involvement in inter-American affairs. Robert Kennedy took control of security issues after the Bay of Pigs, overseeing military aid, counterinsurgency, and police training. The attorney general directed a committee on counterinsurgency, the "Special Group (CI)." Secretary of Defense Robert McNamara did not contest the attorney general's direction of military policies in Latin America. When it came to Latin America, National Security Advisor McGeorge Bundy coordinated rather than made policy. Two aides, Goodwin and Arthur M. Schlesinger Jr., provided the president with copious advice about Latin America. Both favored unwavering support for democracy. Although brilliant, neither man had any special training or expertise in Latin American history and culture. Ralph A. Dungan, another presidential assistant who had no prior experience in inter-American affairs, also worked in the White House on Latin America.

These institutional and personnel developments left President Kennedy at the center of the policy-making process. Despite his inexperience in inter-American affairs, he took up the task with vigor, fulfilling his campaign promise to direct the Latin American policy of the United States. During his 1,000 days in office, he visited Latin America three times and met there or in Washington with most heads of state. Indeed, he entertained a steady stream of visitors that included former presidents, foreign, finance and labor ministers, ambassadors, generals, trade unionists, and Latin American economists like the Brazilian Celso Furtado. He also kept his door open to his U.S. advisors. For example, he met with Assistant Secretary Martin seventy-four times during the sixty-nine weeks that Martin was physically present in Washington. One amazed aide recalled that the president actually discussed with his subordinates ways to recruit secretaries and mobilize typewriters for Alliance programs.[19] The memorandums of these conversations with U.S. and Latin American officials reveal an articulate, educated, refined man who had studied his briefing papers. This picture of Kennedy at work seems remarkably like the public figure that citizens of both continents fondly remember. Kennedy was unfailingly polite with his Latin American visitors, with no hint of the patronizing, condescending attitude that had characterized some of his presidential predecessors. He enjoyed the company of Latin Americans, especially friends like Venezuela's Betancourt. Although cordial, Kennedy also made his case directly and without hesitation, debating for hours with Juscelino Kubitschek, the former president of Brazil, about the nature of the Alliance or with President Roberto Chiari of Panama about the future of the Panama Canal.[20]

President Kennedy carried some core beliefs into his discussions about Latin America. He sympathized with the plight of ordinary Latin Americans, wanted to help, and believed that the United States needed to rectify its past mistakes. As he noted to Goodwin, he liked to think that "those people who threw rocks at Nixon" merely objected to the vice president's "personality." But in fact, they were sending the message that "we can't embrace every tinhorn dictator who tells us he's anti-communist while he's sitting on the necks of his own people." The president's dismay about the historical past led Secretary Martin to suggest that Kennedy had a "guilt complex" about issues like the Panama Canal. Whatever his internal feelings, Kennedy responded quickly to problems. He ordered a financial rescue mission for Bolivia "within a matter of hours" after being told by Press Secretary Pierre Salinger that the State Department had ignored Bolivian pleas for help. While in Costa Rica, he noticed an unoccupied hospital and told aides to find funds to staff it. The Agency for International Development (AID) subsequently granted $130,000 for a children's hospital in San José. And only with great frustration did he approve expenditures for balance of payment purposes and monetary stabilization. He remarked that he wanted Alliance funds to help people, instead of being "really appreciated only by bankers."[21]

The president also showed sensitivity and flexibility on fundamental economic issues. To be sure, he imbibed international capitalism's basic principles of free trade and investment. He denounced the Brazilians for inflation and capital flight, and he told President José Ramón Villeda Morales of Honduras that agrarian reform should not be used to drive the United Fruit Company out of the country. Kennedy understood that the United States had substantial economic interests in the region, with $8 billion in direct investments representing 25 percent of U.S. global direct investments. Trade with Latin America also ranked high, amounting to 20 percent of the international trade of the United States.[22] But the president did not worship at the altar of laissez-faire economics. The Alliance for Progress sanctioned government planning, calling for national development plans. Moreover, Kennedy accepted the principle of compensated expropriation, and he had reservations about U.S. investors dominating a nation's economy, pointing to the role of U.S. copper interests in Chile. He also worried that when U.S. companies owned public utilities and raised rates, Latin American consumers would blame the United States. Kennedy even suggested that Latin Americans not always accede to every demand of the International Monetary Fund (IMF) for streamlined budgets and stringent monetary policies. In a meeting with Argentine Minister of Economy Alvaro Alsogaray, who was negotiating with the IMF, the president "expressed some concern that a too conservative and cautious and deflationary policy would meet the interests and desires of privileged groups and the bankers but not serve the needs of all the people."[23]

Personal political considerations certainly shaped Kennedy's Latin American policies. He labored to keep Latin American issues out of the 1964 presidential campaign. On the emotional question of who should operate and defend the Panama Canal, Kennedy understood the concerns of Panamanian nationalists but demanded that negotiations be postponed. Preparing the U.S. Congress and public for change would take time and hard political work. In mid-1962, he told President Chiari that "1964, 1965, or 1966 would be a better time to go about a 'basic document.'" A year later, he emphasized to Ambassador Joseph Farland "that we do not want an explosion in Panama, we must keep the lid on the next couple of years the best way we can." The president hoped to buy time with "a very active AID program."[24] More important politically to Kennedy, however, was that he not face in 1964 the same charge—losing a Latin American country to communism—that he had thrown at the Eisenhower/Nixon team. For example, he brought extraordinary pressure to bear on Prime Minister Harold Macmillan of the United Kingdom to postpone independence for the South American colony of British Guiana, alleging that it would become a Communist state. At a meeting in London on 30 June 1963, he offered frightening scenarios to Macmillan, prophesying that "the effect of having a Communist state in British Guiana in addition to Cuba in 1964, would be to create irresistible pressures in the United States to strike militarily against Cuba." He even suggested that the prime minister could precipitate the election of a belligerent radical, perhaps Senator Barry Goldwater (R.-Ariz.), and the outbreak of a second Soviet-American confrontation over Cuba. Kennedy reminded Macmillan "that the great danger in 1964 was that, since Cuba would be the major American public issue, adding British Guiana to Cuba could well tip the scales, and someone would be elected who would take military action against Cuba."[25] The British ultimately succumbed to the president's pressure and postponed the colony's independence.

The colloquy with Prime Minister Macmillan underscored what biographer Arthur Schlesinger has identified as his boss's "absolute determination" to prevent a second Communist outpost in the Western Hemisphere.[26] Fighting and winning the Cold War in Latin America was Kennedy's paramount concern. He believed that the Soviet Union's drive for global supremacy included subverting the region. Throughout his presidency he predicted trouble. In January 1961, he told Goodwin that "the whole place could blow up on us." In November 1962, he warned Argentina's General Pedro Eugenio Aramburu to be alert, observing "that the next twelve months would be critical in Latin America with respect to renewed Communist attempts at penetration." In June 1963, Latin America was only "the most dangerous area in the world." In October 1963, less than a month before his death, Kennedy warned that Latin America posed "the greatest danger to us." He even disputed those who claimed the United States was on the road to victory. In June 1962, President Adolfo López Mateos of Mexico observed that "the important thing is to create better economic and social conditions" and that "the Alliance for Progress is the best way to combat Communism." Citing troubles in Colombia, Ecuador, Guatemala, and Venezuela, Kennedy rejected the Mexican's optimism, saying the Alliance would take too long to work. As such, he "returned again and again to his question of what President López Mateos thought was the best way to deal with the obvious danger of an expansion of Communist influence in Latin America." The astonished López Mateos could only promise that he would think the matter over, but he still believed "that rapid economic and social progress was the answer."[27]

Some commentators have charged that President Kennedy's anti-Communist crusade in Latin America transcended international and domestic political issues and involved revenge. The president and the attorney general suffered a painful political defeat when Fidel Castro routed Cuban exiles at the Bay of Pigs in April 1961. The Kennedy brothers allegedly vowed to make Castro and his Communist supporters pay for staining the family honor.[28] Testimony exists to sustain that interpretation of the administration's war against Castro and communism. Under Secretary of State Bowles observed the president and the attorney general's behavior at cabinet and NSC meetings in the immediate aftermath of the collapse of the Cuban expedition. Bowles recorded in his personal notes that Kennedy "was really quite shattered," for "his public career had been a long series of successes, without any noteworthy setbacks." The Kennedy brothers had been "personally humiliated" and were demonstrating a "great lack of moral integrity" in demanding action against Castro.[29] CIA operatives have subsequently alleged that the Kennedys cared more about family honor than national security. They claim that the Kennedy brothers "were absolutely obsessed with getting rid of Castro."[30] Although personal animus toward Castro may have indeed informed the Kennedy administration's Latin American policy, the documentary record does not support the argument that revenge drove U.S. actions. In his private conversations with U.S. officials and foreigners, the president insisted that communism in the Western Hemisphere threatened the United States, impeded the U.S. ability to act elsewhere, and threatened to become a divisive domestic political issue. Those themes are also evident in the verbatim transcripts of the administration's deliberations during the Cuban Missile Crisis.[31] As Robert Kennedy informed his brother on 19 April 1961, Castro's triumph at the Bay of Pigs would lead him to be "more bombastic" and "more and more closely tied to communism." Something "forceful and determined" had to be done, because "our long-range foreign policy objectives in Cuba are tied to survival."[32]

Critical to Kennedy's certain belief that Latin America had become a momentous Cold War battleground was his assessment of Soviet premier Nikita Khrushchev's promise to back "wars of national liberation."

Khrushchev briefly raised the issue in a lengthy speech delivered in Moscow on 6 January 1961. Scholars have subsequently questioned whether Khrushchev intended to provoke the United States; they have suggested that the Soviet leader was addressing doctrinal disputes within the Communist world.[33] In any case, Kennedy ordered his foreign policy team to study the speech. NSC official Walt W. Rostow surmised that Khrushchev intended to promote guerrilla warfare. Ambassador to Brazil Lincoln Gordon decided that Khrushchev, by backing wars of national liberation, had signaled his intention to use Cuba as "a base for military and intelligence activities against the United States" and for further "opportunistic conquests in Latin America." Kennedy drew similar conclusions from his unpleasant meeting with the Soviet leader in June 1961 in Vienna. Upon returning home, the president soberly reported to the nation that his Soviet adversary predicted that in the developing countries "the revolution of rising peoples would eventually be a Communist revolution, and that the so-called wars of liberation, supported by the Kremlin, would replace the old methods of direct aggression and invasion." Kennedy added that it was "the Communist theory" that "a small group of disciplined Communists could exploit discontent and misery in a country where the average income may be $60 or $70 a year, and seize control, therefore, of an entire country without Communist troops ever crossing any international border."[34]

The president and his advisors returned home believing that Khrushchev included Latin America in his master plan. Secretary Rusk informed U.S. diplomats in Latin America that Khrushchev had "voiced Soviet intent to support 'popular' movements against 'rotten and unpopular regimes' " and that elsewhere in his talks he had "expressed his belief that there were a number of governments in Latin America which opposed the interests of his people." Not to oppose the perceived Soviet aggression would imperil the national security of the United States. As revealed in his campaign rhetoric, Kennedy accepted the basic premise of the key Cold War document, National Security Council Paper Number 68 (NSC-68) of 1950. The fate of Western Civilization depended on victory in the Cold War. Moreover, if the United States failed to secure its traditional sphere of influence, other areas of the world would be further endangered. As Rusk once explained to Argentine diplomats, countries on the periphery of the Soviet bloc were watching to see how resolutely the United States handled problems "in our own backyard." Weakness and "a lack of determination on our part," Rusk warned the Argentines, might encourage Soviet aggression in Berlin.[35]

In his report to the nation on the Vienna summit, the president re-assured his fellow citizens that the United States had the talent and resources to win the struggle in the developing world. Despite his pub-lic confidence, however, Kennedy had occasional doubts. He once con-fessed to Rostow that the Soviets had the upper hand in Latin America. Khrushchev, with his $300 million in annual aid, would make Cuba a "showcase" for development. He only had to worry about 7 million Cubans, whereas "I got to be concerned with the future of 200 million Latin Americans. He's bound to do better."[36] Nonetheless, Kennedy threw himself into what he believed was the contest for Latin America. Every decision he made about Latin America's future inevitably in-volved Cold War considerations.

★ Even before assuming office, Kennedy ordered his aides to draw up a battle plan for the Cold War in Latin America. He initially turned to his campaign advisor, Adolf Berle. Berle shared Kennedy's sentiments about the region, especially his alarm about communism. In January 1961, he wrote in his diary that "eight governments may go the way of Cuba in the next six months unless something is done." In his first re-port, which he discussed with the president-elect for ninety minutes, Berle warned that the Communist challenge was more dangerous than "the Nazi-Fascist threat of the Franklin Roosevelt period." Moscow and Beijing appeared to have agreed on a "revolutionary seizure of parts of Latin America." In an addendum to the report, Berle reiterated that Latin America was now "an active Cold War theatre of attack upon the United States" and that by the term "Cold War" he meant "Russian and Chinese stimulation and arming of local political movements to [the] point where they can be converted into civil wars and used to seize and set up governments which will be hostile to the United States."[37] The new president signaled that he accepted Berle's dire outlook by asking him to prepare a second task force report on Latin America and by dispatching Arthur Schlesinger and Ambassador to the United Nations Adlai Stevenson to conduct fact-finding tours of the region.

The numerous reports on Latin America that Kennedy received dur-ing his first six months in office emphasized common themes. All agreed that Latin America suffered from an ancient heritage of poverty, wide-spread illiteracy, and grave social injustice. Indeed, the region's basic social and economic indices made for grim reading. In several coun-tries—Bolivia, the Dominican Republic, El Salvador, Guatemala, and Haiti—malnutrition was widespread, with a totally inadequate daily per capita consumption of 2,000 calories or less and a daily intake of 15 grams of animal protein. In eight other countries, daily per capita consumption only approached the bare minimum of 2,400 calories necessary to sustain people who toiled in fields and factories. By comparison, North Americans daily consumed over 3,000 calories and 66 grams of animal protein. Hungry people predictably had poor health records. Guatemalans had a life expectancy of less than fifty years, twenty years less than for a U.S. citizen. In the Andean nations of Ecuador and Peru, approximately 10 percent of newborns died during their first year of life. Their impoverished parents lacked the knowledge and skills to reduce those infant mortality rates. Even in relatively prosperous nations such as Brazil and Venezuela, adult illiteracy rates ranged from 35–40 percent. In the Central America states of Honduras and Nicaragua, half of all adults could not read. This misery was concentrated in the countryside, where extremes of wealth and poverty were particularly apparent. In Colombia, for example, 64 percent of farmers tilled *minifundios*, tiny plots of land incapable of yielding an income sufficient to sustain, even by regional standards, an adequate standard of living. On the other hand, 1.3 percent of Colombian agriculturists, the rural oligarchy, controlled 50 percent of the land in vast estates or *latifundias*. In Chile, 7 percent of farmers owned 80 percent of the land. Little wonder that desperate *campesinos* were fleeing the countryside and heading for cities such as Bogotá and Santiago. These new immigrants lived in miserable shantytowns on the outskirts of cities.[38]

In the judgment of Kennedy's advisors, instability, agitation, and even revolution might flow from this poverty and injustice because of what they dubbed the "revolution of rising expectations." With dramatic improvements in communication and transportation, the Latin American poor had begun to understand that their dismal lot in life was not preordained. Edwin Martin warned that "cheap Japanese transistor radios are spreading like wildfire, especially in rural areas, thus opening up millions of uneducated and ill-informed peasants to propaganda pressures from the extremists." Under Secretary Ball preferred a more uplifting analysis, noting that "the winds of change are blowing over the continent. Millions of people have come to know that a better life is possible and they are determined to secure it." Unfortunately, the landed oligarchy, as Schlesinger opined, did not understand "the gravity of its own situation." By thwarting change, they fostered the extremism that could lead to proletarian revolution. The task for the United States, then, was to channel those legitimate aspirations away from communism and toward peaceful change, so as to achieve, in Treasury secretary Dillon's description, "a controlled revolution."[39]

In building progressive, socially just, anti-Communist societies, the United States would have to avoid the mistakes of the immediate past. It could no longer support dictators who professed to be zealous anti-Communists. Such strong-armed leaders created "Batista-like" conditions, leaving frustrated Latin Americans susceptible to the appeals of communism. Berle told Kennedy that the United States could no longer purchase short-term security by allying itself with dictators like François "Papa Doc" Duvalier of Haiti, the Somoza family of Nicaragua, and General Alfredo Stroessner of Paraguay. As Berle admonished, "The present struggle will not be won, and can be lost, by opportunist support of transitory powerholders or forces whose objectives are basically hostile to the peoples they dominate." Instead, the United States needed to assist democratic, progressive groups and thereby gain "a political instrument with which to fight the 'Cold War' on the streets, outside the limitations of formal diplomacy."[40]

The historical moment was propitious for reforming Latin American societies. As Schlesinger saw it, the region was "set for miracles." Despite its general poverty, Latin America had experienced meaningful social change in the first half of the twentieth century, with economic growth and development in major urban areas. The new urban middle sectors—doctors, lawyers, teachers, small businessmen, office workers—represented perhaps 25 percent of Latin America's population. Schlesinger speculated that these groups resented oligarchic domination and wanted to "modernize" their societies through a "middle-class revolution." If given power and economic support, they would foster industrialization, economic growth, and such concomitant features of a modern technical society as constitutional government, bureaucratic efficiency and honesty, and social mobility. Their leaders were Betancourt, Figueres, Frondizi, Alberto Lleras Camargo of Colombia, and Víctor Haya de la Torre of Peru. Kennedy's advisors knew, trusted, and even saw themselves in these men. Berle referred to them as members of the "democratic-progressive 'New Deal' movement." Although Latin America's democrats were, like Franklin Roosevelt, on the side of history, they faced formidable opponents in the traditional oligarchy. Schlesinger concluded that the United States needed to promote the middle-class revolution as speedily as possible, for "if the possessing classes make the middle-class revolution impossible, they will make a 'workers-and-peasants' revolution inevitable."[41]

Although predicting that democracy and progressive social change could undermine the appeal of radicals, Kennedy's advisors also recommended that the United States pursue stout anti-Communist policies in the region. Adolf Berle addressed the fears of those who believed that rapid socioeconomic change would lead to disorder by calling for a program of social revolution coupled with anti-Communist policies. As Schlesinger approvingly recalled, Berle imparted "an edge of toughness" to the new approach.[42] The United States was engaged in a political fight and could not "run away from it by hiding behind the doctrine of 'non-intervention.'" Berle and his task force specifically called for mounting a "psychological offensive" in Latin America. The United States needed to fund friendly university professors, journalists, and media personalities. Students and military men should be brought to the United States for education, training, and indoctrination. The United States needed "to own or control in each Latin American country" at least one general circulation newspaper and "one substantial radio chain." In Berle's view, the stakes in this struggle justified using propaganda and presumably the CIA, for the Communists aimed "to enslave the agricultural and industrial masses, as the Soviet Union and Chinese have done, and hold them in slavery for an indefinite period."[43]

In analyzing turmoil in Latin America and in proposing solutions, Kennedy's new experts on Latin America drew on contemporary theories in social science and the lessons of postwar history. When Schlesinger spoke confidently about the U.S. ability to assist a middle-class revolution in Latin America, he was embracing the ideas of prominent colleagues in the academic fields of economics, history, and political science. Scholars such as Gabriel A. Almond, Lincoln Gordon, John J. Johnson, Seymour Martin Lipset, Max F. Millikan, Lucian Pye, Walt Rostow, and Kalman Silvert had enunciated formal theories on political and economic development. They posited a universal, quantitatively measurable movement of all societies from a "traditional" situation toward a single ideal form or "modern" organization. Traditional societies had authoritarian political structures, rural, backward economies, and a lack of faith in scientific progress and the entrepreneurial spirit. A modern society, which would look remarkably like the United States, would be characterized by a competitive political system, a commercialized and technologically sophisticated economic system, mass consumption, high literacy rates, and a geographically and socially mobile population. Contact with the West, especially the United States and the United Kingdom, had spurred the process of change in the developing world. As Millikan wrote, "More than a billion human beings accustomed to life in the setting of a traditional society are now learning to adapt themselves to the requirements of modern life."[44]

With the modernization theory in hand, a social scientist required no special expertise in Latin American history and culture or knowledge of Spanish. "Modernization" implied the obsolescence of area studies. As Almond instructed, "Differences between Western and non-Western political systems have generally been exaggerated." To follow the process of Latin America's political modernization, the student would "have to master the model of the modern, which in turn can only be derived from the most careful empirical and formal analysis of the functions of the modern Western polities." In any case, scholars who specialized in Latin American studies enthusiastically embraced the modernization theory. Professor Johnson of Stanford University identified Latin America's rising urban middle sectors in the influential Latin American nations of Argentina, Brazil, Chile, and Mexico. They valued universal education and supported state policies to promote economic development and social welfare. They also organized into political parties and rejected the old notion of reliance on a strong leader or *personalismo*. Silvert agreed that he saw the emergence of a "modern" person who was a relativist, compromise-minded, and a secularist. In accepting "Western liberal values," middle sector groups rejected the "Mediterranean ethos" of dedication to hierarchy, order, and absolutes. This sense that Latin Americans would inevitably replicate U.S. institutions and adopt Anglo-American values reinforced the traditional North American faith in the existence of natural harmonies and communities of interest in the Western Hemisphere, or, in historian Arthur P. Whitaker's vision, the "Western Hemisphere idea."[45]

The passing of traditional societies seemed certain. But these scholars worried that, if the oligarchs of the old order delayed progress, people who demanded change might turn to "extremist conspiratorial leaders" who advocated the other universalistic social science theory— Marxism-Leninism. Communists were the "scavengers of the modernization process." The United States needed to insure that the transition to modernization proceeded in an evolutionary, not revolutionary, manner. In the late 1950s, Millikan, Pye, Rostow, and others repeatedly called for the United States to declare openly its "interest in the internal stability and development of other nations" and to support that declaration with foreign aid. The social scientists argued that Latin America would need $1.5 billion a year in outside capital during the

1960s and another $1 billion a year in the first half of the 1970s. With this public and private investment, Latin American nations would reach, in Rostow's famous phrase, the "take-off stage," when they began to underwrite their own economic development through internal investment and private borrowing. And, as Gordon noted, the "theory" held that "democracy would have better soil to work in if development were taking place."[46]

President Kennedy gave scholars opportunities to test their theories, inviting several to join his administration. Gordon and Whitaker both served on Berle's task force, and Gordon would become ambassador to Brazil and later assistant secretary of state for Latin America under President Lyndon Johnson. The energetic Rostow served Kennedy both in the White House and in the State Department. He later directed the NSC for President Johnson. Rostow encouraged Kennedy to make the 1960s the "economic development decade." He predicted that with U.S. assistance, Argentina, Brazil, Colombia, Mexico, and Venezuela would reach "complete take-off" by 1970. Within a decade, 80 percent of Latin America's population would be "off the dole."[47]

Sanguine predictions about Latin America's future arose not only from social science models but also from historical experience. Under the aegis of the Economic Cooperation Act (1948), the United States had rebuilt Western Europe in the immediate postwar years with a $12.4 billion investment. Now it was time to start the United States and the world moving once again—to replay the success of the 1940s. The Alliance for Progress would be the "Marshall Plan for Latin America." Occasionally a planner such as Gordon would argue that the Marshall Plan was a "misleading analogy." Overcoming grave socioeconomic inequities might be a more daunting task than "engendering economic recovery in industrially advanced nations temporarily crippled by war."[48] Nonetheless, as Thomas Mann, a veteran State Department officer widely known for his hard-boiled, skeptical outlook, noted, the Kennedy administration worked under an "illusion of omnipotence." The United States had reconstructed Europe; therefore, "it's going to work in Latin America." In the postwar world, the United States was "on the crest of a wave and nobody, literally nobody on the Hill or anywhere else ever questioned our ability to do anything." Mann, who became chief administrator for the Alliance during the Johnson presidency, confessed that in 1960–61 he shared that optimism.[49] Indeed, Gordon swallowed his doubts, telling a Brazilian audience in October 1961 that outside capital available to Latin America would "far exceed the Marshall Plan magnitudes" and that planning and foreign aid would generate economic development in Brazil as it had in southern Italy. As Rostow boasted, "Modern societies must be built and we are prepared to help build them." [50]

The aspiring architects of modern Latin America primarily came from the continental United States, although two men who had served in Puerto Rico, Moscoso and Arturo Morales-Carrión, assisted in the planning process. To be sure, Alliance planners consulted with Latin Americans, and most eagerly welcomed the new U.S. commitment. Since 1945, Latin America's leaders had complained that the United States neglected the region. Two weeks after the Nixon trip, President Juscelino Kubitschek of Brazil wrote to Eisenhower, calling for new hemispheric programs. Kubitschek suggested that the United States pledge $40 billion to Latin America over a twenty-year period. Washington was also aware that democrats like Betancourt and Figueres believed that the United States had foolishly fostered extremism by supporting right-wing dictators.[51] Latin Americans also bolstered the Kennedy administration's anticommunism. Authoritarian rulers like the Somoza family or General Stroessner invariably labeled their opposition as "Communist." But popularly elected leaders also delivered an anti-Communist message. Berle relayed Figueres's observation to the president-elect that "the Cold War is on in Latin America. If the United States is a spectator, she is lost." Rafael Caldera, the head of the Christian Democratic Party in Venezuela, used language reminiscent of Kennedy's Salt Lake City campaign speech when he told a U.S. audience that if Castro succeeded and the Alliance failed, they would see the "inevitable crumbling of Christian civilization." [52]

During the Alliance's formative period, a hint of hemispheric discord appeared over trade issues. Upon returning from his fact-finding tour of South America, Ambassador to the United Nations Stevenson reported that some leaders expressed more interest in trade and commodity price problems than in foreign aid.[53] Such comments reflected the work and theories of Raúl Prebisch, an Argentine economist who directed the United Nations' Economic Commission on Latin America (ECLA). The economies of most Latin American countries depended on the export of raw agricultural goods and minerals. Since the late 1940s, Prebisch had been producing studies that demonstrated that for most of the twentieth century, the "terms of trade" had been moving against producers of primary products like bananas, coffee, copper, and tin. Latin Americans annually paid more for their imported processed foods and manufactures and received less for their exports of raw food and metals. This process had accelerated in the late 1950s and contributed to the region's turmoil. Prebisch's findings questioned a basic premise of international capitalism, widely accepted since the days of Adam Smith, that the wealth of all nations would be increased by trading from comparative advantage. Prebisch met with Alliance planners and generally supported its goals, although he doubted that Latin America could or should replicate the development patterns of the United States.[54] U.S. officials sympathized with this feature of Latin America's plight and agreed to work on stabilizing the price of coffee, Latin America's chief export. But they declined to discuss establishing a fund to compensate for declines in export prices.[55]

Despite the dispute over trade, consensus and harmony characterized most meetings and discussions about the Alliance during the first half of 1961. Perhaps this concord discouraged planners from examining fundamental assumptions and asking hard questions. They presumed that a Castro-style revolution might engulf the hemisphere. They declined to speculate whether pre-1959 Cuba, because of its unusual colonial history, close ties to the United States, and peculiar sugar-based economy, had developed a uniquely fragile set of political, social, and intellectual institutions. The question of whether every Latin American radical possessed the obvious leadership skills and charismatic gifts of a Fidel Castro also went unaddressed.[56] Participants such as Gordon and Schlesinger have subsequently conceded that they badly exaggerated the region's potential for revolution. In Schlesinger's words, "We all underestimated the dead weight of vested interests, of structural rigidities, and of popular inertia." Castro and his compatriots, such as Ernesto "Ché" Guevara, undoubtedly also misjudged the region's receptivity to revolutionary change.[57] Alliance planners failed to analyze closely whether Latin American Communist organizations were vibrant and aggressive or weak and disorganized. They might have recalled that Castro came to power without the aid of either local or international Communists.[58] And they needed to separate Premier Khrushchev's rhetoric from the reality of his nation's capabilities. The issue of whether the Soviet Union had the military and financial resources to pursue a globalist foreign policy and extend its power throughout the Western Hemisphere demanded a sober assessment.

Alliance planners remained similarly uncritical about their economic hypotheses. They drew dubious lessons from the Marshall Plan experience, since what had worked in Belgium might not help Ecuador. Officials also seemingly forgot that the most dramatic political and socio-economic transformations had occurred in West Germany and Japan, countries occupied by U.S. troops for lengthy periods.[59] By the end of 1963, however, administration officials, including the president, were admitting that Latin America could not be readily compared to war-torn Europe. In their eagerness to modernize the region, U.S. officials also implicitly disparaged Latin America's traditions, institutions, and culture. Problems arose because of internal deficiencies, but the U.S. solutions depended on following external models. Self-reliance, individualism, and competitiveness superseded, for example, the Amerindian virtues of community and cooperation.[60] Remnants of the past must be discarded, albeit in an evolutionary manner. As George Ball, the sardonic under secretary of state, later saw it, hubris and arrogance had overtaken good intentions with "the cult of development economics." Nation building, "the most presumptuous undertaking of all," assumed that "American professors could make bricks without the straw of experience and with indifferent and infinitely various kinds of clay."[61]

Whatever its intellectual shortcomings and inherent contradictions, however, the Alliance for Progress came to fruition because President Kennedy had pledged to win the Cold War in Latin America. As he remarked to an aide, "Latin America's not like Asia or Africa. We can really accomplish something there."[62] Many Latin Americans shared the president's international outlook, of course, and the prospect of substantial foreign assistance probably also tempered any objections or doubts that they had about the program. The hemispheric neighbors adopted the charter of the Alliance for Progress at a meeting of finance ministers held at Punta del Este, Uruguay, in August 1961. Secretary of the Treasury Dillon led the U.S. delegation. The president preferred that economic and financial officials, rather than political operatives, control the proceedings, because he did not want Latin Americans to perceive the Alliance in purely Cold War terms. In the aftermath of the Bay of Pigs fiasco, Kennedy feared that they would think "that all we care about is Castro."[63]

At Punta del Este, Secretary Dillon revealed what the president meant in his eloquent message to the conference that "only an effort of towering dimensions can ensure fulfillment of our plan for a decade of progress." By 13 March 1962, the first anniversary of the president's Alliance speech, the United States would provide over $1 billion in public assistance to the region. Dillon further assured the Latin American delegates that over the next ten years they could expect more than $20 billion in public and private capital from the United States, international lending authorities, charitable foundations, and private U.S. investors. With this influx of foreign money and an additional $80 billion from internal investment, Latin American nations would enjoy a real economic growth rate of 2.5 percent a year, approximately double the rate of economic growth during the late 1950s. This sustained growth would underwrite impressive improvements in the health, education, and welfare of the people. Infant mortality rates would decline; life expectancy indices would rise. Common people would have access to potable water and sewer systems. Dillon specifically predicted that by 1970 all Latin American children would achieve literacy by the age of twelve. These pledges far surpassed what U.S. social scientists hoped for in the 1950s when they called on the United States to accelerate the modernization process. As Dillon informed Kennedy, Latin Americans would now understand that the United States was as boldly committed to the development of Latin America as it once was to the reconstruction of Western Europe.[64]

For their part, the economic ministers of Latin America pledged to reform their societies. Their governments would streamline bureaucratic procedures, enact progressive income tax laws, and promote agrarian reform. They would also give special preference to the poor, focusing on areas such as housing and education. U.S. delegates admitted that these promises lacked precision and detail and were cast in general language. What constituted agrarian reform went undefined. But they judged the conference an overwhelming success. Latin Americans finally believed that the United States would promote their welfare. The conference concluded with hearty backslapping and warm *abrazos*.[65]

A Cold War spat slightly marred the U.S. triumph at Punta del Este. The dominant personalities at the conference were Secretary Dillon and the Cuban delegate, Major Guevara. The two men cut strikingly different figures. With his pin-striped business suits and gray herringbone overcoat, Dillon dressed like the investment banker that he had once been. Ché Guevara strode into the conference rooms looking like the dashing revolutionary, with his olive green military fatigues, open shirt, black boots, and trademark beret. In the hot, stuffy rooms, he was the only comfortably dressed conferee. The former Argentine doctor alternately took confrontational and conciliatory stances. In his opening address, he claimed that Latin America's "new age" would be under "the star of Cuba," not the Alliance for Progress. He mischievously added that the Cuban Revolution fostered the new U.S. concern for the region and that whatever Alliance funds Latin America received bore "the stamp of Cuba." Thereafter, he took a constructive approach. In the spirit of reform, he proposed that military barracks be turned into schools. To everyone's amusement, he actually seconded a U.S. resolution that Latin Americans reduce import restrictions. The resolution carried. He emphasized that Cuba would not sabotage the conference, even suggesting that Cuba hoped for Alliance credits.[66] Guevara's diplomatic offensive unsettled the U.S. delegation, and Dillon hastily wired Washington for guidance. The United States dismissed Guevara's overtures; U.S. aid was for the "free world," not countries "under domination of communism." The conference ended in a verbal firestorm, with Guevara alleging imperialism and Dillon accusing the Cubans of inundating the conference "by a flood of falsity and lies."[67]

Ché Guevara accomplished his probable main goal at the conference — to reassure Latin Americans. The U.S.-Cuban confrontation was a bilateral dispute, not a hemispheric issue. He stressed that Cuba did not intend to export its revolution, observing only that "if there are not urgent measures to meet the demands of the people, the example of Cuba can take root in the countries of America." That statement ironically reiterated the position of the United States. As such, Latin Americans, led by Brazil, buried a Peruvian proposal, which was backed by the United States, to rebuke indirectly the Cuban Revolution.[68] After the last session of Punta del Este, Guevara again tried diplomacy, meeting informally with Richard Goodwin for several hours in the middle of the night at a reception. Guevara had previously sent Goodwin a handsomely designed box filled with the finest Havana cigars. Cuba would refrain from supporting revolutionary activity in other countries, he promised, if the United States would stop trying to overthrow the Cuban government by force and lift the trade embargo. Goodwin personally informed President Kennedy of his conversation and circulated a memorandum to national security officials. Predictably, nothing substantive came from the Guevara-Goodwin exchange. The Kennedy administration designed the Alliance for Progress to prevent the spread of communism. An accommodation with Castro's Cuba would have undermined a central purpose of the Alliance. The president's only tangible gesture was to smoke one of Ché's cigars.[69]

✦   With the Alliance for Progress, the United States had a blueprint for building sturdy, self-reliant, anti-Communist societies. But

U.S. officials worried that the reform process would take time and that they would encounter obstacles to change. Latin America faced immediate peril from the international Communist conspiracy. Even before completing work on the Alliance plan, the Kennedy administration had initiated a series of extraordinary measures to contain political turmoil and win the Cold War in the Caribbean region.

2 ★ Gunboat Diplomacy

The John F. Kennedy administration promised that, under the aegis of the Alliance for Progress, the United States would build democratic, socially progressive, anti-Communist societies. But winning the Cold War in Latin America required more than just providing substantial economic assistance to the region. The United States needed reform-minded Latin American leaders who would make hard choices on critical domestic issues like land and tax reform. It also demanded that those leaders unfailingly follow the U.S. lead in the war against international communism. The search for such individuals justified massive interventions in the internal affairs of the Dominican Republic and Haiti. Between 1961 and 1963, President Kennedy and his administration practiced a form of gunboat diplomacy in the Caribbean that had not been seen since the era of Theodore Roosevelt and Woodrow Wilson.

★   When President Kennedy assumed office, the United States no longer had diplomatic relations with Fidel Castro's Cuba. On 3 January 1961, President Dwight Eisenhower had broken diplomatic relations with Cuba, and on 5 January he accepted a Department of State recommendation to urge the incoming administration to invoke the Trading with the Enemy Act and suspend trade with Cuba. One day before leaving office, Eisenhower also privately urged his successor to do "whatever is necessary" to insure the success of the army of Cuban exiles that the CIA was training in Guatemala.[1] But the war against Cuba was not the only diplomatic and military campaign in the Western Hemisphere that Eisenhower bequeathed to Kennedy. The United States had also broken diplomatic relations with the Dominican Republic of Rafael Trujillo and was assisting insurgents who aimed to overthrow the dictator.

Rafael Leonidas Trujillo Molina, the absolute military dictator of the Dominican Republic, was a product of the Dominican National Guard, the constabulary created by the U.S. Marines during their occupation of the country between 1916 and 1924. Trujillo, who was recruited by the marines and rose rapidly through the ranks, seized power in 1930 and used his position as commander-in-chief to maintain for three decades one of the most odious regimes in the history of the Americas. He also cultivated relations with Washington. He promoted U.S. trade and investment and retired the nation's substantial international debt, and with great fanfare, he aligned the Dominican Republic with the United States during World War II and the Cold War. In view of Trujillo's ability to keep his country stable and friendly, many U.S. officials were willing to overlook his gross violations of fundamental human rights. During the 1950s, for example, Trujillo received hearty praise, public embraces from Vice President Richard Nixon and U.S. ambassadors, and approximately $6 million in military assistance.[2]

But during the late 1950s, a heated debate erupted over U.S. policies toward Trujillo. The murderous Dominican strongman extended his tyranny to the United States. He also began to stray from the U.S. position on international issues. In 1956, in New York City, his henchmen kidnapped and murdered Jesús de Galíndez, a Spanish citizen and Columbia University scholar who had written a scathing indictment of Trujillo. Trujillo's men then executed Charles Murphy, an aviator from Oregon who had piloted the plane that took de Galíndez from New York to the Dominican Republic. The de Galíndez and Murphy murders gained national attention through the persistent efforts of Oregon congressman Charles Porter. Trujillo's agents responded to the uproar by arresting and then murdering in prison Octavio de la Maza, a pilot and friend of Murphy. Dominican officials claimed that de la Maza left a suicide note in which he took responsibility for Murphy's death. Beyond fabricating evidence, Trujillo defended himself by having his fifty-four consulates in the United States take out advertisements in newspapers and by planting stories with friendly journalists, reminding readers that he was a staunch anti-Communist. Further, he bribed U.S. officials, including congressmen who sat on committees that allocated a sugar quota to the Dominican Republic. The Trujillo family controlled about 60 percent of the island's sugar industry.[3]

U.S. officials had long recognized that the Dominican Republic's conduct under Trujillo was "below the level of recognized civilian nations, certainly not much above that of the communists." But after Castro's seizure of power in 1959, they concluded that Trujillo had become a Cold War liability. U.S. officials reasoned from analogy. A tyrant in a sugar-producing island had "liquidated and enfeebled" moderate political opponents and polarized the political milieu, thereby providing an opportunity for radicals. The United States could not permit "Batista-like" conditions to develop again. It had to learn the lessons of history to prevent "a domino effect of Castro-like governments" throughout the Caribbean. In November 1959, the same month the Eisenhower administration had decided that constructive relations were over with Castro, State Department officers agreed that the United States would have to bring about the post-Trujillo era.[4]

Throughout 1960, the United States learned about the limits of its power as it applied to Trujillo. The tough old dictator spurned U.S. suggestions that he step down and take up a comfortable exile with a bountiful "trust fund." He also undermined a U.S. plan to cultivate a moderate, middle-class political opposition, ordering a roundup of prominent businessmen, intellectuals, and professionals. And he continued to attack his opponents outside of the Dominican Republic. He despised the region's emerging democratic politicians. On 24 June 1960, his agents attempted to assassinate Rómulo Betancourt, the president of Venezuela, by detonating a bomb planted on a street in Caracas near his passing automobile; Betancourt survived, but his hands were severely burned. The United States responded to this vicious attack by breaking diplomatic relations with the Dominican Republic in August 1960 and by imposing an arms embargo. In January 1961, the Eisenhower administration increased the pressure on Trujillo, banning the export of petroleum products, trucks, and truck parts to the Dominican Republic.

Although the administration closed its embassy in Cuidad Trujillo, the Dominican capital, it left its three consulates on the island open in order to preserve bases for CIA agents. Henry Dearborn, the deputy chief of the U.S. mission, became consul general and de facto CIA chief of station. Since 1959, Dearborn had been a relentless critic of Trujillo, graphically depicting for Washington the dictator's brutality. He once boldly asserted that "if I were a Dominican, I would favor destroying Trujillo as the first necessary step in the salvation of my country." Dearborn's superiors accepted his assessment. In the latter half of 1960, CIA agents discussed transferring weapons to Dominicans who vowed to assassinate Trujillo. On 3 January 1961, President Eisenhower ordered his national security advisors "to do as much as we can and quickly about Trujillo." Nine days later, the 5412 Committee, the special group that oversaw covert activities, ruled that the CIA could send small arms to Dominican dissidents. In the first months of 1961, Consul General Dearborn, through an intermediary, passed pistols and carbines to Dominicans.[5]

Much as he did with the project to overthrow Castro, President Kennedy adopted Eisenhower's scheme to rid the Dominican Republic of Trujillo. The administration judged Trujillo harmful to U.S. interests on several counts. Administration officials agreed that the "paramount interest" was to prevent a "Castro-Communist" takeover of the island. And Dearborn reiterated that "our theme has been that the longer Trujillo continues to dominate the D.R. the more susceptible the country is becoming to leftist extremists."[6] Opposition to Trujillo also provided diplomatic benefits. By denouncing a right-wing regime, the administration could claim that it was not obsessed with communism and that the Alliance for Progress stood for democracy. In his March 1961 speech announcing the Alliance, President Kennedy linked Castro and Trujillo, expressing a "special friendship to the people of Cuba and the Dominican Republic—and the hope that they will soon rejoin the society of free men, uniting with us in our common effort."[7] Anti-Trujillo actions also reassured Latin American democrats like Betancourt about the U.S. commitment to reform and change. Trujillo also earned new U.S. enmity when he began to collaborate with the enemy. Dominican radio stations praised the Cuban Revolution and attacked U.S. "imperialism." Trujillo's henchmen secretly conferred with Cuban and Soviet authorities. Notably, Havana no longer denounced Trujillo.[8]

The administration's first move against Trujillo was a public one. President Kennedy requested that Congress deny the Dominican Republic any "windfall" from Cuba's sugar quota for the last nine months of 1961. In late 1960, President Eisenhower had been forced to impose punitive excise taxes on imports of Dominican sugar when Trujillo's congressional friends tried to transfer the Cuban preference to the Dominican Republic. With unified support from Republican leaders, who had conferred with Eisenhower and Nixon, the administration managed in March 1961 to push legislation out of the agricultural committees and through Congress.

In mid-February 1961, administration officials responsible for national security affairs received a briefing from the CIA on the ongoing covert campaign against Trujillo. On 15 February, Secretary of State Dean Rusk informed the president that the United States had passed small arms and sabotage equipment to Dominican dissidents.[9] In congressional hearings in the mid-1970s and in subsequent memoirs, administration officials claimed that they and the president did not realize until May 1961 that the United States had joined with assassins. They presumably thought the Dominicans wanted the weapons for personal protection.[10] But Consul General Dearborn could not have been more explicit about the motives of the dissidents. On 22 March 1961, he informed Washington that his Dominican contacts viewed "liquidation as the only way to accomplish their ends." He admitted that some conspirators were morally bankrupt, even criminals, but an attack on Trujillo by such men could be justified. Dearborn added: "Political assassination is ugly and repulsive, but everything must be judged in its own terms."[11] White House officials like Richard Goodwin monitored cable traffic, and copies can be found in NSC files. No written evidence exists proving that the president fully understood what Dearborn had reported. As Arthur Schlesinger has pointed out, assassination responsibility arguments come down to "the argument that they must have known."[12] Schlesinger's defense of his boss seems especially ironic in view of President Kennedy's well-known desire to take complete control of U.S. foreign policy. In any case, the CIA did not initially act as if it had been discouraged by the new administration, and it never received criticism or a reprimand for its activities in the Dominican Republic. Agents constantly met with the conspirators, and in April the CIA sent four machine guns and ammunition through diplomatic pouch to the U.S. consulate in Cuidad Trujillo.[13]

Just as President Kennedy was about to launch the Bay of Pigs invasion, his administration made one last attempt to reason with Trujillo. On 15–16 April 1961, at the behest of the president, veteran U.S. diplomat Robert D. Murphy, accompanied by Igor Cassini, met with Trujillo to discuss his future. Cassini was a friend of the president's father, Joseph P. Kennedy, had ties to Trujillo, and acted as an unregistered agent for the generalissimo in the United States. The president knew Cassini's brother, Oleg, who designed dresses for Jacqueline Kennedy. In his lengthy talks with Murphy, Trujillo vowed not to flee his nation as Fulgencio Batista had fled Cuba. Trujillo had previously protested that he had already stepped aside, because Joaquín Balaguer, a prominent Dominican scholar, actually held the title of president. But Balaguer's political independence could be questioned; in his essays he often referred to "God and Trujillo" in the same sentence. Trujillo assured Murphy that he would realign his nation with U.S. international positions. Murphy accepted Trujillo's promises, recommending that the administration reconcile with a traditional Cold War partner. In a covering memorandum, however, National Security Advisor McGeorge Bundy ridiculed Murphy's recommendation, noting that "the Alliance for Progress would be gravely shadowed in the eyes of Latin Americans" by a rapprochement with Trujillo.[14]

Castro's rout of the Bay of Pigs invaders on 17–19 April 1961 caused the administration to hesitate in taking the decisive step against Trujillo. On 25 April, the CIA instructed Dearborn not to pass the machine guns and to inform the dissidents that the United States was not presently prepared to cope with the aftermath of an assassination. At an NSC meeting on 5 May 1961, Kennedy ruled that the United States should not initiate the overthrow of Trujillo before knowing what government would succeed him. He also ordered the U.S. military to be prepared to invade the Dominican Republic to prevent a Communist takeover. The president's ruling left Dearborn incredulous. For a year the United States had been nurturing the effort to overthrow Trujillo; it was "too late to consider whether [the] United States would initiate [the] overthrow of Trujillo." Kennedy clarified U.S. policy for Dearborn. On 25 May, "in view of the reported imminence of an attempt to assassinate Trujillo," he approved a contingency plan that authorized Dearborn to assure friendly Dominicans that they could count on U.S. military support to consolidate their hold on a post-Trujillo government. If "unfriendly elements" seized power after Trujillo's demise, Dearborn had the authority to urge pro-U.S. groups to declare themselves the provisional government and request help from the United States and the OAS. The president's final word, as expressed in a cable he helped write and sent on 29 May to Dearborn, was that the United States wanted to be associated with the removal of Trujillo so as to derive credit among Dominicans and Latin American liberals, but that "we must not run the risk of U.S. association with political assassination."[15]

The next evening, 30 May 1961, members of the "action group" of the Dominican dissidents ambushed and assassinated Trujillo. The aged dictator, traveling only with his chauffeur, was on his way to see his twenty-year-old mistress. One of the assassins was Antonio de la Maza, the brother of the slain Octavio de la Maza of the de Galíndez–Murphy case. The other assassins held similar grievances against Trujillo. The assassins apparently had with them the CIA-supplied pistols and carbines.[16]

President Kennedy and his advisors were perhaps surprised by at least the timing of the attack. The president was in Paris meeting with President Charles de Gaulle and preparing for his meeting with Soviet premier Nikita Khrushchev in Vienna. Press Secretary Pierre Salinger immediately blundered, announcing Trujillo's death before official word came from Cuidad Trujillo. Salinger had inadvertently created the impression that the United States had participated in the assassination.[17] The president both chastised Salinger and ordered Secretary Rusk to stay behind in the United States for a day to survey the situation. Warships, loaded with 12,000 combat-ready marines, patrolled sixty miles off the Dominican coastline. Consul General Dearborn, who was immediately informed of Trujillo's death, reported that it was "highly unsafe" for him to maintain contact with the dissidents. He and CIA personnel were recalled to Washington. The State Department, however, ordered them first to destroy records concerning contacts with dissidents but not to destroy the president's last exculpatory cable of 29 May.[18]

In Washington, White House officials panicked during the first days after Trujillo's death. Uncertain of who now controlled the government in Cuidad Trujillo, they feared that the administration could suffer another foreign policy disaster in the Caribbean. Castro might take advantage of the chaos and team up with evil Dominicans. Attorney General Kennedy, Goodwin, and Schlesinger vehemently argued that the administration should follow the contingency plan formulated in late May and encourage pro-U.S. Dominicans to request a military intervention. According to Under Secretary Bowles, Kennedy even suggested blowing up the consulate to provide the rationale for the invasion. Bowles rallied State Department officers against the idea of sending in U.S. forces "to take over the island without regard for the Organization of American States, treaties, or common sense." To act in a "reckless manner," Bowles added, would only be to compound "the mistake of Cuba." Robert Kennedy, who had heaped vitriol upon the State Department after the Bay of Pigs, again became personally abusive, calling Bowles "a gutless wonder." Bowles resorted to telephoning the president in Europe, asking him to calm his brother down.[19]

Depraved Dominicans indeed seized power after Trujillo's assassination, but they were no friends of Castro. The dictator's security apparatus reacted rapidly and captured or killed all but two of the conspirators. Trujillo's two brothers, who controlled private armies, terrorized political opponents. Trujillo's vindictive son, Rafael Leonidas Trujillo Jr., or "Ramfis," returned from Europe, took charge of the armed forces, and personally supervised the torture and execution of the conspirators. And the Trujillo family maintained its stranglehold on the Dominican economy. As Adolf Berle regretfully told his diary, the new Dominican strongmen "are pretty nearly the lowest form of life in government."[20]

Back from Vienna, President Kennedy reviewed the Dominican situation with aides on 7 June 1961. His brother, in a pacific mood that day, proposed that the administration give Ramfis a chance to fulfill his pledge to move the nation toward democracy. Ramfis had contacted Robert Murphy through Porfirio Rubirosa, the international playboy and sometime Dominican diplomat. Henry Dearborn, also now back in Washington, observed that such promises "were the same moves that Trujillo had always made without any intended impact on the structure of his regime." Dearborn indicated that competent democratic groups existed on the island. In his last report from the Dominican Republic, he had urged that the United States drive the Trujillo family out with military force.[21] The president accepted neither his brother's suggestion of inaction nor Dearborn's aggressive plans. The United States had to focus on winning the Cold War. As Schlesinger recorded, Kennedy listed U.S. policy options for the Dominican Republic. The president said: "There are three possibilities in descending order of preference: a decent democratic regime, a continuation of the Trujillo regime, or a Castro regime. We ought to aim at the first, but we really can't renounce the second until we are sure that we can avoid the third."[22]

Over the next thirty months, U.S. Dominican policy reflected the president's famous descending order of preferences. The State Department sent John C. Hill, the department's longtime liaison with the CIA for Latin America, to replace Dearborn as consul general. In 1954 Hill had helped topple Jacobo Arbenz Guzmán, the alleged Marxist leader of Guatemala. Hill's objectives were first to prevent "Castro/communism" and then to help establish "a friendly government as democratic as possible." Joaquín Balaguer, who remained the nominal president, was informed in July 1961 that Hill had direct access to Kennedy. Kennedy had actually taken time to become "well acquainted" with Hill. What Kennedy considered of "utmost importance" was that the government move toward democracy. But the president wanted Balaguer to know that he was specifically interested in the "progress of anti-Communist laws in [the] Dominican Congress, measures taken [to] exclude [the] return [of] Communist and Castroist exiles, and other actions taken [to] prevent infiltration and agitation by Communist-Castroist elements." The administration also assured Balaguer that the United States would lend military support to stop a "Castroist invasion" of the Dominican Republic. Hill delivered the same message to Ramfis Trujillo in a series of cordial chats with the power behind the throne.[23] This alarm about communism in the Dominican Republic again arose from analogy. U.S. intelligence analysts largely discounted the actual threat.[24]

In deciding to work with the younger Trujillo and Balaguer, the administration assumed that their regime could last until May 1962, when elections were promised. In late August, President Kennedy informed aides that the United States would back Balaguer because he "is our only tool" and because "the anti-Communist liberals are not strong enough." The president wistfully hoped that a Nehru-like figure would emerge who could command popular support, tame the military, and carry out socioeconomic reform. But the president would take no chances. He constantly peppered aides with questions about communism and warned them that "we don't want to have another Cuba to come out of the Dominican Republic." He reportedly predicted that his first year in office would be successful if neither the Congo nor the Dominican Republic was lost to international communism.[25] In the meantime, the United States would wait, in Rusk's words, until it could "persuade the Trujillo family to leave the island in an orderly way that will not result in conditions that might give an opportunity for Castroism." The administration took up Eisenhower's scheme of establishing a trust fund to entice the Trujillos into exile and began to consider lifting some of the diplomatic and economic sanctions against the Dominican Republic. It also established a field-level U.S. military mission on the island in order to strengthen ties with Dominican military officers.[26]

After thirty years of tyranny, Dominicans were disinclined to be patient. They staged massive antigovernment demonstrations when an OAS inspection team arrived on the island in mid-September. Demonstrators pleaded for the OAS to maintain sanctions until the old regime left. U.S. intelligence analysts now understood that the Trujillos leaving the island had "become an obsession" for Dominicans. Dominican democrats were losing faith in the United States, with a concomitant growth of "Castro-minded influence." The Trujillos might not leave, and they might strike a *golpe de estado*, which would only polarize the international and domestic political milieu. The journalist John Bartlow Martin, whom Kennedy sent on a fact-finding mission, concurred, reporting that a renewed Trujillo regime would destroy the middle class, thereby insuring that the next revolution would be "proletarian and leftist."[27]

Confronted with the collapse of his evolutionary scheme, Kennedy acted resolutely. In October he dispatched State Department officer George C. McGhee to Cuidad Trujillo to tell the Trujillos that they must leave the island. When the family balked, Rusk publicly announced on 18 November that the United States would not "remain idle" if the

Trujillos tried to reassert "dictatorial domination." Eight U.S. warships loomed on the Dominican horizon. U.S. fighter jets buzzed the capital's shoreline, and U.S. military attachés encouraged Dominican officers to desert the Trujillos. By 20 November, the Trujillo clan, including Hector and Arismendi, "the wicked uncles," had fled into exile. They left with substantial amounts of money. Ramfis slipped away on his yacht, bringing along his father's refrigerated body.[28]

Both friends like Brazil and enemies like Cuba protested that the United States had violated the nonintervention principle, "the key to the inter-American system."[29] But President Kennedy was undeterred, continuing his remarkable cleansing of the Dominican body politic. In mid-December, Consul General Hill received presidential authorization to demand that President Balaguer transfer power to a council of state. As instructed, Hill couched the ultimatum in the polite language of diplomacy, noting that by stepping aside the Dominican could achieve "a secure position in the history of his country and of western democracy." But he also observed that the United States would not lift diplomatic and economic sanctions until Balaguer left and any delay would do "serious damage to the international reputation of the United States." After Balaguer agreed to U.S. terms, Hill brought the personal congratulations of President Kennedy. Balaguer could only smile, perhaps bitterly, and remark, "After all, it was President Kennedy's plan."[30] When Balaguer resigned, however, political turmoil rocked the Dominican Republic. On 16 January 1962, General Pedro Rafael Rodríguez Echavarría, the right-wing commander of the air force, seized power and ousted the Council of State. U.S. diplomats immediately threatened to break the diplomatic relations that had just been restored and presumably encouraged Dominican officers to oppose their general. On 18 January the *golpe* ended when Rodríguez Echavarría was arrested by his own men. Summarizing the foreign policy of intervention, Hill observed that the United States had earned the gratitude of politically conscious Dominicans for ending the Trujillo dictatorship. It had also created a government unusually "dependent on US in this age of nationalism."[31]

Through 1962, the administration guided the seven-man Council of State toward electoral democracy. The journey proved difficult, for the dominant members of the council were unsavory characters: Luis Amiama Tió and Antonio Imbert Barrera, the surviving assassins of Trujillo. U.S. diplomats constantly reminded all that the United States "would view with grave concern" the overthrow of the council. The administration backed those warnings with a series of naval visits to the

Dominican Republic in order to provide tangible "evidence of our close watch over the situation and of our support for the present Government." Having already invested so much effort in Dominican politics, U.S. officials reasoned that they would "not be unduly concerned about intervention." By intervening, the administration hoped to fulfill the president's goal of a decent regime while simultaneously controlling "the far left (Castro/Communist) and the far right (Trujillistas)." [32] Beyond deploying the U.S. Navy, the administration tried to control developments by releasing the $22 million that President Eisenhower had collected in punitive excise taxes on Dominican sugar and by granting Alliance for Progress funds. So as not to incite the military, it recommended that Dominicans slow the purge of Trujillistas in the armed forces. And it worked to forestall potential leftist agitation. President Kennedy personally ordered aides to improve security by teaching riot control techniques to the Dominican police force. The administration transferred $60,000 in police equipment and brought 500 Dominicans to the United States for police training. Despite this massive effort, the administration was uncertain it would succeed, privately pledging to delay elections if it became "apparent that the results would be contrary to our interests." [33]

In December 1962, Dominicans voted for a presidential candidate acceptable to the United States. Juan Bosch, the leader of the Partido Revolucionario Dominicano (PRD), won 60 percent of the vote, easily outdistancing the candidate of the Unión Cívica Nacional (UCN), a coalition of businessmen and middle-class Dominicans. Bosch, a friend of Betancourt and José Figueres, was another member of Latin America's democratic left. He had spent a most of his adult life in exile, where he helped organize the PRD, the oldest of the anti-Trujillo political organizations. During his presidential campaign, he made populist appeals, promising to address the grievances of Dominican peasants and workers. An intellectual, Bosch had published essays and fiction. He also was a dynamic public speaker. Dominicans particularly admired his dedication, honesty, and frugality. When he took office in February 1963, he was practically destitute.

Although Bosch seemed capable of creating the "decent, democratic regime" that the United States wanted, the Kennedy administration ultimately disdained him. Bosch failed the administration's rigorous anti-Communist test. Relations began well when President-elect Bosch called on Kennedy in January 1963. Kennedy characteristically opened the meeting by asking Bosch "what the United States could do to assist the Dominican Republic" and whether the $40 million in U.S. loans and grants was "effective enough." These Alliance for Progress funds underwrote public works, rural development, and school construction. For example, 28,000 Dominicans worked on projects expanding water supply systems, repairing canals, and constructing gutters, curbs, and sidewalks. Bosch expressed satisfaction with the U.S. aid and further praised Kennedy for his global leadership. He congratulated the president for his triumph in the Cuban Missile Crisis and for having "unmasked Castro in the eyes of many Latin Americans." The two leaders also discussed what methods the United States and Latin American nations could use to overthrow Fidel Castro.[34]

Despite the cordial meeting between the two presidents, administration officials immediately predicted that Juan Bosch would fail to transform the Dominican Republic into an progressive, anti-Communist country. Both Secretary Rusk and Under Secretary Ball judged Bosch an impractical dreamer, lacking administrative skills. Ball judged Bosch as "unrealistic, arrogant, and erratic" and "incapable of even running a small social club, much less a country in turmoil."[35] In truth, Bosch did not always act like a modern North American chief executive. During his brief six months in office, he declined to delegate responsibility, and he spent countless hours listening to the special problems of poor Dominicans. But in the aftermath of thirty years of Trujillo's tyranny, very few Dominicans had administrative or governmental experience. And Bosch spent time with people who had been subjected to unspeakable horrors for decades. In any case, Bosch, who worked sixteen-hour days, accomplished reforms. He shepherded through the Dominican assembly a modern constitution that created a secular state and protected the rights of workers. He also maintained public order, preserved individual liberty, and preached fiscal responsibility. These reforms predictably earned Bosch the enmity of traditionally privileged sectors of Dominican society. Such resistance to change had prompted U.S. intelligence analysts to predict, even before Bosch took office, that "there is a strong possibility that the transition to representative government will break down."[36]

Ambassador John Bartlow Martin relentlessly criticized President Bosch. Martin had earned his ambassadorial appointment in gratitude for his September 1961 analysis of Ramfis Trujillo's regime. Martin had no previous diplomatic experience, having been a freelance journalist who had written campaign speeches for both Adlai Stevenson and Kennedy. He fancied himself a Roman consul whose word should be law in the Dominican Republic. He once informed the State Department that "we should attempt to take his [Bosch's] government away from him." Bosch stood condemned because he declined to take Martin's advice unfailingly.[37] The ambassador's arrogance was superseded only by his verbosity; his reports to Washington ranged from 30 to 100 pages in length. Martin identified with propertied groups in the Dominican Republic who had opposed Trujillo. In December 1962, he had favored the election of UCN candidates. Thereafter, he could not bring himself to report anything positive about Bosch. In January 1963, he even suggested that the incoming president "has been a deep-cover communist for many years."[38]

Martin's primary criticism of Bosch was that he did not outlaw domestic radicals. The new president repealed the U.S.-sponsored Emergency Law of 1962, which controlled the entrance of subversives and permitted their deportation. The Dominican permitted exiled Marxist-Leninists to return home and engage in political activities. He reasoned that this was the proper democratic course to follow and that he could best control radicals when they operated in public. His supporters considered the Emergency Law a Trujillo-like measure. Bosch also judged that the most ominous threat to Dominican democracy came not from the left but from the political right. He did not have effective control over the military or the Dominican police, a force of 15,000 under the control of Antonio Imbert, the right-wing assassin. As such, he could not afford politically to alienate left-wing groups who supported his reform program. Martin was unmoved by such considerations, telling Bosch he must arrest Communists and deport them. He also complained that Bosch did not denounce communism as often as he and Dominican elites would like. In fact, in a speech to the Dominican armed forces, Bosch described communism as meaning "death, war, destruction and the loss of all our properties."[39] In the Martin-Bosch debate, the CIA essentially accepted President Bosch's analysis. It agreed that he was imperiled by a right-wing military *golpe*. Bosch was not, as Martin had speculated, a Communist, and communism was only a "potential" threat in the Dominican Republic. The CIA identified four radical groups with 4,000 members. Because the four groups were not united, "present Communist strength is not formidable."[40]

The CIA and Bosch proved politically prescient, for the Dominican military, backed by Imbert's police, overthrew Bosch on 25 September 1963. The *golpistas* justified their attack with the spurious allegation that Bosch was delivering the nation into the hands of the Communists.

Ambassador Martin opposed the *golpe*, but he immediately told Washington that "I have no desire to return him, or his Cabinet or PRD to power."[41] The ambassador had persuaded his superiors; State Department and NSC officials spoke disparagingly of Bosch, blaming him for refusing "to adopt a firm policy against Communism and Castro, despite repeated warnings from the military and recent well-attended anti-Communist demonstrations."[42] Nonetheless, the administration recognized that Bosch's overthrow had undermined its Dominican policy. Many of the leading *golpistas* had ties to the Trujillo regime. On 4 October, President Kennedy ordered Secretary of Defense McNamara to review contingency plans for a possible military intervention in the Caribbean. The administration also withheld diplomatic recognition, insisting that the new Dominican rulers pledge to hold internationally supervised elections within a year.[43] The *golpistas* rejected the U.S. demand, although they placed three civilians in figurehead positions. By 1 November, Kennedy had essentially decided to resume relations with the Dominican Republic. He no longer wanted to spend diplomatic capital on it, and State Department analysts advised the president that the new rulers seemed amenable to enacting "a Dominican Republic version of our Smith Act" to suppress domestic radicals.[44] The United States restored relations on 14 December 1963, three weeks after Kennedy's death. As the new Johnson administration explained, recognition "will enable us [to] help Dominicans stop possible Cuban arms shipments and strengthen regime's position [to] suppress guerrilla and other extremist-provoked disorders."[45]

The Kennedy administration's inability to force Dominican leaders to schedule an election again demonstrated limits to U.S. power in the Caribbean. Juan Bosch fell from power for domestic reasons. But the administration's wavering commitment to democracy probably encouraged the Dominican military to strike. Ambassador Martin was notably indiscreet. His constant carping about the Communist threat provided credibility to Bosch's conservative critics. Indeed, just three days before the *golpe*, he submitted to Washington a sarcastic assessment of the Dominican president, concluding that Bosch was "a lousy president." And, with his superiors' approval, he maintained close contact with Bosch's enemies in the military and police. He described that policy as saving "an ace in the hole." Men like Imbert and Amiama were offensive, "but we can have no new Castro in the Caribbean."[46] The administration also continued to discourage a purge of reactionary elements in the armed forces, considering them "a major factor in internal stability." Its new police training and counterinsurgency programs actually increased the size of Dominican security forces. It allocated $3.3 million a year to the Dominican military. And during the 1960s, the United States would spend over $3 million on the training and the equipping of the Dominican police. U.S. diplomats conceded that such security programs heightened fears about communism, inevitably increasing tension in the Dominican polity.[47]

U.S. policy toward the Dominican Republic had come full circle by the end of 1963. U.S. officials prepared to deal with men such as Colonel Elías Wessin y Wessin, who trained under Trujillo, pilfered public funds, and indiscriminately condemned all opponents as "Communists."[48] President Kennedy and his advisors seemingly forgot the historical lesson that only enlightened, socially progressive, democratic leaders could undermine the appeal of communism in Latin America. Their fear of Castro and communism tempered their zeal for democracy and reform. As Kennedy had observed, better a Trujillo than a Castro. But this faith in authoritarianism proved as suspect in the 1960s as it did in the 1950s. Trujillo's heirs could not quell demands for political change and social justice. In April 1965, President Johnson responded by sending 20,000 U.S. troops to the Dominican Republic to enforce an anti-Communist stability.

✦   The Kennedy administration's policies toward Haiti followed a pattern similar to actions pursued toward the neighboring Dominican Republic. The United States attacked a hideous dictator who tortured, robbed, and murdered innocent civilians. U.S. officials again worried that desperate Haitians would look to extremist, Castro-like revolutionaries. They searched for leaders dedicated to uplifting the Haitian people and preserving the national security of the United States. When that mission turned out to be impossible, the administration resigned itself to living with a dictator who repressed all opponents, including political radicals.

François "Papa Doc" Duvalier (1957–71) subjected his long-suffering nation to rule that was both savage and bizarre. Born into modest circumstances in the Haitian capital of Port-au-Prince, Duvalier achieved some distinction by completing a medical degree in Haiti, studying public health at the University of Michigan, and directing public health efforts at home. He also became a local expert in native folklore and ethnology. He came to power in October 1957, after a period of political chaos in Haiti. In December 1956, a general strike and the intervention of the U.S. ambassador had helped bring down President Paul Magloire (1950–56), a notoriously corrupt figure. Thereafter, Haiti became increasingly disorderly, with several governments rising and falling. The Haitian military supported Duvalier in a presidential election of dubious legality. When Duvalier's opponents protested the electoral outcome, the military responded by imposing martial law.[49]

Duvalier rapidly built his own base of power, parceling out government posts to sycophants. Emulating the Trujillo clan, he and his family took control of Haitian industries. He groomed his chubby young son, Jean-Claude Duvalier (1971–86), as his successor. He also provided psychological satisfaction to the black masses by lashing out at the French-speaking mulatto elite that had dominated the country. He reminded nationalistic followers that mulattos had collaborated with foreigners when the U.S. Marines ruled the country from 1915 to 1934. Native religious practices were elevated and European faiths, such as Roman Catholicism, were denigrated. Skilled and educated Haitians eventually fled the country in terror. Duvalier further consolidated his hold on power by devising a counterweight to the 5,000-man Haitian National Guard. He created a uniformed militia, or political police, loyal to him. Out of uniform were the Tonton Macoutes, or "bogeymen" in the native Creole slang. Operating out of the National Palace, these 1,000 or so terrorists robbed, tortured, raped, and murdered not only critics of Papa Doc but also peaceful, apolitical Haitians. Duvalier allegedly participated in the beating and torture of dissidents. In mid-1958, one horrified U.S. diplomat reported, with perhaps some sense of irony, that the Tonton Macoutes were "masked night riders reminiscent of the Ku Klux Klan."[50]

Such brutality compounded the miseries of the poorest people in the Western Hemisphere. Haitians had a per capita income of $85. Illiteracy rates were at 90 percent, half the children were malnourished, and life expectancy was forty-three years of age. The small country lacked natural resources other than fertile land. But with 4.3 million people, Haiti had a population density higher than India's. Erosion, deforestation, and environmental degradation threatened Haiti's land and its agricultural output. International assistance helped prevent economic collapse and mass starvation. Haiti was one of the few Latin American countries to receive any U.S. foreign aid in the immediate postwar period. Between 1945 and 1960, U.S. agencies granted Haiti $70 million, primarily in budgetary assistance and donations of food. The United States actually covered about one-third of Haiti's governmental expenditures. In

1961 the Kennedy administration provided approximately $15 million in aid.[51] Despite their wrenching problems, Haitians intensely loved their country, their African heritage, and their history, proudly recalling that their ancestors had thrown French slave masters into the sea and established an independent republic in 1804.

Haiti held little tangible value for the United States. Trade amounted to only $50 million a year, and the United States did not import strategic minerals from Haiti. U.S. direct investments were minuscule. The U.S. military did not have any bases or missile tracking stations there. Haiti did lie, however, in a strategic position along the Windward Passage. In the postwar period, U.S. diplomats focused on keeping Haiti aligned with the United States at the OAS and the United Nations. After 1959, they worried, of course, about communism in the Caribbean.

Duvalier's Haiti became a contested topic in the new Kennedy government. Adolf Berle called upon the administration to dispose of the vicious and venal Duvalier, again arguing that the United States needed to learn the historical lessons of Batista's Cuba and take a stand against dictatorship. He privately met with Haitian exiles, suggesting that the United States would back them if they attacked Duvalier. Career officers in the State Department opposed Berle's plot, sharply questioning the abilities of Haitian dissidents. They predicted that chaos and a struggle for power would follow the overthrow of Duvalier, thereby facilitating "the Castro-Communist penetration into Haiti."[52] On 2 June 1961, three days after the assassination of Trujillo, Secretary of State Rusk, in Paris with the president, temporarily settled the issue. The United States did not need a third crisis in the Caribbean. The administration would continue to live with the Duvalier regime because no acceptable alternative presented itself. Rusk further recommended that the United States should try to help develop Haiti, with the hope that Duvalier "just might have moments when he yearns to be a decent man." The secretary readily conceded, however, that "Haiti is the cesspool of the Western Hemisphere, under a dictator whom we abhor." He also made a remarkable admission for a Cold Warrior. If Haiti went the way of Cuba, "we ourselves cannot in good conscience say that this could be worse for the Haitians however damaging to US and cause of freedom in the Americas."[53]

The secretary of state need not have worried about Communists saving Haiti. The country had the smallest local party in the hemisphere, and the Soviet Union paid no attention to Haiti. U.S. intelligence analysts reported that Haitian peasants were uninterested in communism. The overcrowded country offered no Sierra Maestra where guerrillas could hide. Most Haitians spoke a unique language; any African Communist would have easily stood out in such an insular country. Perhaps a few of the French-speaking elite became acquainted with Marxism in Paris. In any case, Duvalier annihilated opponents. He tolerated the politically conscious only if they stayed quiescent. The political police and Tonton Macoutes so terrified the population that the CIA actually found it difficult to develop sources of information.[54]

Rusk also misplaced his hopes in Duvalier. Scheduled to retire from the presidency in May 1963, Duvalier reelected himself for another six-year term in 1961. He began to speak of divine rights and refer to himself as "president-for-life." He complained about the level of U.S. aid and stole what the Kennedy administration gave. One U.S. officer recalled that he "felt like a doctor transfusing blood into one arm of a failing patient while another M.D.—Dr. Duvalier—had a suction pump on the other."[55] When U.S. officials ignored requests for additional money, he conspicuously met with trade representatives from Poland, and his foreign minister spoke approvingly of Castro. Secretary Rusk personally experienced the brazen nature of the regime. At an OAS meeting in January 1962, Foreign Minister René Chalmers implied to Rusk that he could have Haiti's vote on an anti-Castro measure only if the United States provided a $2.8 million loan to build a jet-capable airport. A philosophical Rusk observed to Ambassador Raymond Thurston that "they tell me I bribed the Haitians. That was just diplomacy."[56] According to one Washington story, State Department officers amused themselves by circulating their boss's apocryphal meal voucher. It read: "Breakfast—$1.85; Lunch with the Haitian Foreign Minister—$2.8 million."

By mid-1962, the Kennedy administration had tired of Duvalier's blackmail. According to Assistant Secretary Martin, President Kennedy fretted more about U.S. relations with Haiti than about those with any other Latin American country. The president hoped that the Alliance for Progress could help the Haitian poor, and he feared the consequences of inaction. His representatives in Haiti also called for action. Exposed daily to Duvalier's politics of squalor, Ambassador Thurston and Colonel Robert Heinl, the commander of the U.S. military mission, grew to despise the Haitian tyrant. In August 1962, the president ruled that the United States would sharply cut back developmental assistance and increase covert contacts with Duvalier's opponents. The Department of Defense strengthened the U.S. military presence off the coast of Haiti and at the military facility in nearby Guantánamo

Bay. Such pressure would presumably convince Duvalier to step down by May 1963, when his presidential term had been scheduled to end. The president opted for a more cautious policy than recommended by Martin and Thurston, who wanted to organize dissident Haitians and perhaps use U.S. military force. But Kennedy questioned the value of "shows of force." And "under present cold war circumstances," the United States needed to be careful. The CIA had not been able to identify a strong, trustworthy Haitian leader. Chaos and confusion might follow the unseating of Duvalier, leading to "a government with Castro-Communist leanings." The president further observed that intervention in the Dominican Republic could not serve as a precedent for an invasion of Haiti because Duvalier, unlike Rafael Trujillo, had not violated international law by attacking a neighbor.[57] Perhaps, the president prayed, Duvalier would resolve the problem by dying. In his mid-fifties, Duvalier had heart disease and diabetes and had nearly died from a heart attack in 1959.[58]

Whatever his physical deterioration, Duvalier's perverse mental abilities remained lively. After the Cuban Missile Crisis, he again took advantage of the United States. The U.S. military needed Haiti's cooperation to carry out the naval quarantine of Cuba. The price Duvalier exacted was that in November 1962 the United States had to sign an agreement to build Haiti a jet-capable airport.[59] This latest swindle had the effect of reminding the administration how much it detested Duvalier. On 5 November 1962, Kennedy sent Assistant Secretary Martin a handwritten note asking "Where are we going now on Haiti?"[60] State Department officers responded in early 1963 with the suggestion that the ambassador or a special emissary should bluntly tell Duvalier to step down. That tactic worked with President Magloire, but Duvalier, like Trujillo, was unlikely to succumb to verbal requests. The CIA again warned that anarchy might follow Duvalier's departure, profiting Castro and Haitian Communists. Ambassador Thurston argued that Duvalier's opponents had to be motivated by the promise of U.S. military intervention. But the OAS opposed intervention on principle, and its Spanish-speaking members ignored Haiti.[61] President Kennedy reacted to all of this by "sharply" expressing his displeasure upon hearing an estimate that it would take fifty-one hours to put U.S. Marines ashore in Haiti. Fifty-one hours was "too long," he told NSC members.[62]

As the target date for Duvalier's departure—15 May 1963—approached, U.S. officials faced critical choices. In early May, Ambassador Thurston warned Washington that it urgently needed "to get this powder keg under control." President Duvalier was in an especially murder-ous mood, for disaffected members of his security forces had recently tried to kidnap his son. Hopes soared when U.S. diplomats received confidential information that Duvalier and his family had airplane tick-ets for Europe, with a departure date of 15 May.[63] U.S. diplomatic pressure seemed to have finally overwhelmed the dictator. On 13 May, Under Secretary Ball testified to senators in executive session that Du-valier was "in a rather psychotic state" and that he was "holed up" in the National Palace with "his hat pulled down over his ears and two guns on the table." The USS *Boxer*, with 2,000 combat-ready marines, waited fifty miles off the Haitian coast. Helicopters could be in Port-au-Prince within one hour.[64] "Friendly Haitians" hopefully would declare a provi-sional government and ask for OAS assistance. The United States would give the OAS a few hours to agree to help but would send the marines within twelve to twenty-four hours of the Haitian request.[65] Duvalier did not flee, however, remaining true to his "president-for-life" title. The European trip may have been a ploy, designed to encourage his enemies to show their hands. On 15 May, the cocky Duvalier held a news conference at which he called on the OAS to investigate violence against African Americans in Birmingham, Alabama.[66]

Unwilling to risk the international opprobrium that would follow a unilateral intervention, President Kennedy ordered the U.S. Navy to withdraw from the vicinity of Haiti. He pursued another option. In mid-June, Ambassador Thurston, who had been declared persona non grata by Duvalier, reminded the president that if the United States did not change the regime within two or three years, "the dangers of com-munist activity were substantial." Because good leaders were leaving the country, the United States needed to organize them abroad. The presi-dent suggested giving President Bosch of the Dominican Republic "a complete green light on building up a Haitian force and giv[ing] the force any help it needs in money or equipment." Two weeks previously, Kennedy had spoken with the Dominican ambassador about "what we were going to do about Haiti" and assured the ambassador that he sup-ported the idea of the Dominican Republic organizing an exile army.[67] Such a scheme presented its own problems, however. Haitians loathed Dominicans, remembering that in 1937 Rafael Trujillo's army had sys-tematically slaughtered 12,000 Haitians who worked in the Dominican Republic.[68] In any case, on 5 August a small force of perhaps 75 to 100 Haitians crossed into Haiti from the Dominican Republic. Duvalier's forces quickly repulsed them. The CIA apparently worked with the exiles but had little confidence in their fighting abilities and did not support the invasion.[69] The fall of the Bosch government in September 1963 quashed any immediate hopes of launching further assaults on the Duvalier regime from the Dominican Republic.

François Duvalier welcomed the overthrow of his Dominican opponent and allegedly later toasted the news of President Kennedy's assassination. Recognizing that its Haitian policy had "failed totally," the administration decided just before the president's death to establish cool but correct relations with Duvalier. It would disassociate itself temporarily from exile attempts to invade Haiti or plots to assassinate Duvalier. It sent a new emissary, Benson E. L. Timmons III, to Port-au-Prince with instructions to take six months to familiarize himself with the country and submit recommendations.[70] During the Johnson presidency, U.S. officials followed the same uncertain course set during the early 1960s. The United States gave some financial assistance to Haiti—about $15 million between 1964 and 1968. The Johnson administration could hardly ignore the desperate plight of the Haitians. At the same time, the CIA halfheartedly supported exile invasions of Haiti, all of which predictably failed.[71] As Secretary Rusk summarized, "We used persuasion, aid, pressure and almost all techniques short of the landing of outside forces, but President Duvalier was extraordinarily resistant."[72] In August 1964, Ambassador Timmons identified the intellectual dilemma that bedeviled U.S. policy throughout the 1960s. The regime's "disregard of human rights is of course most repugnant." But Duvalier controlled Haiti, and the United States had to contain Cuba and the Soviet Union. The United States therefore needed to maintain a "presence against [the] day of inevitable change, and deny [the] country to communists."[73] Such reasoning remained curious, however, because no evidence ever surfaced that any member of the international Communist movement volunteered to assume the problems of Haiti.

✦   The Kennedy administration exerted itself trying to reform the political cultures of the Dominican Republic and Haiti, Cuba's Caribbean neighbors. It attacked the type of right-wing governments that had been traditional allies of the United States during the Cold War. The administration learned, however, that democracy and a commitment to social justice could not be easily transferred to poor nations with unhappy political pasts. But the president and his advisors had not always steadfastly pursued the idealistic goals of the Alliance for Progress. As signaled by President Kennedy's famous listing of his descending order of political preferences, the fear of communism frequently tempered the administration's zeal for peaceful revolution in the Caribbean. Cold War concerns would also be apparent in the administration's response to left-leaning regimes in Central and South America.

3 ✦ Destabilization Policies

The Kennedy administration worked to overthrow dictators like François Duvalier and Rafael Trujillo. It sympathized with the plight of oppressed people, and it believed that constitutional, reformist governments provided the best safeguards against communism. The administration discovered, however, that duly elected Latin American leaders did not always share the U.S. viewpoint on the issues of Cuba, the Soviet Union, and the international Communist movement. During their brief time in office, President Kennedy and his advisors used a variety of political, economic, and military tools to undermine constitutional regimes throughout the Western Hemisphere. The administration demanded unflagging allegiance to its Cold War policies. Despite its public commitment to democracy and reform, the Kennedy administration frequently demonstrated that it preferred anti-Communist authoritarians over left-leaning leaders who respected constitutional processes.

✦   President Arturo Frondizi of Argentina (1958–62) seemingly offered the type of leadership and vision that was compatible with the goals of the Alliance for Progress. Frondizi, a legal scholar and politician, headed the middle-sector Radical Party and received a convincing electoral mandate in February 1958. Argentines fervently hoped that Frondizi could help their nation escape the political and economic turmoil that had gripped it over the past three decades. Since 1930 the Argentine military had repeatedly intervened in the political system, and it had ruled the country from 1955 to 1958. The nation had also experienced the extreme nationalism and erratic behavior of Juan Perón, who dominated Argentine political life from 1943 to 1955. The Argentine strongman had spent the nation's pesos feverishly and had driven away international investors, leaving the country bankrupt and with wild inflation. The Argentine economy, which depended upon the export of meat and grain, also suffered from the vicissitudes of the twentieth-century global economy. Two world wars and the economic depression of the 1930s had disrupted traditional patterns of trade. In

1914 Argentines believed that they had economic prospects as healthy as those of the United States. Forty-four years later, Argentina remained one of the wealthiest Latin American countries, with a per capita income of approximately $800, but it had fallen far behind the Western industrial democracies.

Frondizi took decisive steps to end Argentina's political and economic malaise. To tame inflation, he administered the bitter economic medicine recommended by the IMF. Frondizi devalued the currency, cut public spending, ended subsidies on public services, and fired public employees. The annual inflation rate, which was at 114 percent in 1959, fell to 13.5 percent in 1961. As he stabilized the economy, Frondizi also proceeded with his plans for "developmental reformism," believing that only economic growth and development could restore political and social stability to Argentina. Reversing the nationalistic policies of the past, he welcomed foreign investment, especially in the oil industry. Argentina needed oil to fuel the industrial progress that Frondizi envisioned. U.S. direct investment in Argentina, which was at $472 million in 1960, quickly doubled. Oil production trebled and industrial production went up. By 1960-61, Frondizi's measures began to show tangible benefits, with the nation's economy growing at an impressive 7 percent annual rate. Secretary of the Treasury C. Douglas Dillon, the former investment banker, met with Frondizi in August 1961 in Buenos Aires and came away from the visit pleased with the Argentine's commitment to international capitalism.[1]

President Frondizi also reoriented his country toward the United States. Argentines traditionally identified themselves within the context of European culture. Most Argentines had a European ethnic background, and Europe was where Argentina sold the bulk of its beef and wheat. Trade rivalries complicated U.S.-Argentine relations because the United States similarly exported meat and grains. Argentines had also long resented the U.S. domination of the Western Hemisphere. But Frondizi realized that Argentina needed the outside capital that in 1960 only the United States could afford to grant. Becoming the first Argentine president to visit the United States, Frondizi established a friendship with President Eisenhower and twice met with Kennedy. In an open letter, he lavishly praised Kennedy for launching the Alliance for Progress, comparing it with the heroic U.S. efforts under the Marshall Plan. He thought, however, that Alliance funds should be directed toward financing huge public works projects rather than toward social issues such as land reform. In September 1961, when he met with Kennedy at his retreat in Palm Beach, Florida, he presented a wish list of over $1 billion in public works projects that he wanted the United States to support.[2]

As he pursued his goals, President Frondizi was making formidable enemies both at home and abroad. After overthrowing Perón in 1955, military authorities had proscribed the political activities of his followers. Frondizi had the difficult task of integrating the Peronistas, about one-third of the voting public, back into Argentina's political culture without antagonizing the virulently anti-Perón armed forces. His economic stabilization plan also hit the working-class followers of Perón hard, leading to an unending series of strikes and demonstrations. Nationalists resented Frondizi for welcoming foreign investors. And many in the military flatly opposed a civilian who had no military experience governing the country. Military men frequently labeled the president a "Communist." During his four years in office, Frondizi faced thirty-five crises in the forms of strikes, riots, and threats from the military.[3]

The beleaguered Argentine leader ultimately received little sympathy or support from the Kennedy administration, even though, at a political cost, he wholeheartedly embraced the Alliance for Progress. Frondizi disappointed U.S. officials because he declined to follow dutifully their Cold War policies. Frondizi maintained diplomatic relations with Cuba and opposed a showdown with Fidel Castro. Many in the southern cone countries of Argentina, Brazil, Chile, and Uruguay did not judge Castro to be much of a threat. He ruled a small island country of racially mixed people thousands of miles away from the glittering, European-like metropolises of Buenos Aires or Montevideo. Argentines hardly thought it possible that they could learn from Cubans. Frondizi also feared that a confrontation with Cuba would exacerbate political tensions in Argentina, exciting extremists on both ends of the political spectrum. The Argentine president undoubtedly wanted to restore the respect that Argentina once had in international circles by pursuing an independent, constructive foreign policy. He offered unsuccessfully to mediate between the United States and Cuba.[4] Like other Latin American reformers, he further understood that the existence of Castro meant that the United States would focus on the region's problems. In any case, he accepted the basic premise of the Alliance for Progress that development and reform would defeat radicalism. Latin America, Frondizi argued, should strive for higher levels of social and economic development and ignore "the fate of an extremist caudillo who speaks in favor of a political system that has nothing to do with the reality of our peoples."[5]

President Frondizi's other foreign policy ventures angered the United States. In August 1961, he met for four hours in Buenos Aires with Ché Guevara. He answered criticism of the visit by noting that Richard Goodwin had also recently conversed with the Cuban. His other diplomatic contacts similarly irked the United States. U.S. officials disliked Latin American countries having diplomatic relations with the Soviet Union. They argued that the Soviets would use embassies as a base to promote subversion throughout the hemisphere. Argentina maintained diplomatic relations with the Soviet Union and sold it meat and grains. The balance of trade usually heavily favored Argentina, because the Soviets lacked the advanced technology and industrial equipment that the Argentines wanted.[6] Frondizi also saw commercial opportunity in the People's Republic of China. Noting that the Japanese had told him that they did not consider the Chinese a threat, Frondizi suggested to President Kennedy that Argentina might be able to export its agricultural products to the Chinese. Frondizi's remark drew a tart observation from Kennedy. China, which would soon have nuclear weapons, constituted a "great and unpredictable threat" to the West. It would be "very unfortunate" if Argentina did anything to help such a regime.[7]

The Kennedy administration tried to educate President Frondizi about Cold War dangers. After failing to overthrow Castro in April 1961, the administration campaigned to persuade Latin American nations to break diplomatic and economic relations with Cuba and oust it from the OAS. Six nations—Argentina, Brazil, Bolivia, Chile, Ecuador, and Mexico—resisted U.S. entreaties. In President Kennedy's words, "Argentina was the key to this problem." If Frondizi publicly denounced Castro, others might follow.[8] The administration sent Frondizi a series of covert and overt signals. In September 1961, a staff member who worked in the Cuban embassy in Buenos Aires defected and released documents that allegedly revealed Cuban subversion in Argentina. The State Department managed the disclosure. Frondizi's circle doubted the authenticity of the documents, but the disclosure had the effect of increasing calls in the Argentine military for action against Cuba. Conservative military officers throughout the hemisphere loathed Castro, vividly recalling that the Cuban revolutionaries had dissolved Batista's army and executed officers.[9] U.S. agents apparently urged the military to pressure Frondizi. At a meeting with Kennedy in Palm Beach on 24 December 1961, Frondizi complained that he suspected the pressure from the armed forces for more emphatic action against Cuba "is accentuated by stimulation [from] US intelligence sources."[10] Kennedy neither answered nor rejected Frondizi's allegation.

The administration also brought traditional diplomatic pressures to bear on the Argentine. In September 1961, Kennedy told Frondizi that he understood Argentina's desire to focus on economic development, "but this was not just a U.S.-Cuba conflict but a Soviet one and we couldn't wait." In December, he reminded Frondizi that Castro had just declared himself a Marxist-Leninist. On 11 January 1962, writing "in all frankness," he informed Frondizi of "the importance and urgency" that the United States attached to excluding Cuba from the OAS. He implied that Argentina would benefit from additional economic aid if it voted against Cuba.[11] A week later, Secretary of State Rusk raised the stakes when he speculated to Argentine diplomats that the Soviet Union might be tempted to attack West Berlin if it perceived weakness "in our own backyard."[12] He added that "he had not mentioned this matter to any other Latin American government." Rusk presumably hoped the Argentines did not want to be responsible for the outbreak of World War III.

At the inter-American conclave held again at Punta del Este, Uruguay, in late January 1962, Rusk concentrated his lobbying efforts on the Argentine delegation. Frondizi's Argentina defied the United States, however, when it joined with the five other Latin American nations and abstained on a resolution to exclude Cuba from the OAS. Argentina voted in favor of eight resolutions that denounced Cuba and found communism "incompatible" with the inter-American system. But the six nations, in Rusk's words, "let us down" on the critical exclusion resolution. The secretary especially blamed Argentina, because he did not believe it had domestic leftist groups pressuring it on the Cuban issue as the other countries did.[13] In order to secure the necessary fourteen votes, or bare two-thirds majority, for exclusion, Rusk had to resort to bribing Duvalier's Haiti with the airport loan. Rusk knew he had achieved a dubious victory. The six abstainers represented approximately 60 percent of Latin America's population. As Walt Rostow, a member of the U.S. delegation, saw it, the Argentines had not helped the United States by proposing "a mealy-mouthed anti-Communist compromise resolution." They had acted in a "contemptible manner."[14]

Argentina's abstention precipitated a crisis at home. Military members of the Argentine delegation had refused to sit with their civilian counterparts in protest over the Argentine position on Cuba. On 31 January 1962, the commanders of the air force repudiated the vote to abstain and demanded that Argentina rupture relations with Cuba. In order to forestall a *golpe*, Frondizi agreed to the military demands on 2 February and broke relations six days later. Though obviously pleased by the dramatic Argentine shift, the Kennedy administration now worried about Argentina's future. Rusk noted to the embassy in Buenos Aires that the United States welcomed "foreign policy changes brought about by internal pressures mainly by military" but now believed that "continued and extreme military pressure upon government would be contrary to US interests." The secretary instructed his diplomats to encourage military men to seek moderate solutions. On 25 February, the administration also announced a $150 million Alliance for Progress package for Argentina.[15]

The Argentine military refused to compromise, however, on the subject of Peronism. In mid-March 1962, in clean and honest elections, the Peronists demonstrated their electoral strength, winning 35 percent of the vote, nine governorships, and increased representation in the National Chamber. True to his constitutional sentiments, Frondizi had overseen a free election, although he had mistakenly counted on his party's capturing a plurality of the votes. Argentine military officers excoriated the president for his miscalculation. For ten days, Frondizi frantically negotiated with civilian and military opponents. On 29 March, military officers physically removed him from office, canceled the electoral results, and placed a civilian figurehead, José María Guido, in the Casa Rosada, the presidential office.

The Kennedy administration silently watched the destruction of the democratic process in Argentina. In Assistant Secretary Edward Martin's words, "The best course is to let events take their course." He found it a "close call" whether the United States should defend constitutionalism. The United States resented President Frondizi's maneuverings on Cuba, and, like the Argentine military, it did not want Peronists exercising power again. The United States needed an effective Argentine government that could "meet the challenge which the Peronist forces presented to our mutual objectives." On Martin's instructions, Ambassador Robert M. McClintock, who had just arrived in Buenos Aires, made a few perfunctory calls on key Argentine military officers, recommending that they find a negotiated solution. But his effort was only a diplomatic nicety; he had merely discharged his "moral obligation" to aid Frondizi. He had already informed Washington that it should not cut off Alliance for Progress funds to Argentina when the military struck a *golpe de estado*.[16] Within the Kennedy administration, only Arthur Schlesinger vigorously argued that the United States should issue a statement denouncing military takeovers. But President Kennedy ruled that nothing would be said about Frondizi's overthrow.[17] Secretary Rusk would later acidly imply that Frondizi deserved his fate. In an executive session, Rusk told U.S. legislators that "what led to the overthrow of the Frondizi government was the direct consequence of the attitude of Frondizi toward Castro."[18]

U.S. diplomats were astute enough political analysts to know that the Argentine military hated Juan Perón more than it feared Fidel Castro. But they sought diplomatic advantage by publicly emphasizing the Communist angle. In Ecuador, for example, U.S. officials again encouraged military officers to pressure civilian leaders. CIA agents planted stories with friendly journalists that ascribed Frondizi's overthrow to his reluctance to confront Castro. They also pointed out that the United States had increased its economic aid to Argentina's new anti-Communist leaders. Perhaps this disinformation, known in the spy trade as "gray propaganda," had the desired effect.[19] In April 1962, President Carlos Julio Arosemena Monroy of Ecuador reversed his position and broke diplomatic relations with Cuba.

As CIA agents suggested, the Kennedy administration readily cooperated with Argentina's military leaders. It resumed relations on 18 April 1962 and maintained its economic aid program. In 1962–63, Argentina received over $160 million in long-term economic assistance. The United States also made substantial short-term emergency loans to help the country avoid currency crises. The administration especially appreciated Argentina's new stance on Cuba. Ambassador McClintock argued that the Argentine military "should be regarded as an asset by the United States," because they "are as fervently anti-Communist as we [are]."[20] In November 1962, President Kennedy hosted Argentine strongman General Pedro Aramburu and warmly thanked him for Argentina's support during the Cuban Missile Crisis. He also warned Aramburu to be alert "to renewed Communist attempts at penetration."[21] In January 1963, Kennedy publicly praised Argentina for maintaining good relations with the United States and promised military assistance.

Although the United States had secured a faithful Cold War ally, it ironically no longer had an Argentine leader who believed in the Alliance for Progress and the tenets of international capitalism. President Frondizi had angered Argentine nationalists, including military officers, for limiting the role of the state in the economy and inviting foreign capitalists into Argentina. Rabid nationalism returned when the military permitted a controlled election in July 1963, leading to the election of Arturo Illia, a country doctor from the conservative, anti-Frondizi wing of the Radical Party. Illia shocked the United States when he immediately annulled the contracts of U.S. oil companies. The Kennedy and then Johnson administrations demanded that Argentina compensate the oil companies. President Illia also broke with the IMF, imposed price controls, and granted excessive wage increases to placate Peronist workers. On 22 November 1963, the day of Kennedy's death, Ambassador McClintock cabled that "Illia's new Government has started out on a level of almost guaranteed incompetence." The political scene "was anti-U.S. and anti–Alliance for Progress." The ambassador predicted that a "military *golpe* is inevitable."[22] Indeed, in June 1966 military officers ejected Illia from the Casa Rosada. Two more decades of political and economic chaos awaited Argentina.

The Kennedy administration did not bear primary responsibility for Argentina's political turbulence in the early 1960s. President Frondizi fell from power for indigenous reasons, and his difficulties reflected the larger problems that have beset Argentina for much of the twentieth century. But the administration declined to defend a constitutional leader and friend of the United States at a critical moment, and it exacerbated tensions in a politically volatile country by encouraging the aggressive and ambitious Argentine military to oppose Frondizi over his Cuban policy. As a prominent student of U.S.-Argentine relations has noted, the U.S. pressure on Frondizi on the Cuban issue came "at the cost of playing into the hands of the more extreme nationalists contending for power in Argentina."[23] Defeating Castro and the Communists meant more to the Kennedy administration than preserving democracy and promoting the Alliance for Progress.

✦   Whereas the United States abetted nondemocratic forces in Argentina, it helped organize them in Brazil. The Kennedy administration found fault with Brazil's central governments because they not only conducted relations with Communist nations but also tolerated leftists at home. The administration responded with a concerted effort to shape the international and domestic policies of Brazil. The political and social evolution of Brazil, the largest and most populous nation in Latin America, presumably would help determine whether the United States maintained its traditional domination of the region. As State Department planners noted, "If U.S. policy fails on Brazil, it will become extremely difficult to achieve success elsewhere in Latin America." President Kennedy agreed, adding syllogistically that "Latin

America is critical to [the] West," and "Brazil is [the] key country in Latin America."[24]

As in the United States, a dynamic young politician became president of Brazil in January 1961. Jânio Quadros (1961) had earned a reputation as an energetic, honest administrator, first as the mayor of the industrial center of São Paulo and later as the state's governor. He assumed power in a country with enormous potential and acute problems. As a result of President Juscelino Kubitschek's (1956–61) expansive fiscal and monetary policies, Brazil had experienced economic growth accompanied by inflation, currency fluctuations, and balance of payments deficits. Kubitschek had developed an international reputation as a visionary, both for promoting the building of the futuristic city of Brasília in the nation's heartland and for successfully prodding President Eisenhower into focusing on the need for economic development in Latin America. President Quadros decided that Brazil needed to put its economic house in order, and, like Argentina's Frondizi, he launched a series of tough measures, cutting federal expenditures, balancing the budget, and restricting luxury imports. He also announced that Brazil would develop a foreign policy of "absolute independence" and quickly demonstrated that autonomy by opening contacts with the Soviet Union and its satellites. Quadros's initiatives seemed politically symmetrical, as he simultaneously moved right and left. But his new foreign policy also reflected a long-standing domestic debate on how Brazil could achieve its goal of becoming a prosperous world power consistent with its great size and impressive natural resources. Brazil had traditionally been allied with the United States, with Brazilian soldiers fighting alongside U.S. troops in Italy during World War II. Many Brazilian leaders believed that this alliance had not produced the political and economic benefits that Brazil deserved.[25]

The Quadros administration and its successor, the João Goulart government (1961–64), engaged in an unending debate with U.S. officials about foreign policy in general and Cuba in particular. Brazilians denied the charge that they had become "neutral" in the Cold War. They would not be "systematically neutral," because that meant being "a member of a bloc which always advocated the middle position between the Soviet bloc and the Western bloc." Brazil would reach conclusions on international issues independently and as a reflection of Brazilian national interest. Brazilian leaders could also defend their position by pointing to public opinion polls, which showed strong popular support for an independent foreign policy.[26] In any case, Brazil had hardly become tied to the Communist movement. Brazil established relations with the Soviet Union in 1961, permitted the Soviets to stage a trade fair in Rio de Janeiro in 1962, and signed a commercial agreement in April 1963. Between 1959 and 1963, Soviet-Brazilian trade grew from 5 to 66 million rubles. But that commerce represented only 3 percent of Brazil's trade. The balance of trade favored Brazil, because the Soviets offered goods of poor quality.[27]

On the issue of Castro and Cuba, Brazilians essentially repeated Arturo Frondizi's arguments. They stood firm on the OAS principle of nonintervention, and they argued that sanctions against Cuba "would only serve to push it irrevocably into [the] Sino-Soviet bloc." They further noted that "there had been no known case of Brazilians who had actually been trained in Cuba in subversive activities." Brazilian diplomats reminded U.S. officials like Secretary Rusk that in October 1962, when Cuba had posed a strategic threat to the hemisphere, Brazil and all other Latin American nations had stoutly backed the United States. As President Goulart once put it, Castro had become a "dramatic symbol of revolutionary aspirations of underprivileged masses throughout Latin America." If the United States was patient, the Castro regime would "deteriorate under its own weight." But the United States would do itself a great disservice by agitating the Cuban problem, because "Latin American masses are instinctive[ly] on [the] side of tiny Cuba whenever it [is] menaced by [the] colossus to [the] North."[28]

Brazilians had no more success than Argentines had in trying to cure the Kennedy administration of its obsession with Cuba. In March 1961, a month before the Bay of Pigs operation, Adolf Berle arrived in Rio de Janeiro bearing a $100 million gift for the new Quadros administration to help it import capital goods. After discussing the $100 million loan, Berle predicted an "early explosion" in the Caribbean and asked President Quadros to join inter-American action in the Caribbean. When Quadros declined to help, Berle returned to the subject of the $100 million. As outgoing ambassador to Brazil John Moors Cabot recalled in disgust: "It was obvious it was just a bribe. I mean that's what it amounted to. And Quadros, with increasing irritation, said no."[29] President Kennedy made a similar pitch to the Brazilians. In May 1961, he lectured Finance Minister Clemente Mariani on "political factors" in inter-American relations. The United States had just agreed with the IMF to give Brazil $338.5 million in credits. In the negotiations, "the U.S. Government had completely avoided mention of political factors." But "the United States was interested in the Castro regime because it is a weapon used by international communism in its efforts to take over additional Latin American countries by internal subversion." Castro was "an agent of international communism," not "a traditional revolutionary." Kennedy lamented that it would be impossible to drive Cuba out of the OAS unless the major Latin American nations agreed "on the basic analysis of the situation in Cuba." [30] Quadros again refused to change Brazil's foreign policy, and he further irritated the United States by hosting Ché Guevara and awarding him Brazil's Order of the Southern Cross.

The administration's concern over Brazil grew when Quadros suddenly resigned the presidency on 25 August 1961. Apparently weary of the abuse he had received for imposing his economic stabilization plan, he submitted his resignation to the legislature. Quadros seems to have naively believed that Brazilians would repent and implore him to return. Vice President João Goulart eventually succeeded to the presidency. A career politician, Goulart had also served as vice president under Kubitschek and previously as minister of labor. A fiery speaker and populist, Goulart identified himself, at least rhetorically, with the nation's dispossessed. Goulart had ties to various left-wing groups, including the Brazilian Communist Party. When Quadros resigned, Goulart was in transit on a trade mission to the People's Republic of China. Brazilian conservatives, including military officers, despised Goulart and initially tried to block his ascension to power. Goulart took office on 2 September, after the Brazilian Congress passed a constitutional amendment curbing the powers of the presidency. He regained full presidential powers in January 1963, however, as the result of a plebiscite.

The United States had no love for Goulart. The Eisenhower administration suspected his political leanings, and President Kennedy declined to issue a statement defending the principle of constitutionalism during the succession crisis. As State Department officers saw it, a U.S. statement "would constitute a clear endorsement of the Goulart cause which would be deeply resented by those of our friends who support effort of military to exclude Goulart from presidency on ground [of] his known Communist sympathies." Once Goulart gained power, the embassy in Rio de Janeiro recommended a "watch and wait" policy to see if the Brazilian wished "to live down his fellow-traveling past." But on 25 September, embassy officers worried that "we may be witnessing the early stages of an attempted slow motion coup in which Goulart, wittingly or unwittingly, is paving the way for effective Communist infiltration designed as a prelude to an eventual takeover."[31]

The Kennedy administration never overcame its deep suspicions about Goulart's ultimate goals, interpreting his maneuvers through a Cold War prism. He increased U.S. ire by maintaining Quadros's independent foreign policy and refusing to break relations with Cuba. He exasperated U.S. officials with his fickle and inconstant fiscal and monetary policies, alternately favoring expansion and then imposing restrictions. Inflation and balance of payments deficits swallowed up the substantial U.S. aid, which amounted to over $700 million between 1961 and 1963. Other sins included expropriating U.S. properties, such as the holdings of International Telephone and Telegraph, arousing labor and student groups with inflammatory speeches, and appointing cabinet ministers with politically radical sentiments. He also called for higher prices for primary products such as Brazilian coffee, implicitly suggesting that new terms of trade, not the Alliance for Progress, would generate the economic development and growth that Latin America needed. In short, an irresponsible President Goulart seemingly opposed all U.S. objectives in Latin America. This led Ambassador to Brazil Lincoln Gordon to warn of a "substantial imminent danger" of a Communist takeover. On 30 September 1963, officials in Washington summarized: "Goulart will not be disposed to sacrifice the political support derived from his long-standing ties with extreme-leftist (including Communist) and ultranationalist elements, and he will continue to give them position and opportunity from which they can carry on their anti-U.S., and in some cases Moscow, Peking, or Havana Communist-line, advocacy in Brazil."[32]

Kennedy administration officials had available to them other analyses of President Goulart's intentions. Former president Kubitschek twice met with Kennedy, assuring him that Goulart was not a Marxist, that he supported the Alliance for Progress, and that Goulart had "a genuine liking" for Kennedy. In April 1962, Kennedy had the opportunity to meet with Goulart. Aides characterized their Washington meetings as cordial, warm, and constructive.[33] U.S. intelligence analysts also questioned whether Goulart threatened U.S. interests, noting "there is little reason to believe that he is dedicated to a radical transformation of Brazilian society or to a radical reorientation of Brazil's independent foreign policy." He worked with aides of varying political views, including political moderates. Goulart was "essentially an opportunist" who sought "political power primarily for the personal prestige, popularity, and perquisites to be gained thereby." Scholars have subsequently sustained the CIA's judgment of Goulart.[34] Within the State Department several officers, including Assistant Secretary Edwin Martin, opposed Ambassador Gordon's prediction that Goulart aimed to stay in power beyond his term in office and "take Brazil into the Communist camp." As Martin saw it, Goulart needed the support of the political left because he correctly feared that conservative elements, including military officers, plotted against him.[35] These discriminating interpretations of Brazilian politics failed to persuade the administration to abandon its Cold War verities. As President Kennedy remarked, the situation in Brazil "worried him more than that in Cuba."[36]

The story of how the United States destabilized the Goulart government has been well told elsewhere and only the essential details need be recited here for clarity.[37] On 2 April 1964, Brazilian generals disposed of Goulart and established a military regime that would last until 1985. The Johnson administration approved of the military conspiracy and pre-positioned war matériel and readied a naval task force for duty off the coast of Brazil, in case the generals encountered stiff resistance from Goulart's supporters. Although the overthrow came during the Johnson administration, scholars have agreed that the anti-Goulart campaign began during Kennedy's term. Two critical studies—the Draper Commission Report and the State Department Policy Paper on Brazil—suggested what course the administration was prepared to pursue. The Special Group (CI), the administration's select committee that oversaw counterinsurgency activities, commissioned William H. Draper Jr., a former general, to take national security officers to Brazil and survey U.S. policies there. Draper's report, submitted on 3 November 1962, spoke of Goulart's "perversity" and warned that the Brazilian "would have no personal conviction or inhibition against turning to the Soviet Bloc." Draper recommended that the United States intensify its contacts with the military in preparation for a "more friendly alternative regime." Eleven months later, the State Department task force speculated that the Brazilian military would strike at Goulart. To facilitate "the most favorable possible succession," the task force, which included Ambassador Gordon, called on the United States to continue to cultivate friendly relations and strengthen the "basically democratic and pro–United States orientation of the military."[38]

Interventionist policies proceeded from such recommendations. In December 1962, Kennedy dispatched his undiplomatic brother, the attorney general, to Brazil to confront Goulart over his "putting those leftists and Communists in positions of power." Although the three-hour meeting ended inconclusively, Robert Kennedy decided that the United States could not trust the Brazilian president. Goulart stood condemned because he looked "a great deal like a Brazilian Jimmy Hoffa," the U.S. labor leader whom the attorney general had prosecuted.[39] Beyond lecturing Goulart, the Kennedy administration manipulated the Brazilian political scene. In 1962 the CIA spent $5 million funding the campaigns of candidates for 15 federal Senate seats, 8 state governorships, 250 federal deputy seats, and some 600 seats for state legislatures. The administration further adopted what Ambassador Gordon dubbed an "islands of administrative sanity" approach, funneling Alliance for Progress aid to friendly state governors such as Carlos Lacerda of the state of Guanabara, where Rio de Janeiro is located. By aiding Lacerda, the United States promoted a "rightist extremist" who, in Assistant Secretary Martin's opinion, acted like Senator Joseph McCarthy of Wisconsin. The administration also undercut its social reform programs in the impoverished northeastern states by assisting anti-Goulart oligarchs.[40]

The administration made a special effort to control the Brazilian labor movement. President Kennedy repeatedly complained to Brazilians about the "strong radical, Marxist or communist influence on labor." The administration fought leftist unions with a new Cold War weapon, the American Institute of Free Labor Development (AIFLD). Founded by the American Federation of Labor in late 1961, the AIFLD's mission was to counter "the threat of Castroite infiltration and eventual control of major labor movements within Latin America." The AIFLD rejected the theory of class conflict and preached the benefits of capitalism and "business unionism" to Latin American workers. Between 1962 and 1967, it received $15.4 million, or 89 percent of its budget, from Alliance for Progress funds. For the period from 1961 to 1963, it also reportedly received $1 million from the CIA through conduits like the J. M. Kaplan and Gotham Funds. Such ties, according to one U.S. government study, gave the AIFLD the "appearance of being little more than an instrument of the Cold War." In Brazil the AIFLD instructed trade union leaders on how to organize strikes and demonstrations against Goulart, and it sent ten Brazilians for special training abroad. These men led general strikes against Goulart in April 1964. The AIFLD publicly noted that planning for the overthrow of Goulart went on for months and that it "took pride in the role of its trainees in overthrowing the Goulart administration." AIFLD officials further boasted that they collaborated with the U.S. labor attaché, John Fishburn, and with Brazilian military officers.[41]

As in Argentina, the armed forces ultimately decided the fate of civilian governments. At Ambassador Gordon's request, the administration dispatched a veteran troubleshooter, Colonel Vernon Walters, to Brazil to gather military intelligence. Walters, who had a remarkable facility with foreign languages, had served with Brazilian officers during the Italian campaign of World War II. As Walters later told an interviewer, he recalled being briefed before arriving in Brazil in October 1962 by somebody "high in the Kennedy administration." The president, Walters learned, would not be averse to seeing Goulart overthrown if he were replaced by an anti-Communist who supported U.S. foreign policies.[42] Walters developed a social relationship with General Humberto de Alencar Castello Branco, who led the military conspiracy against Goulart and took control of the presidency on 15 April 1964. Walters also kept Ambassador Gordon apprised of the conspiracy. As such, the Johnson administration developed contingency plans to aid the military men, and it extended diplomatic recognition to the interim government eighteen hours after its installation. Both Walters and Gordon have vigorously denied that they directed the military conspiracy. Scholars have subsequently sustained that plea of not guilty. But they have added that the United States destabilized the Goulart government "by effectively bypassing that government through direct U.S. dealings with and support of other groups, leaders, and institutions in the country and by frequently aligning U.S. assistance with those elements of Brazilian society that eventually overthrew Goulart."[43]

The Johnson administration fulfilled the Kennedy administration's policy for Goulart's Brazil. Privately interviewed in 1964, Robert Kennedy expressed satisfaction with the overthrow, alleging that "Brazil would have gone Communist" if Goulart had not been deposed.[44] In May 1964, while campaigning for a U.S. Senate seat in California, former press secretary Pierre Salinger questioned the Johnson administration's Brazilian policy. National Security Advisor McGeorge Bundy sharply rebuked Salinger, reminding him that Lincoln Gordon, George Ball, and Dean Rusk, "all Kennedy men," supported the policy. The chastened Salinger immediately apologized for his disloyalty.[45]

Castello Branco pleased the United States by breaking relations with Cuba in May 1964 and by sending peacekeeping troops to the Dominican Republic after the U.S. invasion of the island in 1965. In the interests of Brazilian economic growth, however, he maintained, and even expanded, the Quadros-Goulart policy of developing political and economic contacts with the Soviet bloc. Nonetheless, the United States celebrated Goulart's overthrow. Between 1964 and 1966, the United States allocated $950 million in Alliance for Progress funds to Brazil. In May 1964, in a speech to the Brazilian War College, Ambassador Gordon stated "that events in Brazil that spring would be regarded as one of the critical events in the evolution of international relations generally in the 1960s." Assistant Secretary of State Thomas C. Mann seconded Gordon, exclaiming that "the frustration of Communistic objectives in Brazil was the single most important victory for freedom in the hemisphere in recent years."[46] But U.S. officials began to reconsider that victory when military rule persisted in Brazil for twenty-one years. Under the generals, Brazilian security forces carried out gross violations of basic human rights. By 1965, Robert Kennedy was complaining about the U.S. friendship with Brazil.[47] Subjected to withering scholarly criticism, officials like Lincoln Gordon have tried to defend themselves. Gordon has now conceded that neither the Soviet Union nor Cuba wielded any influence in Brazil. Gordon has explained: "What I feared was a 2-stage coup by which Goulart would first assume power in the mold of a Perón or Vargas and then be displaced by a stronger personality—as had happened in Egypt with Neguib and Nasser. That successor, in turn, was likely to copy Fidel Castro in seeking alliance and support from the USSR."[48] Such tortured logic underlay the Kennedy administration's destabilization of the constitutional process in Brazil.

✦ U.S. intervention in the political life of Guatemala took less time and effort than the interventions in the populated South American republics of Argentina and Brazil. Guatemala had a small, impoverished population of approximately 4.5 million people. A few hundred land-owning families controlled the political and economic life of Guatemala. Most Guatemalans struggled to survive as subsistence farmers. The nation's annual per capita income fell below $300. Guatemala's sizable Amerindian population, many of Mayan descent, essentially lived outside of a cash economy.[49] Guatemala's poor expected little from their government. After a decade of socioeconomic reform between 1944 and 1954, conservative elites again held sway in Guatemala City, the capital. Their return to power had been made possible by the CIA intervention in Guatemala in 1954. The Eisenhower administration had directed the overthrow of the popularly elected government of Jacobo Arbenz Guzmán (1950–54) because it feared that President Arbenz might allow the Soviet Union to establish the first Communist beachhead in the Western Hemisphere in Guatemala.

Miguel Ydígoras Fuentes presided over Guatemala when President Kennedy took office. A military officer and civil engineer, Ydígoras had served under Guatemalan strongman Jorge Ubico (1931–44). Between 1944 and 1957, he spent much of his time outside the country, representing Guatemala on diplomatic missions. The reformist governments of Juan José Arévalo (1944–50) and Arbenz kept Ydígoras occupied with diplomacy, preventing him from being a nuisance at home. Elected in January 1958 with 39 percent of the vote, a plurality, Ydígoras promised strong, stable rule. The Eisenhower administration apparently did not favor the sixty-two-year-old Ydígoras, worrying that such an authoritarian figure would further polarize Guatemala's political culture. The administration accepted the archconservative, however, and invited the president-elect to Washington. Ydígoras did not hide his conservative credentials, informing Vice President Nixon that "communism" was the major issue in Guatemala.[50] As president, Ydígoras actually avoided domestic topics, focusing on nationalist concerns. He squabbled with Mexico over border and fishing-rights issues and loudly complained about the United Kingdom's continued control of British Honduras (Belize).

President Ydígoras hardly seemed the ideal man to carry out the reforms envisioned by the Alliance for Progress. The Kennedy administration committed over $27 million in Alliance funds to Guatemala, knowing full well that Ydígoras represented the oligarchic elite. As John Muccio, the ambassador to Guatemala and former ambassador to South Korea, observed, President Ydígoras reminded him of Syngman Rhee, because "he'd say yes to everything, as long as he was on the receiving end." State Department officers used more understated tones in speaking about the Guatemalan, noting that his government suffered "from run-of-the-mill graft, maladministration, and some disregard for personal liberties."[51] Although he was the antithesis of the "decent democrat" called for in the Alliance, the Kennedy administration tolerated President Ydígoras because he fervently supported its Cold War policies. In 1960–61, he permitted the CIA to use a political crony's private estate on the southern coast of Guatemala to train Cuban exiles in preparation for the Bay of Pigs invasion. In February 1961, he wrote Kennedy, urging him to attack Castro and assuring him that "victory will be won." After the Cuban Missile Crisis, he again called for an outright invasion of Cuba. At inter-American conclaves, his delegates publicly ridiculed Cuban representatives, including Ché Guevara. At the January 1962 meeting to consider the exclusion of Cuba from the OAS, the Guatemalan foreign minister made a "sharp and at times telling attack" on the Castro regime, although, as Secretary Rusk dryly pointed out, the effectiveness of the speech was "blunted by length and repetitiveness."[52]

Ydígoras's loyalty earned U.S. support. In July 1960, following domestic disturbances in Guatemala, the Eisenhower administration granted an emergency $9 million loan to help Ydígoras pacify the nation. On 13 November 1960, angry that foreigners secretly trained in their nation, junior Guatemalan officers led by Marco Antonio Yon Sosa and Luis R. Turcios Lima attacked the government. Crying that Castro fomented the rebellion, Ydígoras pleaded for U.S. assistance and began to use the Cubans to suppress the rebellion. The Eisenhower administration responded by dispatching air and naval observation forces to the Guatemalan coast and ordering Ydígoras to keep the Cuban exiles out of the fight. Forces loyal to Ydígoras defeated the junior officers on 16 November, although the insurgents would reappear as guerrillas in the Guatemalan countryside in the mid-1960s. The administration also gave Guatemala an additional loan of $10 million.[53] In March 1962, the United States again went on a military alert when Ydígoras labeled the latest student-led protests as Castro-inspired. The Kennedy administration readied a 1,400-man battle group in the Canal Zone and dispatched ships to patrol sea lanes between Guatemala and Cuba. The U.S. Navy predictably found no evidence of Cuban military intervention. The Guatemalan military, invoking martial law, put down the uprising at a cost of over 500 civilian casualties. Although they saved Ydígoras, Guatemalan military officers exacted a price, taking control of essential government departments. The incident also proved to Assistant Secretary Martin that President Kennedy "was prepared to use U.S. military power to stop the spread of Castroism by force, even in a small Latin American country."[54]

President Kennedy would not need to use U.S. military power to counter what he perceived as a threat to U.S. security interests in Guatemala. Ydígoras's presidential term would end in 1963, and he pledged to oversee a free and open election, which included granting former president Arévalo the right to return from exile in Mexico and enter the electoral contest. Ydígoras's defense of constitutionalism alarmed the Kennedy administration. Since the CIA intervention in 1954, the United States had opposed Arévalo's return to Guatemala and kept close tabs on his whereabouts. U.S. officials blamed Arévalo for Guatemala's leftward drift during the 1940s and early 1950s and resented his bitter critiques of U.S. foreign policy in books such as *The Shark and the Sardines* (1961). In November 1959, for example, the U.S. ambassador informed Ydígoras that the prospect of Arévalo coming to power or even being physically present in Guatemala would be "nothing short of disastrous." In August 1962, Assistant Secretary Martin studied an analysis of Arévalo's political beliefs, concluding that "there was no proof that he was a communist but reason to suspect that he would be more open to both their ideas and party members than we would like a Guatemalan president to be." U.S. officials had second opinions available to them, however. In February 1963, Venezuelan president Rómulo Betancourt assured Kennedy that Arévalo was not a member of the international Communist movement, noting that Castro had publicly denounced him and that Venezuelan Communists burned Arévalo's books. Nonetheless, Kennedy judged Arévalo "quite a risk."[55] Although U.S. officials were uncertain about Arévalo's political intentions, they understood his electoral prospects. Fourteen Guatemalans had expressed an intention to run for the presidency, making it easy for Arévalo to garner an electoral plurality. U.S. officials also knew that Arévalo probably could defeat fairly any political opponent, because many Guatemalans favored his progressive social reforms and, like Arévalo, resented the 1954 intervention.[56]

Why President Ydígoras uncharacteristically contemplated challenging U.S. foreign policy cannot be exactly determined. In conversations with U.S. diplomats, Ydígoras repeatedly argued that Arévalo had a legal right to return to Guatemala and that his political appeal would diminish once he came home. Guatemala should not grant the former president a political martyrdom. Ydígoras opined that it would be best for Arévalo to be defeated in the open, and political leaders existed who could beat him. Other Guatemalans suggested that President Ydígoras wanted to burnish his reputation and repudiate unfair charges that he had been a dictator who ignored democratic procedures. Perhaps Ydígoras also had ulterior intentions. In a multi-candidate election with Arévalo participating, the vote might be splintered, leaving Ydígoras's handpicked candidate with an electoral plurality.[57]

The Guatemalan military and other conservatives vowed not to let Arévalo return. In mid-1962, the Kennedy administration had denounced the Peruvian military for nullifying the election of a left-of-center candidate. In March 1963, Guatemalan officers promised a "Peruvian solution" if Arévalo won the presidency and inquired whether the United States would oppose a *golpe*. When the United States did not respond to that question, army officers further informed Ambassador Bell that the army would find a "bold, forceful solution." And on 12 March 1963, Arturo Peralta, the brother of Defense Minister Colonel Enrique Peralta Azurdia, confidentially told Bell that the army had decided "to force Ydígoras out now and govern for year or so with [a] military junta." Bell also heard the Guatemalan foreign minister disparage his president for being afflicted with a "democracy complex."[58] The highest U.S. officials did not discourage such extreme views. At a meeting of Central American presidents held in San José, Costa Rica, in March 1963, President Kennedy warned Ydígoras that Arévalo "would undoubtedly campaign as an anti-Communist moderate, but he would be dangerous if he won [the] election." At San José, Colonel J. C. King, who directed the Western Hemisphere division of the CIA, also spoke to Ydígoras. Secretary of State Rusk reportedly told the Guatemalan foreign minister that he was aware of the "Arévalo menace."[59] CIA agents in Mexico City kept Arévalo under tight surveillance, and other agents immediately informed U.S. national security officials when Arévalo arrived in Guatemala on 27 March 1963. The Guatemalan flew in by a private airplane from Mexico and landed at a rural airstrip outside the capital. The CIA further reported that Ydígoras had acted duplicitously in not opposing Arévalo's return.[60]

Led by Colonel Peralta, the Guatemalan military overthrew Ydígoras on 31 March 1963, one day after the CIA had predicted it would happen. Ydígoras went to Nicaragua, and Arévalo hastily fled the country. The Kennedy administration went through the motions of public disapproval, briefly suspending diplomatic relations. But on the day of the *golpe*, the administration inquired whether the new regime needed equipment to put down potential public disorders. As Assistant Secretary Martin put it, "We are disposed to want to be helpful." President Kennedy also asked about the capability of the new regime to cope with riots. Ambassador Bell assured Washington that Colonel Peralta and his men had taken power effectively and that they "did so from an honest conviction that such action was required to protect the country from a succession of events which would once again lead it into Communist control." The administration restored relations on 17 April, even though Colonel Peralta ignored U.S. requests to lift the state of siege, suspend military tribunals, and schedule a presidential election.[61]

No evidence yet exists to implicate the United States directly in the Guatemalan military's decision to overthrow President Ydígoras. Like military officers in Argentina and Brazil, Guatemalan military men could make their own decisions. But a fine line runs between knowledge of a conspiracy and complicity in it. Guatemalans knew of the history of U.S. intervention in their country and throughout Latin America. The United States constantly told Guatemalan officials, including military officers, that it abominated former President Arévalo, and it did not discourage those who vowed to stop President Ydígoras from holding an open election. The Kennedy administration had also taken care to cultivate relations with Guatemalan security forces. In September 1961, the president approved military assistance for Guatemala, accepting the finding that it be considered among the "prime targets for Castro-communist subversion." Between 1961 and 1963, the administration sent $4.3 million in military aid, as compared to the $950,000 in military aid that the Eisenhower administration delivered between 1956 and 1960.[62] In April 1963, the Defense Department assured President Kennedy that the new aid would help Colonel Peralta maintain order. U.S. Army Special Forces and Air Commando teams had visited Guatemala, and Guatemalan officers now received counterinsurgency training in a center established in their country. Seven hundred twenty officers a year also took basic police courses and studied riot control techniques under U.S. auspices. The Kennedy and Johnson administrations would ultimately supply the 6,500 Guatemalan police officers and men with all their handguns, 50 percent of their shoulder weapons, and over 6,000 tear gas grenades.[63]

Although the United States wielded significant influence in Guatemala, the Kennedy administration learned again that it could not precisely control the political activities of military men. Like their counterparts in Argentina and Brazil, the Guatemalan military, once introduced to political power, did not easily relinquish it. Ambassador Bell initially deluded himself, predicting that the Peralta regime would favor the socioeconomic goals of the Alliance for Progress, thereby persuading the Guatemalan population to accept the new "autocratic political system." Both Bell and his superior, Assistant Secretary Martin, quickly concluded, however, that the Guatemalan military was no more competent or capable than civilian leaders. In August 1963, Peralta publicly stated that elections could only be held after the resolution of Guatemala's social problems. Embassy officers ruefully commented that they and Colonel Peralta would die of old age before "all urgent social problems" had been solved in Guatemala.[64]

The United States continued the Alliance for Progress in Guatemala, committing over $34 million between 1964 and 1966. But U.S. officials understood that the funds did little social good. In March 1964, Ambassador Bell reported that conservatives in the government, the military, and business blocked social reform. Other analysts pointed out that wealthy Guatemalans labeled land and tax reform and universal public education as "Communist." That resistance to change and the failure to restore constitutionalism, Bell conceded, would inevitably polarize Guatemalan political life and fuel extremism, guerrilla insurgencies, and terrorism. Bell recommended that the United States pressure Colonel Peralta into restoring constitutionalism, leading to the election of a "non-extremist liberal government" and precluding "the election of Juan José Arévalo or any other extremist or pro-Communist candidate."[65] The Guatemalan officer corps eventually scheduled an election, which led to the victory of Julio César Méndez Montenegro, a political moderate, in March 1966. The military permitted Méndez Montenegro (1966–70) to take office but not to rule, refusing to allow civilians to oversee military matters. As Ambassador Bell feared, political extremism had taken hold in Guatemala, with a precipitant rise in guerrilla warfare, urban terrorism, and political assassination. Indeed, Bell's successor, Ambassador John Mein, would be assassinated by left-wing radicals in August 1968. The Guatemalan military bore most of the responsibility for this political violence; it dispatched "death squads" to slaughter anyone who questioned the prevailing social order.[66] Perhaps 150,000 Guatemalans died in political violence between the beginning of the CIA intervention in 1954 and the end of 1996, when the warring factions finally signed a truce.

➤   Cold War imperatives prompted the Kennedy administration to encourage the Argentine, Brazilian, and Guatemalan armed forces to shape their nations' foreign and domestic policies. But these decisions to work with military officers and undercut civilian leaders had ironic results. The Latin American military traditionally allied with conservative elites who denounced the socioeconomic reforms called for by the Alliance for Progress. By bolstering groups that resisted change, the administration also violated its core belief that violence, extremism, and even revolution would ensue throughout the region if Latin Americans did not enjoy political and economic progress. The fear of communism overwhelmed the administration's desire for social justice. Virulent anticommunism similarly characterized the Kennedy administration's policies toward the South American nation of British Guiana, where the administration would take astonishing positions on the issues of colonialism and racism. The administration would further decide that it could no longer abide by the nonintervention principle of the OAS.

4 ★ The Kennedy Doctrine

President Kennedy once observed to Prime Minister Harold Macmillan of the United Kingdom that most foreign policy difficulties "paled in comparison with the prospect of the establishment of a Communist regime in Latin America."[1] By displaying military force in the Caribbean and by intervening covertly in Central and South America, the Kennedy administration labored to prevent a second Communist state in the Western Hemisphere. The administration also resorted to all manner of overt and covert pressures in trying to topple the Castro regime in Cuba. The president similarly demonstrated his "absolute determination" to secure the hemisphere from communism and to bar the influence of the Soviet Union in his approach toward independence for the South American colony of British Guiana.[2] Kennedy's fervent anticommunism would clash with his stated positions on imperialism and racial equality. The experience with British Guiana would further lead Kennedy to declare publicly that the United States could no longer adhere to the nonintervention principles adopted by the inter-American community.

★ British Guiana (Guyana), a small state in the northeastern region of South America, does not share the Iberian heritage of most of the nations of the continent. A former outpost of the British Empire, Guyana is the only English-speaking country in South America. Although initially sighted by Christopher Columbus, the area came under the domination of the Dutch in the late sixteenth century. Those few Amerindian peoples who resided in the area lived at a technologically primitive level. The Dutch took advantage of the warm, wet climate along the coastal plain and developed a sugar-based plantation economy in the seventeenth century. Slaves imported from Africa, who perhaps numbered 100,000 in 1800, produced the sugar cane. At the end of the eighteenth century, during the Napoleonic Wars, the British occupied the Dutch settlements. In 1807 the British abolished the slave trade, and in 1831 they united the former Dutch colonies into British Guiana. It remained a British colony until mid-1966, when it took the name Guyana.

Like most Latin American nations, British Guiana developed a multi-racial society. The British government emancipated all slaves in 1838. Free Afro-Guyanese understandably had no desire to continue working on the sugar plantations, where they and their ancestors had suffered barbarous treatment. Some purchased their own land. Others drifted into urban areas, especially the capital, Georgetown. During the twentieth century, Afro-Guyanese filled the lower levels of the civil service and joined the police force and the military. Desperate for agricultural labor, British entrepreneurs who gained control of the sugar industry imported Chinese and East Indian workers through indentured servitude contracts. Between the 1840s and 1917, 240,000 East Indians migrated to British Guiana. In the mid-twentieth century, most Guyanese of East Indian descent continued to work in the agricultural sector producing rice and sugar for export, although they increasingly aspired to middle-class, urban lives in retail and the professions. The census of 1960 revealed a small but growing population of 560,000 people in British Guiana. The population was growing through natural increase at over 3 percent a year, with East Indians having the largest families. Forty-eight percent of the population claimed East Indian heritage, 33 percent descended from African slaves, and 5 percent came from the pre-Columbian inhabitants. Europeans and multiracial groups comprised the rest of British Guiana's diverse population.[3]

Like its neighbors, British Guiana depended on exports of primary products for its livelihood. Economic activity centered on the production of rice and sugar on narrow strips of land near the coast. Most people lived within ten miles of the ocean. Dense rain forest and jungle covered a good part of the interior. Bauxite production was the key mining industry. British Guiana traded its crops and minerals for processed food and finished goods. The United Kingdom, Canada, and the United States dominated the small British Guianan market. The British and the Canadians controlled most direct investments in the colony. U.S. direct investments, which were principally in bauxite and sugar, amounted to only $30 million in 1960. The economy grew slowly but steadily, at about 2–3 percent a year, in the 1950s. This economic growth gave the colony a per capita income of $384 in 1961, an income level slightly higher than in most Latin American nations.[4]

National independence movements in such far-flung areas of the British Empire as India and Kenya caught the attention of Guyanese patriots. Two men, Cheddi Jagan and Forbes Burnham, led the drive for independence in British Guiana. Jagan, who came from a family of

East Indian sugar workers, lived a notable life. His family invested its life savings in the education of the eldest of eleven children, sending him first from his village to secondary school in Georgetown and then in the mid-1930s to Howard University in Washington, D.C. During the summers, Jagan supported himself by working in the Harlem district of New York City. After graduating from Howard, he attained a degree in dentistry from Northwestern University in 1943. While at Northwestern, he met and married Janet Rosenberg, a student nurse who participated in left-wing political movements, including the Young Communist League of Chicago. Janet Jagan would become her husband's political confidante and partner for over fifty years. Like Cheddi Jagan, Burnham acquired international experience before returning to British Guiana. The son of an Afro-Guyanese schoolteacher, Burnham achieved a brilliant scholastic record in Georgetown. He attained a law degree in London in 1947 and associated with the socialist wing of the Labour Party and the Communist Party of Britain. In 1950 Jagan and Burnham founded the People's Progressive Party (PPP), a political organization that espoused nationalism and socialism.[5]

In 1953 Jagan and his party took partial control of British Guiana. The Colonial Office in London had begun the process of devolution, granting universal suffrage and parliamentary home rule. But six months after the election of Jagan, Prime Minister Winston Churchill sent troops and warships to depose him, alleging that Dr. Jagan and his party were Communists. Propertied interests in British Guiana had protested to London over Jagan's plan to strengthen the union movement. Jagan went on a Gandhi-like hunger strike, and British authorities put him in jail for six months. Controversy has always surrounded the question of what political philosophies Jagan, Burnham, and other members of the PPP actually followed. Leading political figures altered their views endlessly and used the terms "Communist," "Socialist," "Marxist," and "Marxist-Leninist" interchangeably. As one student of the colony's politics noted, one could either say PPP members were loyal supporters of the international Communist movement or nationalists poorly versed in Marxism-Leninism.[6] By the mid-1950s, the British government had stopped worrying about the wavering political proclivities of its subjects in British Guiana. In elections in 1957, Jagan and his wife won cabinet posts. In 1960 the British held a new constitutional conference that established a bicameral legislature and a prime minister for internal affairs. A British governor would control defense and foreign affairs until British Guiana gained its independence. Elections were scheduled for August 1961; independence would presumably follow within two to four years. The government elected in August 1961 would oversee the transition from home rule to independence.

As the colony moved toward independence, an ominous racial division appeared in its political life. In 1955 Burnham broke with Jagan over the leadership of the independence movement and founded his own political party, the People's National Congress (PNC). Burnham apparently tired of doctrinal disputes within the PPP and cared less about international affairs than did the Jagans. As subsequent developments would prove, Burnham also wanted to dominate national life. In establishing the PNC, Burnham signaled that he accepted a racial basis for electoral politics. He made explicit appeals for support to Afro-Guyanese, who feared that the growing numbers of East Indians would want the jobs held by the Afro-Guyanese since emancipation. Burnham understood that his party could never win a free election in which the parties divided along racial lines. He argued for a system of proportional representation. At the 1960 constitutional conference, British authorities rejected Burnham's idea, maintaining the "first across the post" electoral tradition of the mother country.[7]

In the August 1961 elections, Jagan's PPP, Burnham's PNC, and a third party led by Peter D'Aguiar, a man of Portuguese descent who espoused the business community's values, vied for the colony's votes. The elections were fair and free. Although the PPP won only about 43 percent of the vote, it secured twenty of the thirty-five parliamentary seats, because PPP supporters were distributed throughout the colony. Burnham's party won 41 percent of the vote and eleven seats, and D'Aguiar's party secured 16 percent and four seats. If voting continued to break along racial lines, the PPP had a bright future, because the young people of British Guiana were predominantly East Indian in background. The electoral results demonstrated, however, that a system of proportional representation would permit Burnham to form a coalition government with a third party. In any case, Prime Minister Jagan took office in late August 1961. Jagan, who had previously visited Cuba with his wife, praised Fidel Castro and opened commercial relations with the Caribbean island.[8]

The Kennedy administration opposed an electoral system, however free, that would grant Cheddi Jagan the right to exercise power in the Western Hemisphere. Administration officials persuaded themselves that Jagan's British Guiana imperiled Latin America and the Alliance for Progress and threatened the security of the United States. The Jagans were wolves in sheep's clothing who engaged in democratic politics as means to an end. Once free of British colonial rule, they would openly embrace communism and ally with the Soviet Union. The United States would then be confronted with a "second Cuba" on the South American continent. As Attorney General Kennedy saw it, what happened in British Guiana might determine the "future of South America." Kennedy conceded that it was a "small country," but Cuba was also small, and "it's caused us a lot of trouble."[9] Indeed, administration officials constantly saw historical parallels between Jagan and Castro. Deputy Under Secretary of State U. Alexis Johnson reminded British officials that "Castro had originally been presented as a reformer." He added: "We do not intend to be taken in twice." Secretary of State Rusk agreed that, in view of "the prospect of Castroism in the Western Hemisphere," the United States was "not inclined to give Jagan the same benefit of the doubt which was given two or three years ago to Castro himself."[10] President Kennedy also recalled the lessons of history. In a conversation with President Ramón Villeda Morales of Honduras, he observed that "experiences with Jagan, the Chinese, and Castro demonstrate that Communists frequently take over a Government in the guise of enlightened, democratic, revolutionary leaders, and not as Communists per se."[11]

During its first months in office, the Kennedy administration argued that Jagan and the PPP should not be permitted to win the August elections. On 5 May 1961, shortly after the Bay of Pigs fiasco, Kennedy ruled at an NSC meeting that the "Task Force on Cuba would consider what can be done in cooperation with the British to forestall a communist take-over" in British Guiana. Kennedy had previously raised the matter briefly with Prime Minister Macmillan. The president wanted to use covert measures to influence the election.[12] In early August, Rusk speculated that a change in the voting patterns in four or five parliamentary seats could make the electoral result "sufficiently confusing to lay the basis for another election" and "give us a little more time." British authorities deflected the U.S. pressure, seeing no compelling reason not "to allow the normal process of democracy and progress toward self-government to go ahead." They reminded Rusk that the governor for British Guiana would still retain control over defense and external affairs.[13] Despite the British opposition, the administration apparently tried to influence public opinion in the colony. Peter D'Aguiar's party showed U.S. Information Service films with strong anti-Communist and anti-Castro themes on Georgetown street corners. A private U.S.

group, the Christian Anti-Communist Crusade, also tried to turn public opinion against Jagan. The electoral results of 21 August 1961 were,
in Rusk's words, "unpalatable." By the end of the month, the administration had decided to consider courses of action in British Guiana in
the political, economic, and information fields, attaching "importance
to the covert side." [14]

Not all observers of the British Guianan political milieu shared
the conviction of the Kennedys, Rusk, Alexis Johnson, and McGeorge
Bundy that Prime Minister Jagan posed a clear danger to U.S. vital
interests in the region. In 1961–62, special national intelligence estimates prepared under the auspices of the CIA presented uncertain analyses of Jagan and the PPP. The intelligence community thought Jagan
might be a Communist, although he had never declared his affiliation.
Analysts could find no evidence of Cuban or Soviet meddling in British
Guiana. Upon independence, Jagan would align his nation with Asian-
African neutralism and anticolonialism. The intelligence community
expected "his government to be assertively nationalistic, sympathetic
to Cuba, and prepared to enter into economic and diplomatic relations
with the Bloc, although such a government would probably still be in-
fluenced by the desire to obtain economic help from the UK and the
US." Although a Jagan government might "lean in the Soviet direction,"
it also probably would want to join the Alliance for Progress. International issues did not, however, dominate the colony's political life. As
the CIA noted on 11 April 1962, racial conflict between the East Indian
and Afro-Guyanese communities would "continue to be the basic factor
in the political situation in British Guiana." [15] State Department officers
agreed that they could find no evidence of an international Communist
conspiracy in British Guiana. In a 15 March 1962 Department of State
paper, they pointed out that Jagan was the ablest leader in the colony
and that he led its largest and most cohesive political party. They further suggested that the United States would damage its "carefully nur-
tured position of anti-colonialism" among Asians, Africans, and Latin
Americans if it opposed independence for British Guiana. Ambassador
to the United Nations Adlai Stevenson shared that concern.[16] Within
the White House, Arthur Schlesinger initially called for a flexible approach toward Jagan. He suggested that the United States could moderate Jagan through economic aid and invite the independent nation
into the OAS and the Alliance for Progress.[17]

British officials, especially those stationed in the Colonial Office, also rejected the U.S. view that Prime Minister Jagan would make his nation a center of conspiracy and subversion. The British undoubtedly wanted to cut the colonial ties as quickly as possible. The small, unprosperous colony lacked economic potential and was beset by racial tension. The governor of British Guiana, Sir Ralph Grey, fulfilled the stereotype of a condescending colonialist when he claimed that "B.G. in its present condition was hardly a good showpiece for what the 'old imperialism' either had accomplished or what was capable of accomplishing."[18] But the British decision to withdraw from South America also involved principle and thoughtful analyses of the colony's political culture. British diplomats persisted in upholding the sanctity of free elections. Colonial Secretary Reginald Maudling insisted that Britain could not "consistently dislodge a democratically elected government" and that he was not disposed to "make Jagan a martyr." The British also took the high road on the question of imperialism. Foreign Secretary Sir Alexander Frederick Douglas Home puckishly reminded Rusk of the "historic role" of the United States as "the first crusader and prime mover in urging colonial emancipation." Prime Minister Macmillan's cabinet greeted with "pleasure" and "relish" Home's suggestion that the British "might be willing to delay the independence process in British Guiana if the Americans would not insist on expediting it everywhere else." On the floor of the House of Commons, Iain N. MacLeod, a former colonial secretary, pointed to the irony of "America urging us all over the world towards colonial freedom except where it approaches its own doorstep."[19]

The British discounted the Communist threat in British Guiana. "Racialism" was the great danger. Colonial officials worried that if elections were canceled and independence delayed, British Guiana could descend into racial warfare and chaos. As for Jagan, they pointed out that he had acted responsibly since returning to government in 1957. Foreign Secretary Home described Jagan as "a confused thinker" whose mind was "clogged with ill-digested dogma derived from Marxist literature." MacLeod insisted that Jagan was not a Communist but a "naive, London School of Economics Marxist filled with charm, personal honesty, and juvenile nationalism." With economic assistance, the United States could modify Jagan's thinking. Home predicted "that British Guiana may end up in a position not very different from that of India." Jagan depended for his political support on an ethnic community that did not reflexively disdain capitalism.[20] In any case, British officials considered Jagan far more capable than Forbes Burnham. They labeled the Afro-

Guyanese lawyer "an opportunist, racist, and demagogue intent only on personal power."[21] The course of Guyanese history from 1968 to 1985 would subsequently sustain that judgment.

Arguments that emphasized the complex, ambiguous nature of political developments in British Guiana made no real impression on the leading foreign policy actors in the Kennedy administration. They entertained only for a short time the notion of cooperating with Jagan. On 30 August 1961, nine days after the parliamentary election, Schlesinger proposed to President Kennedy that the United States develop a two-track policy toward Jagan. The United States would offer technical and economic assistance to British Guiana and give Jagan a friendly reception and a presidential audience when he visited the United States in October. At the same time, the United States would design a covert program to build up anti-Communist clandestine capabilities.[22] In early September, Secretary Johnson instructed the U.S. ambassador in London, David Bruce, to inform the British that the United States had reluctantly decided to try to "educate" Prime Minister Jagan. But key officials did not believe Jagan could learn an acceptable political philosophy. Johnson warned Ambassador Bruce to keep in mind the possibility that Jagan might be a Communist-controlled "sleeper" who would establish a Castro-style regime upon independence. Assistant Secretary of State Roger Hilsman Jr., who directed the department's Bureau of Intelligence and Research, labeled the prospects of cooperation as a "forlorn hope" and concluded that the United States "would have no reasonable alternative but to work for Jagan's political downfall."[23]

Prime Minister Jagan's visit to the United States provided a significant contrast to Castro's April 1959 tour. During his eleven-day visit, Castro had succeeded in projecting a sincere, progressive image to the U.S. public. Vice President Richard Nixon, who interviewed Castro for three hours, suspected his ideas but came away from the meeting impressed with the Cuban's leadership abilities. Castro surprised U.S. officials by not asking for economic aid. He apparently wanted to demonstrate to his public that he would be the first Cuban leader not dependent on U.S. goodwill.[24] Jagan's October 1961 visit, however, proved politically disastrous for him and the colony. On interview programs on radio and television, he refused to denounce the Soviet Union and took an aloof stance on the Cold War. U.S. officials pressed him on doctrinal and ideological issues, asking him to comment on the views of Marxist intellectuals like Harold Laski, Paul Sweezy, and Paul Baran. Jagan avoided being drawn into such a discussion, although he conceded that he was a socialist. Jagan emphasized to President Kennedy, however, that he believed in democracy, an independent judiciary, and an independent civil service "in the British tradition." What Jagan wanted from the United States was economic aid for domestic development so as to buttress his political position. He called U.S. assistance "a political necessity for him." He envisioned receiving $40 million, which, on a per capita basis, would be far more than the United States offered any Latin American country under the Alliance for Progress. As a rule, Kennedy never discussed specific sums of money with foreign leaders. He assured Jagan that the United States cared more about a country's international stance than its domestic arrangements, noting that the United States assisted Communist Yugoslavia. Kennedy cautioned Jagan not to become economically dependent on the Soviet bloc if British Guiana decided to exchange its bauxite for bloc commodities. Jagan left the United States with a sense of failure. He had not made a "satisfactory 'political' impression." Kennedy declined to see him a second time, and he obtained only a vague promise of a $5 million aid package.[25]

After October 1961, the Kennedy administration probably had more CIA operatives in British Guiana than economic development specialists. In early January 1962, Under Secretary George Ball, citing administrative difficulties, ruled against giving British Guiana any immediate economic assistance. The decision, which undoubtedly had the support of Rusk, suggested, in Schlesinger's view, "the evisceration of the British Guiana action program." Schlesinger complained to his boss, and Kennedy ordered Fowler Hamilton, the administrator of the Agency for International Development, to expand technical assistance to the level of $1.5 million.[26] In an informal talk to State Department employees, Kennedy expressed his disgust that the department had "been fiddling" with the question of sending an aid mission to British Guiana. Without a U.S. economic presence, it would be "easy for Jagan to bring in aid from the Communists and also to inform the population of our hostility to them."[27] Despite this ambivalence, the president ultimately sided with his senior foreign policy advisors and against Schlesinger. According to Schlesinger, the president agonized over British Guiana, conceding that Jagan had an impossible task in trying to reconcile a polity torn by factionalism and racism.[28] But working with Jagan involved unacceptable international and domestic political risks. On the day he told Hamilton to expedite aid, Kennedy also demanded an intensification of the covert program in British Guiana. Jagan had not taken a proper Cold War stance during their October meeting. The president's conservative political supporters, like Senator Thomas Dodd (D.-Conn.) and Senator George Smathers (D.-Fla.), denounced Jagan. In March 1962, the State Department reported that since Jagan's visit it had received 113 letters from U.S. legislators opposing cooperation with him.[29] U.S. labor leaders accused Jagan of "pro-Communist activities."[30] Such political pressure influenced President Kennedy's thinking. In Attorney General Kennedy's revealing language, the president "was convinced that Jagan was probably a Communist."[31]

U.S. policy for British Guiana became unequivocal on 19 February 1962. Dean Rusk informed Foreign Secretary Home that he had concluded "it is not possible for us to put up with an independent British Guiana under Jagan." He alleged that the United States had not succeeded in establishing a basis for economic understanding with Jagan. Rusk declined to add that he opposed any economic assistance to the colony. The secretary darkly noted that the "events of 1953" might be repeating themselves. The colony, Anglo-American harmony, and the inter-American system would all face "disaster" if Jagan continued in office. Rusk called for "remedial steps" leading to new elections.[32]

In his message to Lord Home, Rusk noted the ongoing disorders in Georgetown. The Kennedy administration had already launched its campaign to overthrow Jagan. Between 12 February and 19 February 1962 a general strike, demonstrations, riots, and looting disrupted life in the capital. The agitators succeeded in burning the center of Georgetown to the ground. The violence took on ugly racial overtones, with protesters attacking East Indian shops. Jagan had to resort to calling in 2,000 British troops to restore order. The protests, in which Burnham, D'Aguiar, and their followers participated, came in reaction to Prime Minister Jagan's proposed austerity budget, calling for significant reductions in government spending and higher taxes on the wealthy. Colonial authorities ridiculed the idea that Jagan had presented a Marxist program. They called it a "Crippsian" budget, referring to the severe 1948 budget that Chancellor of the Exchequer Sir Richard Stafford Cripps of the Labour Party had given the United Kingdom during its postwar hard times.[33]

Although it is difficult to document precisely, because the CIA has reportedly destroyed its British Guiana records and because some White House deliberations on British Guiana remain classified, it is now known that the CIA, working through U.S. labor unions and foundations, financed the protests and concomitant violence.[34] A London-based union, Public Service International, and its representative, William

Howard McCabe, funneled CIA money into British Guiana. The Public Service International obtained the money through its U.S. affiliate, the American Federation of State, County, and Municipal Employees (AFSCME), and CIA-funded organizations like the Gotham Foundation. McCabe sent money to Richard Ishmael, who led the Trade Union Council, a conservative labor organization in British Guiana. The Trade Union Council used the money to provide food and supplies to strikers. Ishmael and his associates received training from the American Institute of Free Labor Development, which received virtually all of its public funding from the U.S. government. According to police reports cited in parliamentary debates in London, Ishmael carried out bombings and arson attacks against government buildings in Georgetown. A CIA operative, Gene Meakins, worked for the Trade Union Council, editing a weekly newspaper and a daily radio program that put out a constant barrage of invective aimed at Jagan.[35]

In Washington and London also, the Kennedy administration intensified its assault on Jagan and the PPP. On 8 March 1962, Kennedy issued National Security Action Memorandum (NSAM) No. 135; Rusk's letter to Home was now official policy.[36] In May, administration officials hosted Forbes Burnham in Washington. Burnham successfully garnered official support. He stressed his anticommunism and commitment to racial harmony and made a series of wild public charges about Cuban influence in British Guiana. In June, Schlesinger gave up the battle for a cooperative approach to Jagan. In a letter to the president, Schlesinger recognized that Burnham "would cause us many fewer problems" than Jagan. Jagan's heart was with the Communist world. He was not a disciplined member of the Communist Party, "but then neither is Castro." Schlesinger understood that British Guiana would become a Cold War casualty. He questioned whether Burnham believed in racial equality and thought "that British Guiana would be worse off with Burnham than with Jagan." In July, Schlesinger further informed the White House that the CIA plans for British Guiana made him "nervous."[37]

The British tried to resist the U.S. pressure to undermine Prime Minister Jagan. In a 30 May 1962 letter to Kennedy, Prime Minister Macmillan pointed to the need to uphold the Western position on colonialism at the United Nations. He hoped to persuade Kennedy to provide economic support to British Guiana if "Dr. Jagan's party is the choice of the people." But the British had begun to weaken their defense of free elections. Macmillan conceded that developments in British Guiana held "special concern" for the United States. Another official granted that the colony lay within the U.S. "sphere of influence."[38] Analyzing the British reaction, U.S. officials decided that the Colonial Office exercised too much influence over British policy. They believed that the Foreign Office appreciated U.S. hemispheric and global responsibilities and that talks about British Guiana should be held in Washington rather than London. National Security Advisor Bundy urged the president to become engaged personally on the issue, questioning whether Secretary Rusk could overawe the British.[39] Indeed, on 21–22 July 1962, Kennedy met with Ambassador David Ormsby Gore at the family compound in Hyannis Port, Massachusetts, and told him Jagan could not be won to the side of the West. Kennedy added that the United States could not "afford to see another Communist regime established in this hemisphere."[40]

In their Washington meetings with British officials, administration officials disclosed their covert plans. The president authorized Richard Helms, deputy director of the CIA, to impress upon the British "the urgency of taking action."[41] The CIA seized the moment on 22 April 1963, sponsoring a second general strike in British Guiana that would last eighty days. The pretext for the strike was a bill that Jagan introduced into parliament that would give the government the power to certify unions. Jagan argued that organizations like the Trade Union Council represented the sugar industry rather than the sugar workers. In the 1950s, Forbes Burnham had supported the labor legislation. The CIA reportedly spent $1 million on the strike and perhaps supplied arms to Burnham's supporters. Six graduates of the American Institute of Free Labor Development sat on the strike committee. Gene Meakins of the CIA actually negotiated with Jagan. U.S. oil companies refused to deliver petroleum to the colony.[42] Open racial warfare between Afro-Guyanese and East Indians broke out, leaving over 300 people dead. The two strikes, in one scholar's view, left a legacy of racial hatred that "permanently scarred" the national psyche of the Guyanese population. Per capita income fell from $384 in 1961 to $312 in 1963. The violence subsided only when Jagan relented and allowed the labor bill to lapse.[43]

Having demonstrated its ability to generate chaos in British Guiana, the Kennedy administration moved to remove Jagan from office. The U.S. consul general in British Guiana, Everett K. Melby, warned that Jagan enjoyed solid support from his party and that it was wishful thinking to hope that his government would fall through traditional parliamentary procedures. Melby recommended the scheme that Burnham had been espousing since 1960—proportional representation.[44] An electoral system that proportioned parliamentary seats would give Burnham, with about 40 percent of the electorate behind him, an opportunity to form a coalition government with D'Aguiar. Colonial authorities, in opposing proportional representation, worried that the scheme would make voting along racial lines more certain. The Kennedy administration liked the solution of proportional representation. It offered the promise of ousting Jagan, while ostensibly leaving the United States in the position of supporting free elections and the end of colonialism. President Kennedy brought the idea with him when he traveled to England in mid-1963. Rusk had previously warned the British that Kennedy wanted his talks with Macmillan to focus on British Guiana. The United Kingdom must not leave behind a country in the Western Hemisphere with a Communist government. British Guiana was "not just a Colonial problem but one with the highest foreign policy implications."[45]

President Kennedy's 30 June 1963 discussion with Prime Minister Macmillan, Foreign Secretary Home, and other members of the governing Conservative Party at Birch Grove, England, must surely rank as one of the most extraordinary exchanges of views during the history of the Cold War. Kennedy politely listened as Colonial Secretary Duncan Sandys listed the colonial, racial, and parliamentary issues that bedeviled the government's relationship with British Guiana. Kennedy congratulated Sandys on his presentation and immediately shot back "that if the UK were to get out of British Guiana now it would become a Communist state." Kennedy raised the stakes by then adding that independence for the colony could precipitate war in the Caribbean and presumably a global conflict. A second Communist state in the region would "create irresistible pressures in the United States to strike militarily against Cuba." Embellishing the theme, Kennedy implied to Macmillan and his advisors that they had the power to prevent the election of a belligerent, rash person in the 1964 American presidential race. Kennedy repeated "that the great danger in 1964 was that, since Cuba would be the major American public issue, adding British Guiana to Cuba could well tip the scales, and someone would be elected who would take military action against Cuba." In case the British failed to grasp the gravity of the issue, Kennedy instructed them that "Latin America was the most dangerous area in the world." The president promised that the United States would take a sympathetic approach to British problems with colonies such as Southern Rhodesia, but the British needed "to drag the thing out" when it came to independence for British Guiana. Kennedy recommended that the British cite "instability and the danger of racial strife" as rationales for delay.[46]

At Birch Grove, Kennedy did not receive an explicit commitment from the British, and Macmillan and Home did not comment directly on the president's lecture. They were perhaps stunned by the president's direct attack on British policy. But much as happened in the late 1890s when Lord Salisbury, the prime minister, tacitly conceded the U.S. position on the boundary dispute between British Guiana and Venezuela, the British again succumbed to intense presidential pressure. In 1963 the United Kingdom had neither the power nor the will to challenge the United States in the Western Hemisphere. As President Grover Cleveland and Secretary of State Richard Olney would have it, the United States was "practically sovereign" in the region, and "its infinite resources combined with its isolated position" rendered it "master of the situation." President Kennedy had been almost as blunt with his friend, Prime Minister Macmillan.

The British undermined Jagan and sacred parliamentary procedures on 31 October 1963. In mid-October, Jagan, Burnham, and D'Aguiar attended an Imperial Conference called by Colonial Secretary Sandys. The parties predictably deadlocked. Jagan wanted the continuation of parliamentary home rule, a date set for independence, and the lowering of the voting age from twenty-one to eighteen. His adversaries demanded proportional representation, new elections, and a delay in setting the independence timetable. On 26 October, Jagan made a critical mistake when he signed an agreement permitting Sandys to resolve the dispute. The colonial secretary shocked Jagan when he accepted all of Burnham and D'Aguiar's demands. Sandys established a proportional representation electoral system, set new elections, and postponed setting a date for independence until after the new elections. He also rejected Jagan's idea of lowering the voting age. The governor general of British Guiana subsequently announced that he would not be bound by the British tradition of asking the leader of the largest party to try first to form a government. Even under proportional representation, Jagan and the PPP could be expected to win the most parliamentary seats.[47]

Jagan tried to conciliate the Kennedy administration, even as the United States and the United Kingdom plotted to spoil the fruits of his electoral victories. On 16 April 1963, just before the onset of the second general strike, Jagan sent a lengthy, impassioned letter to Kennedy. He pleaded for economic assistance, citing the several cases in which the United States had made preliminary promises of help and then reneged on loans. The only new money in British Guiana came from the American Institute of Free Labor Development, which built homes for members of the anti-Jagan Trade Union Council. The prime minister praised the Alliance for Progress and noted that he carried out the types of fiscal, tax, and agrarian reforms called for in the charter of the Alliance. He stated he wanted a mixed economy for his country and that his party had no plans to nationalize the key bauxite and sugar industries. He denied that the economy of British Guiana had become closely tied to "any international conspiracy." In fact, the colony continued to sell most of its primary products to the industrial democracies. Jagan also reaffirmed his commitment to parliamentary democracy and his respect for the rights of citizens as guaranteed in the U.S. Constitution.[48] In September, Jagan tried an oral approach, asking Consul General Melby what could be done to improve relations with the United States. He felt that the United States had adopted a policy of "Jagan must go." The prime minister asked for U.S. understanding and assistance in realizing his ideal of a "socialist state created by non-violent means." Melby sent an account of his conversation with Jagan to Washington. Secretary Rusk instantly dismissed the overture, instructing Melby that "we wish to avoid creating any impression, or enabling PPP to do so, that there exists real possibility of improving relations between the PPP and USG."[49] The Kennedy administration had convinced itself that Cheddi and Janet Jagan were determined to align their party and nation with the international Communist movement.

Jagan and the PPP lost control of the government in late 1964. Jagan's followers protested the decisions of Sandys, launching their own general strike between February and August 1964. Violence again ensued, with over 1,000 casualties. The strike failed to change the new electoral arrangements. Governor General Richard Luyt, a South African and tough anti-Communist, sided with Burnham and D'Aguiar's parties during the strike and arrested PPP legislators. In the 7 December 1964 elections, the PPP won 45.8 percent of the vote but, under the new scheme, only twenty-four of the fifty-three parliamentary seats. Burnham's PNC won 40.5 percent and twenty-two seats, and D'Aguiar's organization captured 12.4 percent and seven seats.[50] At the governor general's request, Burnham formed a government with the support of D'Aguiar. The coalition oversaw the colony's independence, which came on 26 May 1966.

The Johnson administration fulfilled Kennedy's policy on British

Guiana. In 1964 the British opposition Labour Party had criticized proportional representation, arguing that it would heighten racial tensions. Harold Wilson, the leader of Labour, labeled the Colonial Office's plan a "fiddled constitutional arrangement."[51] In October 1964, Labour took power in the United Kingdom, but Prime Minister Wilson did not challenge the U.S. prescription for British Guiana. After Secretary of State Rusk reiterated the U.S. position on Jagan to Foreign Secretary Patrick Gordon Walker, the new government agreed to respect the judgment of Sandys on proportional representation. It also rebuffed Jagan when he traveled to London and requested a postponement of the election.[52] The Johnson administration rushed economic assistance to the new Burnham government, sending it $12.3 million in 1965. Between 1966 and 1968, the United States provided an additional $25 million. By comparison, between 1957 and 1964, the United States gave the Jagan government only $4.9 million. Burnham initially pleased the United States by severing commercial ties with Cuba and by voting against the admission of the People's Republic of China into the United Nations.[53]

The British decision, made under duress, to give its colony a system of proportional representation and schedule new elections effectively resolved the Kennedy administration's problem with British Guiana. Perhaps reflecting his own distaste for the harsh treatment of Jagan, Arthur Schlesinger offered an ambiguous assessment of U.S. policy in his 1965 biography of Kennedy. "With much unhappiness and turbulence," Schlesinger wrote, the British colony "seemed to have passed safely out of the Communist orbit."[54] The administration's Cold War victory did not, however, relieve British Guiana of its unhappiness and turbulence. Proportional voting solidified the country's racial divisions. As one historian opined, the imperatives of the Cold War distorted political and racial relationships within British Guiana. As such, "the struggle for independence became transformed into an internal struggle for power, one that resulted in the racial polarization of Guyanese society."[55] Schlesinger came to share such a judgment. In 1990, at a forum attended by Jagan, Schlesinger confessed to feeling "badly about my role thirty years ago." He offered excuses for the Kennedy administration, arguing that the intense domestic fear of communism warped the administration's thinking. He also accused the CIA of being too eager "to show its stuff." But Schlesinger admitted that "a great injustice was done to Cheddi Jagan."[56]

Injustice and discord marred Guyana during its first twenty years of independence. The British proved prescient about the nature and character of Prime Minister Forbes Burnham. The 1964 election, which the British supervised, was the last without widespread voting irregularities. In 1968 and 1973, Burnham's party, the PNC, conducted fraudulent elections. Burnham, who dominated Guyanese life until his death in 1985, encouraged a personality cult. He authorized the physical surveillance and wiretapping of his political opponents, and he made racial appeals to his supporters. After 1969, Burnham also shocked the United States by pushing Guyana leftward. He posed as a leader of the Third World in opposition to capitalist imperialism. He attended conferences in Havana. Burnham also spoke of "cooperative socialism," and in 1976 he stated he wanted Guyana to become a Marxist-Leninist state. In the 1970s, he nationalized the bauxite and sugar industries, giving the government control over 80 percent of the economy. Skeptics suggested that Burnham ordered the nationalization less out of ideological conviction and more out of a desire to create opportunities for plunder for himself and his political cronies. By the mid-1980s, Guyana ranked as one of the poorest countries in the world.[57]

Cheddi Jagan stayed in political opposition for nearly three decades. At times, he and the PPP grudgingly accepted some of Burnham's economic policies. In 1992, with his country verging on an economic breakdown, he captured 54 percent of the vote in an honest election. He preached racial harmony to his citizens. In the post–Cold War era, he also promoted a mixed economy and invited foreign investment to Guyana, although he still upheld his socialist beliefs. Jagan conducted cordial relations with the administration of President Bill Clinton, although the administration blundered diplomatically in 1994, when it proposed nominating a former enemy of Jagan, William Doherty Jr. of the American Institute of Free Labor Development, to be the U.S. ambassador to Guyana. Jagan protested, wryly observing that "maybe President Clinton doesn't know our history but the people who advise him should at least know their own history."[58] In March 1997, while still in office, Dr. Jagan died in Washington of a heart attack, after undergoing heart surgery at Walter Reed Army Hospital. In December 1997, Guyanese voters chose Dr. Jagan's seventy-seven-year-old widow, Janet Jagan, to lead the country.

✦   The Kennedy administration's campaign against independence for British Guiana prompted it to pronounce a new doctrine for Latin America. In 1948 the U.S. Senate had ratified the charter of the OAS, which prohibited any state from intervening "directly or indirectly, for any reason whatever, in the internal or external affairs of any other state." The United States had accepted as binding the nonintervention pledge associated with the Good Neighbor policy of Franklin D. Roosevelt and Secretary of State Cordell Hull. The ratification signaled the U.S. acceptance of the juridical equality of all states, a principle espoused by nineteenth-century Latin American jurists like Andrés Bello and Carlos Calvo and twentieth-century diplomats like Argentine foreign minister Luis Drago, who in 1902 had protested the naval bombardment of Venezuela by Europeans over a debt issue. The ratification of the OAS charter also represented a repudiation of the foreign policy of Theodore Roosevelt. In 1904 Roosevelt had claimed that the United States, as the dominant regional power, had the obligation to exercise "international police power" to insure that Latin Americans paid their international debts and respected foreign lives and property. Under the aegis of the "Roosevelt Corollary" to the Monroe Doctrine, the United States had repeatedly intervened in the internal affairs of Caribbean and Central American nations during the first third of the twentieth century, incensing Latin Americans and badly straining inter-American relations.

The United States found it difficult to reconcile its commitment to respect the national sovereignty of Latin American nations with its Cold War concerns. In light of historical experience, many Latin Americans regarded the nonintervention principle as sacred and inviolable. They also believed that the United States exaggerated the threat of communism, confusing it with indigenous brands of revolutionary nationalism. Although it never systematically examined the dilemma, the Truman administration first grappled with the problem of how to defeat communism in the region and still adhere to the nonintervention pledge. In 1952 the administration accepted the proposal of Anastasio Somoza García of Nicaragua that the two countries work together to overthrow the allegedly pro-Communist regime of Jacobo Arbenz Guzmán of Guatemala. President Truman authorized the CIA to provide Guatemalan exiles with weapons and funds. But the operation lasted only five weeks, and the administration canceled it in October 1952. The CIA had apparently been unable to maintain the confidentiality of the operation.[59]

President Eisenhower never authorized an overt attack on a Latin American government, relying on CIA-backed covert interventions, most notably in Guatemala, to fight communism. But his administration quietly prepared to ignore U.S. treaty commitments. To basic policy statements on Latin America, which were developed by the NSC and approved by the president, the administration attached a section on "exceptions to non-intervention." A staff study had found that "it is probable that the majority of Latin American governments do not yet favor even limited multilateral intervention." It speculated that collective action "would probably be supported" only if a "clearly identifiable communist regime should establish itself in the hemisphere." The study concluded that "overriding security interests" required the United States to consider acting unilaterally, recognizing "that this would be a violation of our treaty commitments, would endanger the Organization of American States . . . and would probably intensify anti-U.S. attitudes in many Latin American countries." Eisenhower and the NSC accepted that hard bargain. In policy paper NSC 5613/1 (1956), the Eisenhower administration vowed that the United States would take any political, economic, or military action "deemed appropriate" to sever ties between a Latin American nation and the Soviet bloc.[60]

President Kennedy made explicit the Eisenhower dictum. In late May 1963, at the president's direction, a special NSC task force, working outside of normal channels, began preparing a declaration to be known as the "Kennedy Doctrine." As National Security Advisor Bundy explained it, the president wanted "a declaration or doctrine which would put the Russians and the Latin Americans on notice that the U.S. would not accept a second Castro in this hemisphere." The development of the Kennedy Doctrine came during the period when the administration was pressuring the United Kingdom to delay independence and establish an electoral system of proportional representation in British Guiana. In fact, Bundy opined that the easiest way to disclose the new policy would be in the context of a crisis, like British Guiana, in which "our decision to act would be generally approved."[61] The task force realized, however, that OAS members would not welcome a public statement reiterating the U.S. right to exercise international police power in the Western Hemisphere. Latin Americans did not share the administration's anxiety about subversion and "another Cuba."[62]

The president decided, however, not to spare Latin American feelings. His assessment of regimes in British Guiana, Brazil, and elsewhere led him to defend the U.S. resolve to take any measure necessary to defeat communism in the hemisphere. On 18 November 1963, in the middle of his last speech on inter-American affairs, the president took up the issue of "international responsibility." Communism ceaselessly struggled for world domination and menaced the Alliance for Progress. The American states needed to confront the challenge by coming "to the aid of any government requesting aid to prevent a takeover aligned to the policies of foreign communism." Kennedy advised: "My own country is prepared to do this." "Every resource at our command" must be used "to prevent the establishment of another Cuba in this hemisphere."[63] The Kennedy Doctrine attracted little public comment, for, as Bundy explained to Attorney General Kennedy, the president's declaration "was blanketed almost immediately by his death."[64] Bundy advised President Johnson to make a similar public statement, "taking a more vigorous line than we have in the past."[65] North and South Americans learned about this feature of U.S. policy in the spring of 1965, when President Johnson ordered 20,000 U.S. troops to invade the Dominican Republic and then pronounced his Johnson Doctrine. Johnson agreed with President Kennedy that "the American nations cannot, must not, will not permit the establishment of another Communist government in the Western Hemisphere."

✦   The Kennedy administration's policies toward British Guiana had ironic overtones. As a senator, Kennedy had earned international acclaim for denouncing French colonialism in Algeria. Yet he insisted that the British "drag out" the independence process in their South American colony. On 11 June 1963, the president gave an eloquent, moving address to a national audience on the moral dimensions of civil rights and promised to introduce legislation that would outlaw discrimination against African Americans. Even as Kennedy spoke, U.S. agents inflamed racial tensions in British Guiana. The president spurned Cheddi Jagan, a leader who welcomed the Alliance for Progress, and embraced Forbes Burnham, an authoritarian and demagogue. As a presidential candidate, Kennedy identified with President Roosevelt and the Good Neighbor policy. His experience with British Guiana convinced him, however, to repudiate the nonintervention principle, the essence of the Good Neighbor. Kennedy's fear of the international and domestic consequences of the expansion of communism in the Western Hemisphere led him to take such extraordinary steps. But the administration did not reject all reform leaders and movements. Political leaders who espoused constitutionalism, reform, and anticommunism existed in Latin America, and the administration firmly supported them.

5 ✳ Constitutional Defenses

The Kennedy administration took seriously its professed view that the United States had an obligation to promote social justice, the rule of law, and respect for basic human rights in Latin America. Administration officials cherished those principles and further believed that equitable, law-bound societies would be resistant to the appeals of communism. Several Latin American politicians agreed with the U.S. prescription for progress and justice and eagerly embraced the Alliance for Progress. Some of these Latin Americans also accepted U.S. leadership in the Cold War. The Kennedy administration vigorously defended such national leaders, putting U.S. diplomatic power and prestige behind their constitutional aspirations.

✦   President Kennedy and his advisors favored Rómulo Betancourt's Venezuela over other Latin American leaders and countries. As the president once publicly proclaimed, President Betancourt represented "all that we admire in a political leader," and his reform programs served as "a symbol of what we wish for our own country and for our sister republics."[1] Kennedy exceeded diplomatic niceties because he trusted the Venezuelan, enjoyed his company, and knew that Betancourt believed in the Alliance for Progress. He also judged Betancourt to be a fellow Cold Warrior under assault from the international Communist movement. President Kennedy always found the time and resources to support those types of Latin American leaders.

President Betancourt (1959–64) traveled a tumultuous path to reach Venezuela's highest office. Born in 1908 to a rural family of modest circumstances, he attended public schools and the Universidad Central in Caracas. With other idealistic university students, he joined in 1928 in an unsuccessful protest against the vicious and venal regime of General Juan Vicente Gómez (1908–35). Gómez sent Betancourt for a stay in his dungeon and then exiled him. While in Costa Rica, Betancourt briefly associated with the Communist Party. He later helped organize Acción Democrática (Democratic Action), a secular political organization dedicated to transforming Venezuelan society. In 1945 he and fellow party members helped oust the latest general ruling the nation. Betancourt headed the junta which oversaw Venezuela's first free election, held in early 1948. But Venezuela's democratic experiment ended late that year, when military officers again seized power and established another military dictatorship, principally under Colonel Marcos Pérez Jiménez. Betancourt spent the time from 1948 to 1958 living in Costa Rica, Cuba, Puerto Rico, and New York. He found little support from the Eisenhower administration; Eisenhower's advisors were comfortable with military rule in Venezuela, and they suspected Betancourt's youthful radicalism. While in exile, Betancourt exchanged ideas with Latin American reformers like José Figueres and Juan Bosch and U.S. liberals such as Adolf Berle. He kept in contact with Acción Democrática officials who operated clandestinely in Pérez Jiménez's Venezuela. He also wrote his *Venezuela: política y petroleo* (1956), a scathing indictment of Pérez Jiménez and the foreign oil industry. When mass protests toppled Pérez Jiménez in early 1958, Betancourt returned in triumph and secured an overwhelming electoral victory.

The Eisenhower administration only reluctantly embraced Venezuela's new democratic, anti-Communist leader. In November 1960, President Eisenhower confided to aides that "it was strange that he used to think of Betancourt as a leftist and now he was beginning to look like a rightist in relation to pro-Castro, pro-Communist attacks against him."[2] But a strong personal bond quickly developed between Betancourt and Kennedy. As Assistant Secretary Martin noted, "A personal electricity seemed to flow" between them. On the surface, the relationship might have seemed unusual, for the two men came from different worlds. Unlike the elegant, charismatic U.S. leader, Betancourt was short, plump, balding, bespectacled, and "sometimes sloppy." He also had been badly scarred by the assassination attempt ordered against him by Rafael Trujillo. As National Security Advisor McGeorge Bundy observed, Betancourt was "an insignificant looking man" who proved "the point that appearances don't count for much."[3] Perhaps Kennedy liked Betancourt because he saw in the Venezuelan the characteristics that he believed a leader needed. Twenty years of exile and constant combat with political enemies had taught Betancourt that a tough, pragmatic attitude would help him in addressing domestic and international problems.

President Kennedy undoubtedly enjoyed Betancourt's hospitality. The Venezuelan responded to the Alliance for Progress speech by declaring that Kennedy spoke "a language that has not been heard since the days of Franklin Delano Roosevelt."[4] The U.S. president also relished the tumultuous welcome that Betancourt arranged for him when he visited Venezuela in December 1961. The large, friendly crowds he met served as a delicious counterpoint to the violent demonstrators encountered by his political rival, Richard Nixon, when he arrived in Caracas in May 1958. Betancourt gave the president another splendid "photo opportunity" by having him participate in a land redistribution ceremony in the village of La Morita. Both Venezuelan and U.S. officials worked hard to ensure that Kennedy had a safe and happy visit. Twenty thousand bayonet-wielding Venezuelan troops stood at the ready. And presidential aide Richard Goodwin actually suggested that Catholic priests read a pastoral letter to their Venezuelan parishioners urging them to welcome the first Catholic U.S. president. Nonetheless, Kennedy approached the visit with trepidation. As he prepared to leave the plane at the airport in Caracas, he wryly speculated on Goodwin's future "if this doesn't work out." Presidential assistants Kenneth P. O'Donnell and David F. Powers armed themselves with revolvers and stayed close to the president.[5]

President Kennedy reciprocated Betancourt's kindness. He put on a grand ceremony for Betancourt when he came to Washington in February 1963. He also rewarded Betancourt with a direct telephone line between the White House and Miraflores, the Venezuelan presidential palace. Whereas Kennedy frequently flattered Latin American leaders by asking them for their views on regional issues, Kennedy took Betancourt's advice seriously. He informed him about all key decisions on Latin American policy and consulted with him about men such as Juan José Arévalo, Juan Bosch, and Salvador Allende, the Chilean socialist. The presidents spoke frankly. Betancourt repeatedly complained about bureaucratic delays in administering Alliance funds, and he objected to the prices Venezuela received for its chief exports, petroleum, coffee, and cacao. President Kennedy refused to subscribe to the so-called Betancourt Doctrine. Betancourt believed that it was "nonsensical" to denounce totalitarian regimes in Asia or Europe and to tolerate despotic governments in the Western Hemisphere. Betancourt wanted Kennedy to refuse to recognize Latin American military governments on principle and as a way of warning the Venezuelan military not to strike another *golpe*.[6]

U.S. officials also admired Betancourt because he seemed to be the living symbol of the Alliance for Progress. He would presumably show Latin Americans how a progressive, enterprising, dynamic middle class could create a modern, egalitarian society. Alliance planners placed their faith in a man who had become a cautious, evolutionary reformer. The years of exile had taken their toll on Betancourt. He concluded that his Acción Democrática party had alienated Venezuelan elites by pushing too hard and fast for reform during the *trienio*, the period between 1945 and 1948. Popular support and electoral mandates could not guarantee success; Betancourt judged that he would have to mollify the traditional centers of power—the landed oligarchy, the military, the church, and the foreign oil industry—if he wanted to consolidate a constitutional system and pursue reform. He subsidized church activities, and he bought military officers new weapons. He also tempered his commitment to change. During the *trienio*, Acción Democrática had passed an agrarian reform law that encouraged local peasant organizations to determine the pattern and pace of land redistribution. By comparison, the agrarian reform law of 1960 created a centrally controlled, planned process that would parcel out land only as support services, such as roads, homes, and marketing facilities, were in place. The state would compensate the original landowners, and it would also provide subsidies to commercial farmers.[7]

Critical to Betancourt's plan of working around and through traditional power holders was the foreign oil industry. In 1960 Venezuela ranked third in world oil production, giving it a per capita income of $800, higher than other Latin American countries except Argentina. U.S. and British-Dutch companies produced the petroleum. U.S. investments in Venezuela amounted to over $2.5 billion, accounting for over 30 percent of U.S. direct investments in Latin America. But Venezuela's relative wealth, as particularly revealed in Caracas's stunning skyline, misled casual observers; in fact, most Venezuelans lived poorly. Although he had written about how foreign oilmen had colluded with the corrupt Gómez and unsavory Pérez Jiménez, Betancourt accepted their continued role in Venezuelan life and dismissed talk of expropriation or nationalization. Needing increased revenues in order to finance economic diversification and social reforms, Betancourt and his party resorted to imposing new taxes on the oil industry. Unfortunately for Venezuela, the declining price of oil on global markets in the 1960s sharply limited its income and curtailed Betancourt's reform plans.[8] In any case, by defending constitutionalism, respecting international capitalism, and preaching restraint, Betancourt earned the respect of Kennedy administration officials. They approvingly placed him within the moderate reform tradition of the Democratic Party of Roosevelt, Truman, and Kennedy. They dubbed him a "New Dealer."[9]

Betancourt's moderation infuriated young Venezuelans, many from Acción Democrática, who had stayed home in the 1950s and resisted the Pérez Jiménez regime. They charged that President Betancourt had forfeited his moral authority and the opportunity for meaningful reform by appeasing elites. For these young radicals, the Cuban Revolution provided the answer. As they saw it, Betancourt had been talking about revolution for thirty years, whereas Castro, after two years of hard fighting, immediately transformed Cuba. They further alleged that, in declining to nationalize the oil industry, Betancourt and his followers acted "like cowards" who feared "Yankee pressure, imperialist pressure." These Venezuelans threatened the Betancourt government with violent antigovernment demonstrations in Caracas in late 1960. Many joined the Movimiento de Izquierda Revolucionaria (Movement of the Revolutionary Left), or MIR. In 1962 the Venezuelan Communist Party, which claimed 20,000 members, decided to support the armed insurrection.[10] For much of the 1960s, Venezuela's constitutional authorities confronted leftist agitation, guerrilla warfare, and urban terrorism.

To U.S. officials, President Betancourt's struggle against Venezuelan leftists seemed part of the global war against the international Communist movement. In the 1961 task force reports, Adolf Berle judged Venezuela "the point of greatest attack" and a "hinge to the situation." Citing CIA reports, Berle warned that a successful Communist uprising in Venezuela would fan regional "brushfire wars." Walt Rostow drew parallels between U.S. military involvement in South Vietnam and Betancourt's defense of his presidency. In April 1963, intelligence analysts advised the Standing Group, the counterinsurgency task force, that if guerrillas triumphed in Venezuela, Castro's tactics would be vindicated. But if Betancourt survived, Castro's influence would decline throughout Latin America.[11]

Kennedy administration officials believed that Communists especially targeted Betancourt because he was Latin America's most blunt and credible critic of Fidel Castro. Betancourt and Castro came to power at the same time, and both competed for the hearts and minds of Latin Americans. In January 1959, Castro made a triumphant tour of Venezuela. When he met with Betancourt, Castro surprised the new president by asking for a $300 million loan and oil shipments at discount prices. The amused Betancourt initially characterized Castro as young and naive. But his attitude hardened when Castro began to criticize Latin Americans who were not revolutionaries. In March 1959, for example, Castro insulted José Figueres, Betancourt's friend and mentor, at a rally in Havana. Thereafter, he publicly questioned Venezuela's reformist path and celebrated the growing, violent opposition to Betancourt's government by political leftists.[12] From Radio Havana flowed a steady stream of invective and derision. The "tyrant of Venezuela" foolishly opposed "the heroic struggle waged by the people of Venezuela against the outrages committed by the present government." As Castro told a Cuban audience, Betancourt "could mobilize 100,000 students only if he gave them permission to organize a demonstration against him."[13]

Betancourt did not turn the other cheek when it came to Castro. He reportedly knew about and approved of the planning for the Bay of Pigs operation. He broke relations with Cuba in late 1961 and supported the U.S. crusade to drive Cuba out of the OAS. In October 1962, Venezuela held a seat on the U.N. Security Council. Its representative firmly defended the military quarantine of Cuba, and Betancourt sent two destroyers to assist the U.S. Navy in enforcing it. Betancourt also permitted Cuban exiles to operate in Venezuela. As he told President Kennedy, the "resistance movement in Cuba must be strongly supported and Venezuela is so doing within its resources."[14] Assistant Secretary Martin has also stated in his memoirs that in August 1963 Betancourt informed the U.S. ambassador that he favored the assassination of Castro and that he would finance it and encourage José Figueres, "an able conspirator," to arrange the assassination.[15]

The Kennedy administration vowed to do anything "within reason" to support Betancourt, because he was Castro's "number one target." Officials accepted Betancourt's argument that "victory or defeat of this government experiment in Venezuela will have a real significance, good or bad, depending on its results, for all of Latin America."[16] President Kennedy personally oversaw the defense of Betancourt's government. He met with Venezuelan political figures, such as Christian Democratic leader Dr. Rafael Caldera, and congratulated them for affirming democratic processes. In the Oval Office, Kennedy hosted Brigadier General Antonio Briceño Linares and pointedly observed to the military man that "he was aware of the support given by the Armed Forces to President Betancourt." The White House also issued public statements applauding Betancourt when he suppressed insurrections. Embassy officers assisted by advising Venezuelan leaders how to use television and radio to dramatize the government's fight against radicals.[17]

The administration put money behind its verbal support of Betancourt. In early 1961, it rushed an emergency aid package of $100 million to help Betancourt calm impoverished urban areas, where leftist organizers flourished. Between 1962 and 1965, the United States provided an additional $140 million. It also backed Venezuela's requests for assistance, which amounted to another $200 million, from international lending agencies such as the World Bank and Inter-American Development Bank. Betancourt put the money to work on public housing and public works projects, although he believed the United States could do more. In 1961 alone, he asked for $220 million. When he tired of filling out loan applications, Betancourt teasingly prodded Kennedy by reminding him that he fought against those seeking to "establish in Caracas a branch office of Habana."[18]

U.S. military assistance came along with Alliance for Progress funds. Venezuelan authorities remained ambivalent about that feature of U.S. involvement. They wanted the military to protect the government from armed insurrection, but they feared, in light of Venezuela's history, that the armed forces would again seize power. Venezuelan ambassador José Antonio Mayobre told President Kennedy that training programs for Latin American officers would "inevitably stimulate their interest in taking political power." The president answered "that close association with the American military, who understood so well the need to subordinate the military power to the civilian, would be helpful in deal[ing] with the problem with which the Ambassador was concerned."[19] Although the president believed his own answer, he and his advisors sought additional objectives. They too wanted the leftists routed, but they also wanted a strong Venezuelan military as a safety measure. In Kennedy's words, "The Armed Forces were essential to prevent the radical Left or Right from taking over." Ambassador to Venezuela C. Allan Stewart agreed with his president, noting that "U.S.-oriented and anti-Communist armed forces are vital instruments to maintain our security forces in Caribbean region." Stewart recalled that the military preserved Guatemala from communism in 1954, whereas Castro triumphed because the Cuban military disintegrated.[20]

The Kennedy administration made sure that the Venezuelan military remained intact. Between 1961 and 1965, the United States supplied over $60 million in credits and grants for military equipment and training, twice the amount of military aid supplied during the 1950s. In 1961–62, seven Venezuelan officers attended Special Warfare School at Fort Bragg, North Carolina, and eighty-three officers took counterinsurgency courses at Fort Gulick in the Canal Zone. In June 1962, the administration rushed pistols and submachine guns to the Caracas police force. A year later, it sent seven helicopters to help the government with its surveillance program of university students. The U.S. military mission, which was the largest in Latin America, trained men in antiguerilla tactics and, as in South Vietnam, assigned U.S. personnel to advise in combat operations against insurgents.[21] To insure coordination of its economic and military assistance programs, the administration sent to Venezuela an interdepartmental task force headed by Henry Byroade, the former ambassador to Afghanistan. The task force, which arrived in September 1962, was modeled after the Taylor-Rostow mission to South Vietnam in 1961. It studied how to save President Betancourt, defeat the Communists, and build a nation.[22]

As it did in South Vietnam, the Kennedy administration assumed that the international Communist movement instigated terrorism and violence in Venezuela. President Betancourt did not dissuade administration officials from that assumption, for he usually blamed Castro for Venezuela's troubles. The Venezuelan found it difficult, however, to provide the United States with concrete evidence of Castro's treachery, other than to cite Havana's endless tirades against him. For example, he complained to Kennedy in December 1961 about arms being smuggled into Venezuela, but he blamed the Panamanian National Guard for the aggression.[23] Venezuelan members of MIR undoubtedly traveled to Cuba and returned home with ideas, training, and money. The Venezuelan Communist Party perhaps received funds from the Soviet Union. In the previous four decades, the Soviets had, at times, financially supported Latin American Communist parties. But Venezuelan Communists only joined the insurgency at the end of 1962 and quit by 1965. They engaged in bitter disputes with MIR and Castro, proclaiming that they rejected "the role of revolutionary 'pope' which Fidel Castro arrogates to himself."[24] Despite the outside assistance MIR may have received, it remained an indigenous organization. In 1965 a CIA study concluded that MIR members "ran their own shows," were a "home-grown revolutionary organization," and could be described as an "extreme-nationalist, revolutionary nationalist movement."[25] Whatever their origins, Venezuelan guerrilla fighters, who numbered between 1,000 and 2,000, created havoc in the country. The government reported that over 400 people died in revolts joined by Venezuelan marines at Carúpano and Puerto Cabello in mid-1962.

President Kennedy tried to help his Venezuelan friend find damning evidence against Castro. While in Washington in February 1963, Betancourt publicly denounced Castro, advising the National Press Club that "we should continue constantly and unremittingly our actions against this regime in Cuba to encircle it, to cut it off without ceasing and failing."[26] After meeting with Betancourt, the president wrote to CIA Director John McCone that "it is obvious that the Communists in Venezuela support Castro. Do we have any information that could be presented in a public forum, such as the OAS, that would indicate that the link between the anti-Betancourt terrorists and Castro is direct?"[27] That link surfaced on a Venezuelan beach in November 1963, when Venezuela announced that it had discovered a cache of Cuban arms, consisting of eighty-one rifles, thirty-one machine guns, and ammunition for heavy weapons. These arms were allegedly left for insurgents determined to disrupt the upcoming Venezuelan presidential election. CIA officers brought one of the rifles in the cache to Robert Kennedy, who then sent it on to his brother. The president was shown where the Cuban coat of arms was sanded off the rifle. According to Richard Helms, a pleased president said: "Great work. Be sure to have complete information for me when I get back from my trip [to Dallas]. I think maybe we've got him now."[28]

The Cuban intervention surprised intelligence analysts in Washington, for Castro had not previously exported arms, although they also noted that Castro reportedly stated "he would like very much to get rid of 'Betancourt and company.'"[29] In fact, some have subsequently questioned the validity of the discovery. Joseph Burkholder Smith, who had previously served as the CIA chief of station in Caracas, has implied that CIA operatives, responding to presidential pressure, engaged in a form of "black propaganda" and planted the arms. Philip Agee, a former CIA agent who turned against the agency, also recalled that he immediately suspected that the Caracas station, working with Venezuelan agents, planted the arms. But neither man had hard evidence to sustain his suspicions. As Agee recorded in the diary he reconstructed, "For the sake of discretion I haven't asked." Perhaps predictably, Fidel Castro charged that the CIA had "faked" the evidence. Soviet premier Nikita Khrushchev seconded the Cuban's allegation.[30]

The arms cache incident provided an opportunity for the Johnson administration to intensify, in McGeorge Bundy's words, "our present nasty course" against Cuba. CIA Director McCone showed President Johnson "the evidence that proved absolutely that arms had been imported into Venezuela from Cuba."[31] The administration, through the U.S. Information Agency, launched a massive anti-Cuban campaign throughout Latin America. Venezuela lobbied Latin Americans, telling them that serial markings on the weapons and intercepted messages provided irrefutable proof that Cuba had violated the nonintervention principle of the OAS charter. In July 1964, the OAS acted on the Venezuelan complaint; by a vote of 15 to 4, it called on member states to break relations and impose economic sanctions on Cuba. Cuba was effectively ostracized from the inter-American community, with only Mexico ignoring the sanctions.

If he had lived, President Kennedy would have been heartened not only by the OAS vote but also by the Venezuelan presidential election. For the first time in its history, Venezuela had a peaceful transfer of power from one popularly elected leader to another. On 1 December 1963, over 90 percent of the electorate voted, ignoring threats from leftists to shoot anyone who came to the polling stations. Raúl Leoni, Betancourt's political associate, secured a plurality of the vote and was inaugurated on 11 March 1964. Betancourt's transfer of the presidential sash to Leoni set the nation on a course of orderly transfers of power.

Reflecting on Betancourt's constitutional success, Attorney General Kennedy claimed that the Special Group on counterinsurgency that he directed "was responsible for the preservation of the democratic system in Venezuela." Without U.S. assistance to the military and police, "Venezuela would have been taken over by the Communists."[32] Indeed, President Betancourt put U.S. security assistance to vigorous use. He authorized the military and police to conduct mass arrests of leftists and to combat radicals in the streets. He also permitted security forces to arrest MIR and Communist Party members who held legislative seats and to subject them to military tribunals. Betancourt suspended constitutional guarantees five times, 778 out of the 1,847 days he was in office. His decisions remain controversial in Venezuela. Betancourt believed that his crackdown on leftist agitators forestalled another right-wing military *golpe*. With historical hindsight, he might argue that he spared Venezuelans the bloody nightmare of military rule that terrified the citizens of Argentina, Brazil, Chile, and Uruguay for over two decades.

By choosing not to raise issues such as tax reform with Venezuela's entrenched elites, Betancourt probably ensured that he could never fulfill the lofty goals of the Alliance for Progress. He and Leoni worked diligently for the poor, resettling approximately 160,000 families on their own farms, allocating budgetary expenditures to health and education, and cutting unemployment. But Venezuela never hit the Alliance's target of an annual growth of 2.5 percent a year, and 75 percent of Venezuelan youth still did not complete the sixth grade. Revenues to do good were scarce because the price of a barrel of oil fell below $2 in the 1960s; Venezuela collected less in taxes per barrel than it did in the 1950s.[33] During the "energy crisis" of the 1970s, the price of oil zoomed to over $30 a barrel, providing the Venezuelan treasury with unprecedented revenues. Subsequent Venezuelan governments squandered that bonanza. Despite these setbacks, U.S. officials would have judged Venezuela one of the few successes of the Alliance for Progress. It established a constitutional system, carried out some reform, crushed local radicals, and proved a good soldier in the war against Castro and communism.

★   The Kennedy administration also planned that Chile, like Venezuela, would serve as a "showcase" for the Alliance for Progress. The South American republic had already committed itself to many of the Alliance's ideals. Chile had maintained, except for brief interruptions, a constitutional system since 1833. Chilean elites gradually extended the right to vote to ordinary people. The electorate grew from 500,000 in 1938 to 2.5 million in 1963. Chileans perceived themselves as living in an urbane, literate society that took art, literature, and political philosophy seriously. They similarly took pride in noting that they had generally avoided the violent confrontations that had marred their neighbors' histories. Like the advanced European nations, Chile developed a twentieth-century social welfare state. Under the leadership of Arturo Alessandri Palma (1920–25), Chile adopted a social security system and a labor code that protected the rights of urban workers.

Despite this seemingly happy past, Chile had grave social and economic problems. Since 1930, the population, growing at 2.5 percent a year, had more than doubled to 8 million people. Food production had not, however, kept up with the population spurt. Prior to 1930, Chile had been a net exporter of food; in the early 1960s, its imports of food exceeded its exports by $100 million. Inefficiencies and injustices in the agricultural sector of the economy accounted for this poor performance. Seven percent of landowners controlled 80 percent of the land. Most of Chile's 400,000 rural families were landless. Many landowners did not put their holdings to productive use. Chile had fewer cattle in 1960 than in 1910. Per capita agricultural production actually decreased in the late 1950s. The desperate rural poor migrated to urban centers such as Santiago. They dwelled in shantytowns, known locally as *campallas*, or "mushrooms," on the outskirts of cities. Perhaps 25 percent of Chileans lived in absolute poverty.

Global economic developments compounded Chile's problems. Chile traditionally had relied on foreign investors to exploit its natural resources. In the nineteenth century, the British had developed the nation's nitrate resources. In the twentieth century, U.S. firms such as the Anaconda and Kennecott corporations produced Chilean copper for world markets. By 1960, U.S. direct investments in Chile amounted to an impressive $700 million. But like the prices of other primary products, the price of copper, which accounted for over 60 percent of Chile's foreign earnings, had been unstable in the post–World War II period and had generally fallen in the 1950s. The price of copper oscillated from sixteen cents a pound to over fifty cents between 1950 and the mid-1960s. With such instability, national economic planning became virtually impossible. Chile tried to diversify its economy by nurturing "infant industries" with high tariffs. The Chilean domestic market was, however, too small and poor to make that a viable economic strategy. The economy scarcely grew at the rate of 1 percent a year during the 1950s. Desperate to maintain the nation's generous social compact, Chilean authorities responded to the mounting crisis with monetary expansion, foreign borrowing, and deficit financing. Annual inflation rates of 30–40 percent were the predictable results of those decisions. Then, in 1960, Chile suffered a devastating earthquake that created over $200 million in damages.[34]

Economic instability and growing poverty had the effect of fracturing the Chilean political system. The polity divided roughly into thirds. Wealthier Chileans trusted in the political parties and solutions of the past, believing Chile should rely on foreign investment and trade and maintain its social safety network by spending money on public works and social welfare. In the middle stood the Christian Democratic Party, a new, growing organization modeled on the Christian Democratic movement that flourished in West Germany and Italy. Christian Democrats, who took their inspiration from the encyclicals on social responsibility of Pope Leo XIII and Pope John XXIII, believed in evolutionary change, emphasizing land, tax, and educational reforms. Communists and socialists, led by Salvador Allende Gossens in the Frente de Acción Popular (Popular Action Front), or FRAP, offered Marxist solutions for Chilean problems. Allende and his supporters favored the nationalization of the copper industry and the radical redistribution of land. They became fervent admirers of Fidel Castro and the Cuban Revolution. In the presidential election of 1958, Allende nearly won the presidency, finishing only 3 percent, about 34,000 votes, behind the conservative choice, Jorge Alessandri Rodríguez, the austere, sixty-two-year-old bachelor son of the former president. Eduardo Frei Montalva of the Christian Democrats came in third in the presidential race.

For U.S. officials, Chile under President Alessandri (1958–64) presented several dilemmas. The Eisenhower administration initially welcomed Alessandri's election, predicting that he would establish "a businessman's government." The administration had unsurprisingly opposed the Marxist Allende's election, although it is uncertain whether it intervened in the Chilean electoral process. In mid-1959, it arranged a $100 million economic rescue package of public and private loans to help Alessandri cope with Chile's staggering financial problems. But by mid-1960, U.S. embassy officials advised Washington that the United States would need to cultivate reform-oriented political parties; President Alessandri declined to attack vigorously Chile's social and economic problems. If Chile achieved little progress, Allende's political appeal would inevitably grow.[35] The Kennedy administration also grew frustrated with the pace of change in Alessandri's Chile. It showed its displeasure by delaying an invitation for Alessandri to visit Washington and President Kennedy. When the president finally welcomed Alessandri in December 1962, he departed from prepared public welcoming remarks to note puckishly that Alessandri's populist father would have enthusiastically supported the Alliance for Progress.[36]

President Alessandri also disappointed on the Cuban issue. Chile opposed the Bay of Pigs operation, and in January 1962, Chile joined its neighbors, Argentina and Brazil, in declining to exclude Cuba from the inter-American community. Chile shared the perception that a Caribbean island could not possibly pose a strategic threat to a southern cone nation. Like Argentina, Chile also believed that its unique geopolitical position gave it a special role in international relations. During World War II, for example, Chile waited until early 1943 before siding with the Allies. Chile's aloofness did not, however, infuriate U.S. officials. They believed that, unlike Argentina, Chile had compelling domestic reasons for passing on the Cuban issue. Salvador Allende and his supporters, which included fifty-three Chilean legislators, made clear that "any aggression against Cuba is an aggression against the small nations of the world, against Latin America, and against Chile."[37] Secretary Rusk conceded that such factors were "obviously dangerous and important" in explaining Chile's abstention. President Alessandri also took care to assuage U.S. officials. He privately condemned Nikita Khrushchev for his "irresponsibility and demagoguery," noted that Cuba had unjustly treated the United States, and supported the United States during the missile crisis. Alessandri further offered, in a private conversation with President Kennedy, to have staff in the Chilean embassy in Havana collect information on Cuba and pass it on to the United States.[38]

As outlined by State Department officers, the United States had developed an inconsistent policy toward Alessandri's Chile. The Kennedy administration wanted a success story for the Alliance for Progress in South America, and between 1961 and 1963, it allocated almost $350 million to Chile. Indeed, during the 1960s Chile would receive over $1 billion in Alliance-generated funds, the highest amount in South America on a per capita basis.[39] This support inevitably tied the United States to a Chilean leader in whom it had little confidence. The United States backed Alessandri, even though he resisted financial and economic reforms, because it feared that a crisis in Chile would benefit Allende. As officers noted, "We are not prepared to risk a Socialist or FRAP victory, for fear of nationalization of U.S. investments, the consequences of that action, and the possible Communist influence in a Socialist (or FRAP) government." What the United States needed was a political party that would satisfy the "aspiring elements" of Chilean society.[40] In Venezuela, the Kennedy administration had found satisfaction in Rómulo Betancourt and his Acción Democrática party. The administration decided to replicate that experience by bolstering Eduardo Frei and his Christian Democratic movement.

President Kennedy agreed with State Department analyses of Chilean political culture. In March 1962, he asked aides to send him information on the Christian Democrats. He also asked for reports on Chile's economic performance. As Ambassador to Chile Charles Cole recalled, Kennedy became particularly well informed about Chile. The president concluded that electoral victories by the Chilean Christian Democrats would augur well for the rest of Latin America.[41] As he observed to Chilean ambassador Walter Mueller, socioeconomic reforms would diminish the appeal of FRAP. The president agreed with Ambassador Cole that U.S. aid projects "should be carefully chosen, for production of rapidly visible results, and to encourage the people, giving them hope of economic and social progress and justice without a turn to the extreme left."[42] Kennedy further argued that the outcome of Chile's elections would have global consequences. He informed President Alessandri that it would be "a major setback for us if the Communists were to win an election in a democratic country when we have said that communism can remain in power only by building a wall." In order to prevent that diplomatic defeat, Kennedy met with Frei in Washington in September 1963. He also told aides he wanted to visit Chile so as to have "maximum possible impact" on the Chilean presidential election, scheduled for September 1964.[43]

Although President Kennedy focused on promoting the Christian Democrats, he developed contacts with other Chilean politicians. In inviting Alessandri to Washington, the president overruled his advisors, thinking that the Chilean should be given the opportunity to explain his problems.[44] After receiving the invitation, Alessandri somewhat mollified the United States by concluding an agreement with the International Monetary Fund and passing an agrarian reform law that empowered the central government to purchase unused land. Only about 1,200 rural families, however, received land under Alessandri's law. The Chilean leader probably sensed that Kennedy and his advisors preferred a Christian Democratic government. Kennedy also hosted Julio Durán, the leader of the Radical Party, a group of moderate conservatives. The president did not appreciate Durán's comparing Eduardo Frei to the Communists.[45]

In backing Frei and the Christian Democrats, the Kennedy administration signaled that it could accept a major change in the copper companies' privileges in Chile. Frei proposed a "Chileanization" of the copper industry. Chile would purchase part ownership of the companies; the companies, in turn, would be expected to use the proceeds of the sale to increase production and establish processing and fabricating facilities in Chile. Chile would presumably increase export earnings, and workers would find new employment opportunities. The administration found no major problem with Frei's plan, which resembled the public-private business relationships that had existed for foreign companies in Mexico since the 1930s. President Kennedy believed that the success of the Alliance for Progress partially depended on increased foreign investment. He complained to President Alessandri that U.S. companies invested too much of their money in Europe and not enough in Latin America.[46] But Frei's plan preserved private capital and might take questions about Anaconda and Kennecott out of the arena of partisan politics. As a State Department study noted, copper production was an explosive issue in Chilean politics, because the companies were "quite foreign in character." They were wholly owned U.S. subsidiaries that declined to offer stock for sale locally. Managers who resided in New York City made the decisions that determined the basic economic health of Chile.[47]

As was revealed in congressional hearings in the mid-1970s, the Kennedy administration went beyond publicly praising evolutionary reformers and providing public funds for economic development in its quest for constitutional leaders who would transform Chile and defeat the Marxist left. It conducted a massive covert intervention in the Chilean political process. In April 1962, the Special Group on counterinsurgency secretly approved a $50,000 expenditure to strengthen the Christian Democratic Party, and in August it authorized an additional $180,000 expenditure for the next year. The Special Group hedged U.S. bets by giving a total of $50,000 to the Radical Party. After the Christian Democrats had a spectacular showing in the April 1963 municipal elections, the Special Group enthusiastically supported Eduardo Frei, allocating $3 million for the upcoming presidential election. The CIA actually spent $2.5 million on Frei, which represented more than half of his campaign fund. The United States apparently did not inform Frei about the intervention. CIA agents in South American countries busied themselves "laundering" money for the Frei campaign. The CIA agents in Chile spent the money on polling, posters, advertisements, and anti-Communist projects designed to win over student, labor, and women's groups. They also made special efforts organizing slum dwellers and peasants. In September 1964, Frei enjoyed a landslide victory, taking 56 percent of the vote. Allende took second place with 39 percent of the vote. Frei's chances of achieving an electoral plurality were always excellent. The 1964 election was essentially a two-man race, because conservative forces, fearful of an Allende victory, did not sponsor a viable candidate. Nonetheless, the CIA boasted that U.S. intervention enabled Frei to win a clear majority in the 1964 election.[48]

The Kennedy administration had similarly intervened in the 1962 Brazilian congressional elections. But it probably drew a sharp distinction between that intervention and its support of the Christian Democrats of Chile. In Brazil it wanted to destabilize a constitutional government that it considered dangerous, whereas in Chile it hoped to move beyond the reliable but undynamic Alessandri administration. Chile needed to address its socioeconomic problems in order to undermine the appeal of FRAP. U.S. officials were certain that political radicals like Salvador Allende intended to abridge Chilean constitutional guarantees. They accepted Ambassador Cole's warning that FRAP would end democratic government in Chile and "would be so dangerous for U.S. interests in Chile and in all Latin America that U.S. policy should be to strive to prevent it."[49] Cold War verities apparently kept administration officials from seeing the irony in their calculations and actions. As one student of U.S.-Chilean relations has observed, "The covert manipulation of the democratic process by massive secret funding and efforts to divide and weaken political parties clearly violated the principle of popular sovereignty."[50] The covert intervention may have also weakened the democratic process by urging Chileans to view political opponents as mortal enemies. The CIA financed a "scare campaign"; it depicted, via films, posters, leaflets, and wall paintings, images of Soviet tanks and Cuban firing squads. It also disseminated "disinformation" and "black propaganda," planting false stories in an attempt to turn the Chilean socialists and Communists against one another.[51]

The Kennedy and Johnson administrations made a good bet in placing U.S. money on the Christian Democrats. President Frei (1964–70) proved a progressive and an advocate of the Alliance for Progress. He resettled 27,000 families on their own farms, and his administration built over 400,000 low-cost homes. He also had some success taming Chile's inflationary fires, lowering the annual rise in prices from 80 percent in 1964 to 17 percent in 1966. U.S. Ambassador to Chile Ralph Dungan, a former aide to President Kennedy, openly backed these reforms. In the view of the U.S. Agency for International Development, Frei's Chile had become "one of the few countries in Latin America where substantial social and economic change is taking place without civil discord, interruption of normal constitutional government or serious political instability."[52] The Johnson administration responded to this good news by providing an additional $500,000 in covert campaign funds to help Christian Democrats in congressional races. The CIA spent additional money organizing interest groups on behalf of the Christian Democrats.[53] Such support did not make President Frei a slave to U.S. interests. He accepted the 1964 OAS decision to exclude Cuba from the inter-American community. But he established diplomatic relations with the Soviet Union, and in 1967 he signed a trade agreement with the Soviets. Like other Latin American leaders, he also increasingly complained about the terms of trade between the industrialized world and the producers of primary products.[54]

Despite some notable achievements, President Frei and his Christian Democrats failed to create the conditions for long-term economic growth and development. He faced constant obstructionist tactics from both ends of Chile's political spectrum. The structure of Chile's constitutional and legal systems also gave Frei's opponents numerous ways to delay reform. Frei had hoped, for example, to resettle 100,000 rural families during his term. His "Chileanization" scheme did not produce as much copper or as many new jobs as planned. The price of copper on world markets continued to fluctuate wildly. During the 1960s, Chile's economy grew at an annual rate of 1.9 percent, well below the 2.5 percent Alliance target. Between 1966 and 1970, the economy grew only at a 1.3 percent annual rate.[55] This economic decay and political polarization set the stage for Chile's descent into political chaos and confusion and ultimately into two decades of appalling political repression under General Augusto Pinochet Ugarte (1973–90). The Kennedy administration's public policies, at best, only delayed this Chilean tragedy; its covert actions may have made it more likely.

✦   The Kennedy administration's most dramatic defense of constitutionalism came in mid-1962, when it angrily denounced the Peruvian military for annulling the presidential elections and seizing power. On 19 July 1962, President Kennedy issued a remarkable statement, charging that the Peruvian military had violated the charter of the Alliance for Progress and that the cause of democracy in Latin America had suffered "a ruinous setback." The president broke relations with Peru, recalled Ambassador James Loeb Jr., and suspended economic and military assistance programs. The U.S. pressure seemingly forced Peruvian military officers to reconsider their *golpe*. By August, they agreed to restore civil liberties, schedule a new presidential election, and permit OAS officials to monitor the election. In June 1963, Peruvians elected a civilian, Fernando Belaúnde Terry, in a reasonably fair election.[56]

Prior to the *golpe*, U.S. officials viewed Peru as a reliable Cold War partner that might enact the fundamental social and economic reforms called for by the Alliance for Progress. In 1962 Manuel Prado y Ugarteche (1939–45, 1956–62) was completing his second presidential term. President Prado and his prime minister, Pedro Beltrán, were moderate conservatives who provided Peru with dignified, albeit uninspired, rule. They represented Peruvians of European heritage who lived in coastal areas and traditionally held sway over Peru's people of mixed racial heritage (*mestizos*) and the Amerindian groups who resided in the Andean highlands. These descendants of the Incan empire, who comprised about 50 percent of Peru's 11 million people, lived on the margins of existence. Although Peru had a small Communist Party and no active insurgent movement, U.S. officials worried that Peru's dreadful inequities "provided one of the best illustrations of a 'potential for social revolution'" in Latin America.[57] In fact, violent, radical protest movements would briefly appear in the mid-1960s and explode throughout Peru in the 1980s. Despite their misgivings about the government's inertia, Kennedy administration officials respected Peru's leaders, because they promised to oversee a peaceful, constitutional transfer of power in 1962.

The United States also appreciated Peru's diplomatic support. During World War II, President Prado had faithfully sided with the United States against the Axis powers and became a friend of President Franklin Delano Roosevelt. Prado continued to support U.S. Cold War positions, and he and Beltrán were among the hemisphere's harshest critics of Fidel Castro. Less than two weeks before the Bay of Pigs invasion, Prime Minister Beltrán urged Secretary of State Rusk to take "quick and decisive action" against Castro and not to worry about outcries of intervention from Latin Americans. He added that "the adverse reaction would not last and that the event would soon be forgotten as a live issue, as in the case of Guatemala and the assassination of [Patrice] Lumumba." President Prado told Kennedy that Peru would consider recognizing anti-Castro Cubans as a legitimate government in exile. In January 1962, at the inter-American meeting called to denounce Cuba, Rusk confessed that his "sharpest difficulty" might be to persuade President Prado "to take a firm but reasonable rather than an extremely belligerent view" toward Castro.[58] Such loyal support earned President Prado the honor of being the first Latin American president that Kennedy hosted in the Oval Office. While in Washington, Prado assured a joint session of Congress that Peru stood with the United States in the struggle against the international Communist movement and that "whatever measures you may be required to take to combat it, you will find my country at your side."[59]

U.S. officials believed, however, that they could improve on President Prado. They looked forward to the election of Víctor Raúl Haya de la Torre, leader of Alianza Popular Revolucionaria Americana (American Revolutionary Popular Alliance), or APRA, as Peru's next president. The APRA movement, which was founded by the dynamic Haya while in exile in Mexico in the mid-1920s, presented an eclectic approach to Peru's and Latin America's problems. Borrowing from the Mexican Revolution, Marxism-Leninism, and European socialism, APRA initially called for the end of imperialism, nationalization of land and industry, respect for Amerindian people, and the internationalization of the

Panama Canal. In Peru the Aprista party, which Haya also established, took a populist approach but also expressed sympathy for the plight of middle-sector groups. It also became distinctly anti-Communist. Although it developed strong electoral support, the Apristas had difficulty gaining political power. From 1931 on, the Peruvian oligarchy, particularly the military, overturned Aprista electoral victories. The military never forgave the Apristas for a 1932 insurrection that led to the execution of military officers. The military, in turn, carried out wholesale executions of Aprista followers. Haya and other Aprista leaders spent years in jail and exile. In 1956 the Apristas supported Prado's election, because he had not persecuted them during his first presidency. President Prado allowed the Apristas to organize between 1956 and 1962.

However confused, inconsistent, and baffling the Aprista platform may have been, Kennedy administration officials convinced themselves that Haya could fulfill the goals of the Alliance for Progress. Like Betancourt and Figueres, Haya had met and impressed U.S. liberals who espoused anticommunism and social reform. Senator Hubert H. Humphrey (D.-Minn.) called Haya's party a "worthy representative of the democratic, non-Communist left."[60] Ambassador Loeb, who formerly presided over the liberal, anti-Communist organization Americans for Democratic Action, also had confidence in Haya. The Peruvian seemed the epitome of middle-class evolutionary reformer envisioned by the architects of the Alliance for Progress. In February 1962, Assistant Secretary of State Robert Woodward called the Aprista party "the strongest anti-communist force in Peru." His successor, Assistant Secretary Martin, agreed that it was "an unusually effective agent of change but firmly anti-communist, the kind of party we wanted everywhere in Latin America but rarely found." Reports from U.S. field officers who worked with Aprista members in organizing student, labor, and farm groups substantiated those views.[61]

Two other major candidates, besides Haya, presented themselves for the national election, which was scheduled for 10 June 1962. Manuel Odría (1948–56), the former general who had seized power in 1948, ran on a vague platform of national unity. Running for a second time for president was Belaúnde, a U.S.-trained architect who represented the aspirations of educated middle-sector Peruvians. He also spoke about massive public works projects, such as a trans-Amazon highway. Although it publicly stated it could work with the winner, the Kennedy administration suspected both of Haya's opponents. Odría had been a dictator, and Belaúnde declined to repudiate the Peruvian Communists who supported him. Haya's organization, on the other hand, was "the only political party in Peru which had taken a firm stand against the communists." [62]

During the first half of 1962, the administration worked hard to ensure that Peruvians would accept the results of the presidential election. In February and March, the highest-ranking Peruvian military officers explicitly told Ambassador Loeb that they would not serve under an Aprista president. They could not forget the past, and they detested Haya. At Loeb's suggestion, the State Department recalled him to Washington so that he could take back to Lima the president's personal views. Kennedy authorized Loeb to inform the Peruvian military that the United States "was committed in the hemisphere, and in the eyes of its own people and Congress, to the support of non-communist constitutional governments throughout the hemisphere." Ambassador Loeb could further warn them that he had discussed these matters with the president and that the United States would find it "impossible" to recognize a military government.[63] To insure that Peruvian officers understood the U.S. position, the administration dispatched a retired U.S. military officer, who had previously served in Peru, to speak to the military men. It also ordered the U.S. Information Agency to launch a propaganda campaign in favor of constitutionalism in Peru. As the election took place, President Kennedy instructed Loeb to convey privately to President Prado appreciation for his firm stand on behalf of constitutionalism. Two days after the election, in a public ceremony in Washington honoring the visiting Panamanian president, Kennedy toasted Peruvian democracy.[64]

The Peruvian national elections did not produce, as the United States had hoped, a decisive electoral mandate for Víctor Haya de la Torre. The Aprista leader finished less than 1 percent ahead of Belaúnde and only 4 percent ahead of Odría. His party had, however, captured a significant plurality of congressional seats. The Peruvian Congress would have to choose a president in late July. Leaders and parties negotiated from mid-June to mid-July 1962, with the military apparently again warning Haya to step aside. The surprising result of the talks was that the Apristas agreed to support the election of Manuel Odría as president and an Aprista leader as vice president. During his dictatorship, Odría had imprisoned scores of Apristas and forced Haya to hide in the Colombian embassy. Odría presumably now promised to respect constitutional processes and support a reform program. The Kennedy administration nervously watched these maneuvers. It rejected Ambassador

Loeb's suggestion that it publicly warn that it would refuse to recognize "any government imposed by force." But President Kennedy again privately thanked President Prado for his "gallant efforts" and offered to consider sympathetically and urgently any request for assistance.[65]

On 18 July 1962, Peruvian military officers used a U.S. Sherman tank to batter down the gate to the presidential palace and then arrested seventy-three-year-old President Prado. They established a twelve-man junta under the direction of General Ricardo Pérez Godoy. The Kennedy administration and the U.S. public found the military's attack on President Prado outrageous. President Kennedy's blistering denunciation of the *golpe* won him hearty praise at home but only limited support abroad. Venezuela and Costa Rica warmly applauded the president and suggested that the OAS meet to condemn the Peruvian action and all illegal changes of government. But the larger Latin American nations, led by Mexico, rejected the views of Rómulo Betancourt and José Figueres; they upheld the nonintervention principle of the OAS charter. The U.S. business community in Peru also opposed the break in relations, arguing that it endangered their $450 million in direct investments.[66] Kennedy's denunciation surprisingly failed to evoke much reaction among Peruvians. Large-scale strikes and demonstrations did not follow the military *golpe*. U.S. officials had perhaps misjudged the Peruvian political milieu, analyzing the struggle between the military and Haya as a fight between reaction and reform. The *golpe* could be viewed as another episode in a three-decade-long blood feud.

President Kennedy quickly regretted having become personally identified with the Peruvian fight. He complained to aides that "he had got himself, as President, too far out in an exposed position in this regard." He further observed that "power was an important factor" and that "one had to work with governments in power."[67] The United States could not be seen as having diminished prestige and influence in the hemisphere. As Ambassador to the OAS DeLesseps Morrison saw it, "Such flip-flops in foreign relations are humiliating and do us little good."[68] After the junta released President Prado and permitted him to seek exile in Paris, the administration quickly came to terms with the Peruvian military men. It accepted their pledge to hold a new election in June 1963, after failing to force them to agree to a February or March election date. It requested that the military vigilantly watch for any expansion of Communist influence in the labor movement.[69] The administration pleased the Peruvian junta by managing to kill the Venezuelan proposal for an OAS meeting on constitutionalism.[70] On 17 August 1962, less than one month after the break, the United States restored diplomatic relations with Peru and resumed its economic aid programs. The administration also agreed not to send Ambassador Loeb, who had become popularly identified with the Apristas, back to Lima, choosing instead J. Wesley Jones, a career foreign service officer, as the new ambassador. To demonstrate that it still disapproved of the military *golpe*, the administration withheld military assistance. But the administration capitulated on that issue also when, in October 1962, President Kennedy overruled a State Department recommendation and ordered the resumption of full military assistance. As explained in a joint State-Defense telegram, which was sent to the embassy in Lima on 23 October 1962 in the midst of the Cuban Missile Crisis, the United States needed "solidarity in face Cuban-Soviet threat to hemisphere security."[71]

The Peruvian military transferred power to a civilian in mid-1963, when Belaúnde defeated Haya and Odría in another close election. Perhaps some Peruvians, fearing another showdown between the Apristas and the military, switched their votes from Haya to Belaúnde. Both the Kennedy administration and the Peruvian military had saved face. The United States had upheld the principle of constitutionalism, and the military men had again prevented their enemies from taking power. During Belaúnde's (1963–68) tenure, U.S.-Peruvian relations soured, as disputes broke out over the contractual rights of the International Petroleum Corporation, a subsidiary of Standard Oil of New Jersey, and the rights of tuna-fishing vessels, such as the *Chicken of the Sea*, to fish within the 200-mile territorial limit claimed by Peru. Belaúnde also proved ineffective in implementing the goals of the Alliance for Progress. In Peru over 1 million rural families were landless or owned minuscule plots of land. Belaúnde's agrarian reform program managed to help about 9,000 families.[72] As U.S. intelligence analysts noted in a May 1963 survey of Peru, "Unless the forces of moderation are able to bring about orderly change, radical leadership will probably get the chance to try its methods."[73] President Kennedy would not live to see the various radical political groups that would attempt to break up the existing Peruvian social and economic structure. Nonetheless, as always, he fretted about Peru's and Latin America's place in a world of international communism. Before sending Ambassador Jones off to Lima, the president reminded him that Latin America occupied "a primary place in our policy considerations. Europe was relatively secure and prosperous while the situation in Latin America required our best efforts and attention."[74]

As Kennedy had astutely realized, the United States had made a tactical error in publicly confronting the Peruvian military and then accepting an unsatisfactory solution. Other Latin American military men quickly surmised that they could wait out the United States. Unless the issue involved communism, the Kennedy administration would not again risk U.S. prestige to save a constitutional regime.[75] Indeed, in late 1963 a replay of the Peruvian imbroglio occurred in the small Central American nation of Honduras. On 3 October 1963, Colonel Oswaldo López Arellano overthrew the popularly elected government of Dr. Ramón Villeda Morales (1957–63) and canceled the national elections scheduled for 13 October. Colonel López and his conservative friends opposed the probable election of Modesto Rodas Alvarado; they alleged that Rodas would not show proper respect toward the Honduran military. Throughout 1963, U.S. officials stationed in Honduras had advised Colonel López that the United States favored elections and that the Honduran presidency was "not a job for the military." The administration also judged that Dr. Villeda and his Liberal party had done "a relatively good job" in support of the Alliance for Progress. In late 1962, President Kennedy had a cordial meeting with the Honduran leader in Washington.[76] The Kennedy administration broke relations and suspended aid programs after the *golpe*. But the cocky Honduran officer predicted to Ambassador Charles Burrows that the United States would ultimately accept his seizure of power and that it would resume its aid within six months. The ambassador knew that Colonel López calculated correctly.[77] López promised to schedule an election and made the appropriate noises about being a good anti-Communist. By 1 November, a disgusted President Kennedy had privately decided to restore relations. On 14 December 1963, the Johnson administration announced the restoration of diplomatic relations with Honduras. Colonel López dominated Honduran political life for the next twelve years, giving his nation unsavory and unenlightened rule.

The unhappy Peruvian and Honduran experiences, combined with the overthrow of Juan Bosch by the Dominican military, prompted Kennedy to order Assistant Secretary Martin to issue a statement on U.S. "policy regarding military governments in Latin America." The president read drafts of the paper and explicitly approved the final statement, which appeared on 6 October 1963 in the *New York Herald Tribune*. The United States would not adhere to the Betancourt Doctrine, which called for the rejecting of all unconstitutional governments. The administration had found that it could not presently attain the Alliance's goal of development within the framework of democracy in every country, because "in most of Latin America there is so little experience with the benefits of political legitimacy." The United States would continue to oppose the overthrow of constitutional governments, but it would use force only against "intervention from outside the hemisphere by the international Communist conspiracy." In any case, the United States had learned that it was beyond U.S. power to "create effective democracy" or to keep "a man in office by use of economic pressure or even military force, when his own people are not willing to defend him."[78]

As administration officials interpreted it, Martin's public statement represented a critical shift in policy. Presidential advisor Arthur Schlesinger sent the president an impassioned three-page memorandum alleging that Martin's statement seemed "unduly cold and condescending" and might suggest "to sensitive Latinos an unconscious paternalism and contempt in American policy." Schlesinger feared that the statement signaled that the United States had lost faith in progressive democracy and that the administration now looked "to military rule to produce progressive regimes." As Schlesinger requested, President Kennedy struck a note of reassurance at his next press conference, suggesting that the United States had not reversed its position on constitutionalism.[79] But the administration published Martin's statement in the *Department of State Bulletin* and repeated it to all Latin American diplomatic posts. U.S. diplomats were told that the new policy had been cleared "at highest levels" of the U.S. government.[80] Other administration officials agreed that the president meant what Martin wrote. Presidential advisor Theodore Sorensen opined in his memoirs that Kennedy had come to recognize "that the military often represented more competence in administration and more sympathy with the U.S. than any other group in the country."[81]

★   The Kennedy administration preferred constitutional leaders and democratic political movements over military regimes. It took extraordinary measures to bolster Rómulo Betancourt, Eduardo Frei, and Víctor Haya de la Torre and their respective political parties. These men accepted the Alliance for Progress and the need for the United States to wage Cold War against the Soviet Union and its Cuban ally. The administration also gladly worked with Costa Rica, the democratic Central American nation that had established progressive policies. And military *golpes* in Peru, the Dominican Republic, and Honduras disappointed the administration. But it quietly rejoiced when, in July 1963, the Ecuadorian military overthrew President Carlos Julio Arosemena Monroy, an inept alcoholic who allegedly did not take the Castro threat seriously.[82] The administration also assisted the Argentine, Brazilian, and Guatemalan armed forces in their pursuit of political power. President Kennedy and his advisors valued stability and anticommunism over the rule of law in Latin America. The administration's pursuit of an anti-Communist stability would also be evident in the new military doctrines it exported to Latin America.

6 ⭐ Counterinsurgency Doctrines

The Kennedy administration took an active, aggressive approach toward inter-American affairs. It tried to transform the social and economic structures of Latin American nations through the Alliance for Progress. It constantly intervened in the political processes of its southern neighbors, trying to create responsible, reform-minded, anti-Communist leaders, parties, and institutions. And it conducted an unrelenting war against Fidel Castro's Cuba. The administration also dramatically changed the U.S. relationship with the Latin American military. It scrapped the notion that the armed forces of Latin America had a responsibility to defend the hemisphere from outside attack. Instead, it used military aid as an incentive to persuade military officers that they should concentrate on internal security and national development. Counterinsurgency, civic action, and public safety were to be the new missions of Latin American security forces.

✦   The Kennedy administration inherited a military aid program for Latin America that was a legacy of World War II. The experience of the war had caused U.S. defense planners to want Latin America to be militarily dependent upon the United States. Prior to the war, South American nations had purchased their arms and accepted military training missions from Europe, including the Axis nations of Germany and Italy. In order to exclude foreign influences and promote U.S. ideas on peace and security, officials proposed an arms standardization policy for the hemisphere. The United States would provide arms if Latin America would cooperate in postwar hemispheric defense, make its military bases available to U.S. air and naval forces, and agree not to purchase equipment and training from foreign sources. In both 1946 and 1947, the Truman administration submitted a military aid package to Congress but did not secure funding. Congressional critics managed to delay legislation, arguing that military aid was wasteful, would bolster authoritarian regimes, and would trigger a hemispheric arms race. The Truman administration did not press the issue; it kept busy fulfilling the military needs of Cold War allies in Western Europe, Greece, and Turkey, and in China.

In the aftermath of the Korean War, which intensified U.S. fears of an international Communist conspiracy, the Truman administration persuaded legislators to include Latin America in the global military aid program. In 1951–52, Congress appropriated almost $90 million in direct military aid for Latin America. The administration commenced signing bilateral military agreements with the individual Latin American republics. The Eisenhower administration continued the program, providing an additional $400 million in military assistance during its eight years in office. It transferred heavy equipment, such as combat aircraft, warships, and tanks, to the Latin Americans. Neither the Truman nor the Eisenhower administrations precisely explained the costs and benefits of military aid. The questions that skeptical legislators had initially raised about the dangers of arming poor, weak, undemocratic nations remained unaddressed. How this military alliance would actually work also went unexamined. The United States spoke about a multilateral defense of the hemisphere but negotiated bilateral agreements. In any case, providing Honduras or Ecuador with tanks would probably not deter the Soviet Union from launching a nuclear attack. At an NSC meeting, President Eisenhower conceded that the Latin American armed forces could contribute little to hemispheric defense. In executive session, Senator John F. Kennedy agreed that military aid produced no military value. What military aid accomplished was to help the United States cultivate diplomatic relations with the military dictators who dominated Latin America during the 1950s. As a U.S. military official once noted in defending military aid to Anastasio Somoza's Nicaragua, "The Latin American officers who work with us and some of whom come to this country and see what we have and what we can do are frequently our most useful friends in those countries."[1]

Such reasoning became suspect by the end of Eisenhower's second term. In the political tumult that followed Vice President Nixon's trip to South America, concerned citizens and political aspirants, like Senator Kennedy, denounced the Eisenhower administration for arming dictators. Administration officials also questioned the wisdom of past policies as they analyzed the Cuban Revolution. During the 1950s, the United States had given Cuba $16 million in military assistance and trained over 500 Cuban officers. But Castro's forces, using guerrilla-style tactics, had humiliated Batista's army. Defense planners wondered whether other Latin American armed forces would succumb to guerrilla insurgencies. Moreover, they now conceded that money spent on heavy military equipment might be better dedicated to alleviating the poverty and frustration that were generating revolutionary ferment in the region. During its last year in office, the Eisenhower administration began to reorganize its military aid program for Latin America. It wanted smaller, more mobile forces capable of maintaining internal security against civil disturbances or insurrection. Latin American officers would need to learn new combat tactics to counter the threat of Communist guerrillas. The administration further hoped that Latin American soldiers would contribute to their nations' development through "civic-action" programs, building dams, roads, and other public works projects under the direction of a military corps of engineers.[2]

Whereas the Eisenhower administration began to use words like "counterinsurgency," "civic action," and "internal security," President Kennedy aggressively pushed to make such concepts essential parts of his Latin American policy. His analysis of Nikita Khrushchev and Fidel Castro's intentions, based on the "wars of national liberation speech," the Bay of Pigs experience, and the Vienna summit, convinced him that the United States needed to take new military actions to prevent the Cuban Revolution from spreading throughout the hemisphere. As he warned the U.S. people a week after the Bay of Pigs invasion, "We are opposed around the world by a monolithic and ruthless conspiracy that relies primarily on covert means for expanding its sphere of influence— on infiltration instead of invasion, on subversion instead of elections, on intimidation instead of free choice, on guerrillas by night instead of armies by day."[3] President Kennedy made good on his vow to respond to that challenge. He had NSC officials read Khrushchev's boast about wars of national liberation, and, at his first NSC meeting, he told Secretary of Defense Robert McNamara that he wanted an emphasis placed on counterinsurgency doctrines. On 27 February 1961, Kennedy instructed the Joint Chiefs of Staff to study what the United States could do to build antiguerrilla forces around the world, but especially in Latin America. He asked his generals to find out "how these military Latin Americans feel about Castro; from a military viewpoint, what would they do from their countries to offset his regime; and does Castro represent a threat to their countries?"[4] In early September, he issued NSAM No. 88, ordering the secretary of defense to explore what steps could be taken "to increase the intimacy" between the U.S. and Latin American armed forces. Latin Americans needed to be taught, the president opined, "how to control mobs and fight guerrillas." To insure that his concerns received constant attention, the president subsequently issued NSAM No. 124, appointing a committee, the Special Group (CI), to oversee counterinsurgency efforts. General Maxwell D. Taylor, the president's military representative, and Attorney General Robert Kennedy headed the Special Group, which focused on Southeast Asia and Latin America. The president further ordered civilian and military officers assigned to Latin America to attend a five-week interdepartmental seminar on "Problems of Development and Internal Defense."[5]

Although Kennedy's initiatives were born of fear of Communist subversion, they also reflected the contemporary belief among some scholars that military organizations could contribute to the social and economic development envisioned in the Alliance for Progress. Professor John J. Johnson of Stanford University argued that Latin American military officers no longer came from or represented the oligarchy. Like civilian middle-sector groups, they wanted administrative order and efficiency, industrial development, and technological progress. These new military men were as "competent as any other group concerned with national policy" and could serve as a "bulwark of order and security in otherwise anarchical societies." Lucian W. Pye of the Massachusetts Institute of Technology theorized that modern militaries, which were "modeled after industrial-based organizations," could serve as "modernizing agents," strengthening the administrative functions of developing nations. Pye's colleague, Max Millikan, suggested inviting more military officers to the United States to study the "potential uses of the army in economic and social development." Samuel P. Huntington of Harvard University predicted that as modern militaries focused on professional concerns, such as training and weapons systems, they would no longer interfere in daily political life.[6] These scholarly judgments led an "action intellectual" like Walt W. Rostow to assure a graduating class of U.S. Special Forces, or "Green Berets," that a trained soldier's role in the modernization process could be compared to that of a doctor, teacher, or agricultural expert.[7]

The concept that development and security could be achieved through a "modernizing military" became a central feature of the Kennedy administration's approach to Latin America. Policymakers worried that the habitually repressed sectors of Latin American societies, once uprooted from the traditional order, might choose communism over democracy. As a joint State-Defense Department report observed, over the short term "the reforms generated by the Alliance for Progress are likely to weaken, rather than strengthen the fabric of society in most

Latin American countries." Communists and other "left-wing political factions" could be counted on to exploit the turmoil. The United States would need the Latin American military to preserve internal security until the masses realized the benefits of the modernization process. The Latin American officer corps traditionally supported conservative political institutions. "Today, however, the same factors which are revolutionizing the civilian environment are affecting the military establishments of Latin America." The "rising generation of younger officers" favored social and economic reform. The United States needed to secure the loyalty of these modernizing officers and train them to cope "with uprisings or guerrilla actions in rural areas." The State-Defense report recognized that a policy that strengthened military forces was "fraught with hazardous political consequences." The United States would have to take care to preserve the principle of civilian control and avoid being identified "with any step backward either to repressive dictatorship or military intervention in political life."[8]

In a comprehensive report on 30 November 1961, the Joint Chiefs explained to President Kennedy how the United States could use military assistance to achieve the objectives of the Alliance for Progress. Through the rapid provision of equipment, training, and matériel, the United States could shift the Latin American military's focus away from hemispheric defense and enhance "the capability of indigenous forces to conduct counter-insurgency, anti-subversion, and psychological warfare operations." An expanded educational program would give U.S. officers the chance to teach democratic values to their Latin American counterparts. The Joint Chiefs recommended that Latin Americans fill available quotas in U.S. military schools. Close contact with the Latin American officers would also give the United States the opportunity to demonstrate the potential of military services to support social and economic development. The Joint Chiefs foresaw Latin American soldiers waging civic-action campaigns, constructing village schoolhouses, and conquering illiteracy. The Joint Chief's optimistic, even idealistic, report left the president "favorably impressed."[9]

By mid-1962, President Kennedy had transformed U.S. military actions in Latin America. The United States now conceded the obvious: the Soviet Union had neither the capability nor the intention to invade Latin America. Latin Americans needed to concentrate on internal security and recognize the threat posed by "Castroism and communism in general." The president dispatched interagency teams, consisting of representatives from the State and Defense Departments, CIA, and Federal Bureau of Investigation (FBI), to the region to assess the dangers of Communist infiltration and subversion and the capacity of the Latin American military and police to respond. Perhaps predictably, the teams found security deficiencies everywhere.[10] Kennedy responded by expanding U.S. military assistance to the region. Between 1961 and 1964, U.S. military assistance averaged $77 million a year, a 50 percent increase over the average of the Eisenhower years. During the mid-1960s, military assistance exceeded $100 million a year.[11] By expanding military assistance, Kennedy broke promises he made during the presidential campaign and in his presentation of the Alliance for Progress to restrict arms expenditures. The president also ordered that the new aid should be dedicated to enhancing internal security in Latin America. He routinely used his presidential authority to waive congressional restrictions on military aid for internal security. In 1959 Senator Wayne Morse (D.-Ore.) had successfully attached an amendment to the Mutual Security Act that barred military aid for internal security, because he worried that the United States would become identified with forces repressing legitimate dissent. The Morse amendment permitted presidential exemptions, however, and Kennedy always found that Latin American countries were "considered prime targets for Castro-communist subversion." The president and his aides confidently assured Congress that the aid would not be used "to deter legitimate popular expressions of aspirations for greater social justice and political freedom."[12]

As the president wanted, the administration also worked on "increasing the intimacy" with the Latin American armed forces. General Lyman L. Lemnitzer, the chairman of the Joint Chiefs, personally informed Kennedy that in fiscal 1961 the Defense Department had reserved for Latin Americans in U.S. war schools 360 spaces for riot control training, 344 spaces for counterinsurgency training, 160 spaces for a course on psychological operations, and 77 spaces for civil affairs training, at a cost of $650,000.[13] In fiscal 1962, the peak year, the United States trained nearly 9,000 Latin American officers and enlisted personnel. Overall, during the 1960s an average of 3,500 Latin American officers and men annually attended military schools such as the U.S. Army Caribbean School in the Canal Zone, renamed the "School of the Americas." Select Latin Americans trained at the Special Warfare School at Fort Bragg, North Carolina. At the School of the Americas, military instructors taught courses in Spanish. Latin Americans studied topics on clandestine operations, communism and democracy, defoliation, the use of informants, interrogation of prisoners and suspects, handling mass rallies and meetings, intelligence photography, and polygraphs.[14] Students presumably left U.S. military schools with a knowledge of counterinsurgency doctrines and an appreciation for U.S. institutions and values. U.S. officials certainly tried to make Latin Americans feel welcome. In an extraordinary gesture, President Kennedy took time in the midst of the Cuban Missile Crisis to greet Brazilian military officers touring the United States. The Brazilians left deeply impressed by the president's hospitality.[15] CIA operatives also met with Latin Americans. They believed that they had an excellent opportunity to recruit Latin American officers who studied in the United States.[16]

The Kennedy administration expanded the internal security program to include Latin American police forces. In 1961 Robert Kennedy informed his brother that FBI agents confidentially reported to him that they questioned whether the Latin American police could control rioting mobs. Other security teams delivered similar assessments.[17] In August 1962, the president issued NSAM No. 177, establishing a police assistance program, the Office of Public Safety, under the aegis of the Agency for International Development. He further directed the Special Group on counterinsurgency to oversee the police program's development. Kennedy ordered that the new agency be given a separate "internal security" budgetary line "so it would not be cut with economic development projects." During the 1960s, more U.S. technicians would work on police projects than worked in health and sanitation programs. The Office of Public Safety had the authority to expedite deliveries of equipment to imperiled countries in order "to deny the police assistance field to the Communist bloc."[18]

U.S. officials carried out NSAM No. 177. During the 1960s, the United States spent $43.6 million on the Latin American police and brought over 3,000 officers to either the Inter-American Police Academy at Fort Davis in the Canal Zone or the new International Police Academy in the Georgetown section of Washington, D.C., for three to six months of training and indoctrination. U.S. police officers also traveled to Latin American cities, offering both course work and field training to Latin American police.[19] The administration judged the police program a public relations success and a wise investment. The program had the effect of "civilizing" internal defense. As one report noted, "The sometimes repressive image of Latin American military forces is ameliorated by shifting part of the internal defense burden to civilian police forces who are trained to maintain law and order without unnecessary bloodshed and an obtrusive display of tanks and bayonets." Police assistance also proved cost effective, for "the total cost of a 225-man riot control company fully equipped with Willys personnel carriers, tear gas, batons, hand arms and a tank car for spraying crowds with indelible dye comes to only $58,000."[20] During the course of the program, the Brazilian police, for example, received 36 patrol cars, 52 jeeps, 260 portable radios, 800,000 rounds of pistol ammunition, 540 riot batons, 122 gas masks, 20,000 gas grenades, 20 fingerprint kits, and a $137,000 computerized information-processing system.[21] President Kennedy wanted even more, issuing another NSAM in late 1962 ordering "that careful consideration be given to intensifying civil police programs in lieu of military assistance where such action will yield more fruitful results in terms of our primary internal security objective."[22]

While the police maintained order in Latin American cities, the Kennedy administration hoped the army would pacify the countryside and engage in nation building. In 1962 the administration allocated $9 million for civic-action programs, primarily for Central America. The civic-action program would eventually receive $54 million in funding.[23] Infantrymen would put down their rifles and pick up hammers and shovels. In President Kennedy's words, the Latin American military could do more than defend their countries: "They can, as we have learned through our own Corps of Engineers, help to build them."[24] As they constructed roads and irrigation systems, Latin American soldiers would be refurbishing the government and military's image among *campesinos* and undermining the appeal of radicals. Civic action, Secretary McNamara judged, would serve as "an indispensable means of establishing a link between army and populace."[25]

Although administration officials used the modern language of "pacification," "civic action," and "counterinsurgency" to describe their military initiatives in Latin America, they in fact implemented policies previously tried. During the first third of the twentieth century, when U.S. forces occupied Cuba, the Dominican Republic, Haiti, and Nicaragua, the United States attempted to organize an apolitical constabulary loyal to the government and in service to the people. U.S. Marines engaged in civic action, overseeing the building of roads and communication systems in Central America and the Caribbean. In the late 1920s, U.S. armed forces also conducted a counterinsurgency campaign of sorts in Nicaragua, chasing after the Nicaraguan nationalist, Augusto César Sandino. Kennedy administration officials did not, however, ponder the historical lessons of those earlier experiences.

The Kennedy administration vigorously defended its new military policies, brushing away concerns on how military spending related to democracy and social and economic progress. Secretary McNamara assured U.S. senators that "the exposure of the military officers of those nations to our schools acquaints them with democratic philosophies, democratic ways of thinking, which they, in turn, take back to their nations." The president repeated the same argument to a worried Venezuelan ambassador. General W. A. Enemark, who oversaw military assistance to the region, further explained that "well disciplined and well-trained Latin American forces led by U.S. trained and oriented leaders of moderate views will provide the stability and degree of internal security which are necessary to economic and social development and to the success of the Alliance for Progress." And because Latin American officers frequently became political figures, it was, in McNamara's opinion, "beyond price to us to make friends of such men." In 1962, Secretary of State Rusk even suggested to a skeptical Senator Morse that since World War II the Latin American military had generally "been a force for good," because military men had "played a leading and often decisive role in unseating dictators."[26] Rusk perhaps exaggerated; in the late 1950s, mass popular uprisings, not military *golpes*, led to the ouster of military dictators like Venezuela's Marcos Pérez Jiménez. In 1963 McNamara even went so far as to claim that he knew "of no instance in which our military assistance program has acted to support undemocratic or nondemocratic oriented individuals in power or in efforts to achieve political power." Senator Morse reminded him that the Peruvian *golpistas* trained in the United States and used U.S. tanks to assault the presidential palace. Possibly chastened by the six military *golpes* that occurred between 1962 and 1963, McNamara modified his defense of military aid. In 1964 he testified that "the essential role of the Latin American military as a stabilizing force outweighs any risks involved in providing military assistance for internal security purposes."[27]

Although the administration appeared publicly confident and untroubled by questions about its military initiatives, some officials privately objected to the new emphasis on internal security. During his year as undersecretary of state, Chester Bowles repeatedly warned that "we are failing to build into our training programs for foreign military personnel an understanding of the values and practices of a democratic society." Bowles asked whether aid to countries such as Nicaragua should be conditioned on the accomplishment of specific reforms in police and judicial procedures.[28] Other officials predicted that providing additional equipment would inevitably raise the maintenance and operation costs of the Latin American armed forces. Local governments would have fewer resources to devote to economic development. The Bureau of the Budget questioned the whole process that established that subversives threatened Latin America. Speaking of the report submitted by the team that assessed conditions in Central America, bureau officials complained that "the process of evaluation and the rather hasty manner in which the evaluations appear to have been made do not inspire our confidence." The report "was a rather narrow inquiry to establish deficiencies in military armed strength against stereotyped or presumptive findings of threats to internal security."[29] To calm the doubters, the State Department ordered U.S. ambassadors to consult with "pro-US, anti-communist civilians" in Latin America who could assess whether the new military programs imperiled democracy. But as Arthur Schlesinger later pointed out, the U.S. ambassadors lacked the authority to suspend aid if a Latin American military or police unit abused citizens.[30]

U.S. officials developed the new programs on internal security and counterinsurgency with little advice or consent from Latin Americans. But most Latin American military leaders readily accepted the training and equipment. Military men knew the history of the Cuban Revolution; Castro had dismantled Batista's army and executed officers. Latin American officers had on their own begun to develop counterrevolutionary doctrines. In their war college, the Escola Superior de Guerra, Brazilian officers discussed nation building, counterinsurgency, and an active political role for the military.[31] Authoritarians like the Somozas of Nicaragua readily welcomed civic-action programs, believing that they would accrue to their political advantage. New roads gave the appearance of progress in Nicaragua even as the Somozas ignored the social and economic changes, like land reform, called for in the Alliance for Progress.[32] Ambassador to Honduras Charles Burrows recalled that the Honduran military similarly used civic-action funds to impress their countrymen. But the roads they built "didn't go anyplace."[33] Although Latin American officers supported the new U.S. programs, they did not give up their fondness for the prestige equipment associated with the older hemispheric defense program. U.S. military aid to the region increased rapidly in the 1960s in part because Latin Americans wanted both warships and tear-gas canisters. For example, the Johnson administration engaged in a fiery debate with Peru over its demand to purchase combat aircraft. President Kennedy pointed to the problem when he asked in NSAM No. 206 whether jet aircraft are "really justifiable items for the internal security mission, or are they included essentially for political reasons?"[34]

✦ Because of Cold War security concerns, the Kennedy administration went ahead with a counterinsurgency initiative "fraught with hazardous political consequences." Guerrillas operated in the Colombian, Guatemalan, and Venezuelan countrysides. Urban terrorists also operated in Venezuela. In mid-1961, Central American foreign ministers warned the administration that their nations could expect to receive the "brunt of Castro-Communist attack and subversion." They spoke of discovering both arms caches and "plans of subversive elements to overthrow governments." Such evidence fed the U.S. belief in an international Communist conspiracy. In early 1962, U.S. intelligence analysts estimated that some Caribbean countries "may fall under Communist control." In South America, administration officials feared that U.S. interests were threatened "by growing social unrest and [the] avowed intent of [the] Castro-Communist movement, in alignment with [the] Sino-Soviet bloc, to use this unrest to seize political control by indirect aggression."[35] Cubans and their Soviet allies constantly plotted against the United States. In mid-1962, one administration report alleged that 17,000 Latin Americans, including 14,000 Cubans, would receive Communist-directed training and indoctrination in 1961–62. Havana had opened a special school for Latin American youth; "such a school could have graduated a total of 2,000 students by the end of 1961." Women, trade unionists, and professionals also "reportedly" took six-month courses. Moscow joined in the subversion by bringing thirty Latin American Communists and hundreds of Cuban Communists to the Soviet Union for party training.[36] Even if U.S.-Soviet relations improved, the United States needed to keep up its Cold War guard. On 31 August 1963, Secretary of State Rusk cautioned U.S. diplomats in Latin America not to misinterpret the successful negotiation of the Test Ban Treaty on nuclear weapons. "For the foreseeable future," Rusk observed, "USSR, world communism, and local communist parties must continue to be considered in Latin America as enemies both of existing order and of efforts through the Alliance for Progress to accomplish major improvements in it." The Soviet Union still held to its ideology of backing "national liberation movements of oppressed people."[37]

The Soviet Union assuredly hoped to extend its influence in Latin America. As one respected authority on Soviet foreign policy toward

Latin America noted, the Soviet leadership was "irrevocably committed to national liberation movements and the ultimate achievement of socialism in America."[38] Moreover, the Soviet Union directly challenged the United States and threatened Latin America when it placed missiles with nuclear warheads in Cuba in 1962. But outside of protecting their Caribbean client state, Soviet policymakers placed a low priority on relations with Latin America during the 1960s. Latin America received only about 6 percent of Soviet foreign aid for the non-Communist developing world. Soviet policymakers faced formidable obstacles, as another scholar observed, in realizing "the maximum ideological/strategic goals so often emphasized in the literature." The Soviets understood that the United States dominated the Western Hemisphere. Challenging that domination entailed significant costs and enormous diplomatic risks, as evidenced during the Cuban Missile Crisis. Physical barriers, such as distance, impeded communication between the Soviet Union and Latin America. The Soviets also learned that they had little to offer economically to the region. As producers of raw materials and primary products, the Soviet Union and Latin America were economic competitors, not natural partners. Latin Americans understandably preferred the finished goods of the United States, Western Europe, and Japan over the shoddy wares offered by the Soviets. During the 1960s, Soviet trade with Latin America, excluding Cuba, accounted for a minuscule percent of the Soviets' global economic activity. The balance of trade always overwhelmingly favored the Latin Americans. During the 1970s and 1980s, Argentina sold massive quantities of wheat to the Soviet Union. But this growth in trade reflected the dire state of Soviet agriculture; the balance of trade favored the Argentines by an incredible factor of 50 to 1. During the Cold War, the Soviet Union never managed to establish a lasting, satisfactory relationship with any Latin American country except Cuba.[39]

The Soviet Union's primary assets in the region were the Latin American Communist parties, whose memberships ranged, according to Department of State estimates, from 150 in Panama to 50,000 in Argentina. Latin American Communists traditionally hewed closely to Moscow's line and engaged, when possible, in legitimate political activity, trying to build a mass political movement of workers. Most countries prohibited Communists from openly organizing. Latin American Communists eschewed violence and subversion, because they and Moscow judged the revolutionary potential, or "balance of forces," in the individual countries as unfavorable to them. The Cuban Communists notably did not join Castro's guerrilla movement, and in 1966 the Bolivian Communists declined to support Ché Guevara's visionary plan to make a revolution in their nation. Latin American Communists also provided no help to Castro during the missile crisis. In the 1960s, Colombian, Guatemalan, and Venezuelan Communists briefly backed insurgencies in their countries. But these revolutionary nationalist movements, such the Movement of the Revolutionary Left in Venezuela, arose outside of the international Communist movement. By the end of the 1960s, Latin American Communists lined up solidly behind Moscow's call for establishing normal political and economic contacts between the Soviet Union and Latin American nations. Indeed, Latin American Communists never led a revolution. Fidel Castro derided party members, alleging that they feared revolutions; he labeled them "political posers," "paper shufflers," and, most damning, "bureaucrats."[40]

Castro favored promoting revolution through armed struggle. In part, he justified insurrection as a necessary defensive tactic. As Castro explained to Soviet authorities, "The United States will not be able to hurt us if all of Latin America is in flames."[41] The United States had not taken seriously the peace overture that Ché Guevara had made at Punta del Este in August 1961. Between 1961 and 1962, the Kennedy administration had carried out Operation Mongoose, a massive campaign of terrorism and sabotage against his island. Castro further knew that the CIA devised plots to kill him. And on 19 June 1963, the president, known in CIA parlance as the "Higher Authority," approved a new sabotage campaign against Cuba. Ten days before his death, Kennedy approved additional sabotage operations.[42] Castro also despised those leaders in countries such as Colombia, Peru, and Venezuela who orchestrated the anti-Cuban movement in the inter-American community. Beyond seeking revenge, Castro concerned himself with Latin American affairs because he believed that he and his Cuban Revolution had solutions for Latin America's economic and social inequities.

But the realities of both Cuba's poverty and international politics helped tame Castro's revolutionary fervor. Cuba lacked the money and equipment to assist revolutionaries; it could only provide inspiration and training. Prior to 1966, the United States had no hard evidence of direct Cuban support to insurgent groups, other than the dubious Venezuelan arms cache incident of November 1963.[43] Castro depended on the Soviet Union for war matériel, and the Soviet Union had to weigh its support for Castro against its long-term interests in improving relations with the United States and Latin America. In May 1963, in the aftermath of the missile crisis, Castro visited the Soviet Union and learned from Premier Khrushchev that the Soviets would not support armed insurrection in Latin America and that Castro should not attempt to dictate the policies of Latin American Communists. That party line became manifest at the Havana Conference of Latin American Communists held in November 1964. Although the conferees cloaked the final communiqué in militant language, Castro had to concede that Latin American parties could, as Moscow advised, pursue separate, non-violent paths to power. To be sure, at the January 1966 Tricontinental Conference, also held in Havana, Castro asserted that "the battle will take on the most violent terms." Such brave talk led to Ché Guevara's pathetic adventure and his eventual capture and execution in Bolivia in 1967. Bolivian *campesinos* declined to become the sea in which the foreigner Guevara could swim.[44] As a State Department official happily summarized in 1967, "The confident predictions of sweeping Communist victories which have often emanated from Havana have not been borne out."[45]

Guevara's disaster in Bolivia pointed to another barrier to the expansion of "Castro-communism" in the region—Latin American nationalism. Whether they were governmental leaders, radicals, or *campesinos*, Latin Americans questioned doctrines exported from either Moscow or Havana. During the Cold War, only three nations—Argentina, Mexico, and Uruguay—continuously maintained diplomatic ties with the Soviet Union, and only Mexico always kept its embassy open in Cuba. When Latin American governments denounced statements made at the Havana and Tricontinental Conferences, the Soviets quickly disavowed any association with interventionism. These mainly Catholic countries also harbored suspicions about Marxism-Leninism. Moreover, the labor movement in Latin America had not developed according to classical Communist theory, evolving instead toward state-sponsored or corporatist forms of organization. The political traditions of strongman, or *caudillo*, rule and populism also remained prevalent in Latin America. Perhaps Cubans became "Fidelistas" before they became Communists.[46]

Policymakers in both the Kennedy and Johnson administrations had available to them analyses that outlined the ambiguities of the Communist threat and the complexities of internal security. In early 1962, U.S. intelligence officers predicted the "growth of indigenous, non-Communist, radical nationalism." In late 1962, they concluded that Castro and Cuba served primarily as "symbols of revolution" and that "Castro's influence in Latin America had waned by the time of the missile base crisis." In mid-1963, a State Department officer responsible for internal security called it "a distortion of concept" to blame left-wing guerrillas for turmoil in countries such as Colombia and Guatemala. Counterinsurgency tactics would be useless against the ills of "rural banditry" and "chronic instability." [47] In the week after Kennedy's assassination, the State Department's Bureau of Intelligence and Research dismissed the notion that Castro and Soviet bloc countries controlled the clandestine arms traffic in Latin America. Arms were readily available in Latin America, and even right-wing dictators marketed them.[48] In early 1964, the CIA received an account of a source's conversation with Cuban foreign minister Raúl Roa. Roa said that Castro believed Khrushchev wanted nothing to do with Latin America and "would never send a single revolver" to the region. For his part, Castro reportedly stated that he wanted to be "left in peace" and that, if his neighbors stopped conspiring against him, he would not aid any revolutionary movements in Latin America.[49] By the end of the year, analysts claimed that insurgents did not threaten any Latin American government and that Latin American Communist parties, which were weak, adhered to Moscow's line of peaceful coexistence and largely ignored Castro. As a CIA study speculated, "If the International Communist Movement continues in its present disunified state, these home-grown revolutionary organizations are likely to become more significant." [50]

Kennedy and Johnson administration officials ultimately discounted nuanced analyses of insurrection in Latin America and trusted in their fears, and in the familiar certainties of policy documents such as NSC 68 (1950), that the Soviet Union orchestrated the world's troubles. On 18 January 1962, the day that he created the Special Group, President Kennedy revisited Khrushchev's "wars of national liberation" speech. He called it "one of the most important speeches of the decade." The president reminded NSC members that Khrushchev "had made clear the pattern of military and paramilitary subversion which could be expected under the guise of 'wars of liberation.'" On 13 September 1963, he instructed Ambassador Llewellyn Thompson to call on Khrushchev and deny recent Soviet charges that the United States had again assisted Cuban exiles who attacked the island. Instead, Kennedy accused the Soviet Union's client, Cuba, of fomenting insurgencies throughout the hemisphere. Speaking for the president, Ambassador Thompson claimed that "information available to us shows a direct connection between terroristic activities in Venezuela and the Castro regime."[51] During their time in the executive branch of government, the president and his brother never lost faith in their counterinsurgency, civic-action, and public-safety programs. In 1964 Robert Kennedy boasted that the Special Group "was responsible for the preservation of the democratic system in Venezuela." If not for the police training provided, "Venezuela would have been taken over by the Communists." The attorney general also suggested that the Special Group saved Colombia and the Dominican Republic.[52]

President Johnson preserved intact the counterinsurgency and internal security features of his predecessor's Latin American policy. Assistant Secretary of State Thomas C. Mann, Johnson's point man on Latin America, reaffirmed the Kennedy administration's commitment to internal security and its faith in the Latin American armed forces. Mann told U.S. ambassadors in Latin America that the military was "a potent political force" that had "been friendly to the United States, anti-Communist, and conservative, preferring stability but increasingly supporting orderly economic and social reform and progress." In mid-1967, Johnson's committee on counterinsurgency issued a directive to U.S. ambassadors in Latin America "stressing the President's concern over Communist insurgency and asking them to give special attention to 'preventive medicine' action which might be taken now to build up internal security capabilities." Johnson's aides also sent him what Walt Rostow tagged "a lively memo" on counterinsurgency that "will give you some satisfaction." In August 1967, the Venezuelan police had killed or captured the leaders of a fifty-man "Strategic Sabotage Command," and in Nicaragua the Guardia Nacional, or National Guard, had "wiped out 14 Castro-oriented guerrillas." The memorandum concluded that "August 1967 has been a vintage month for the COIN (counterinsurgency) forces in Latin America."[53]

Although it is difficult to measure their effect precisely, the counterinsurgency policies developed by the Kennedy administration contributed to internal security in Latin America. With substantial U.S. economic and military assistance, the Betancourt and Leoni governments managed to calm Venezuela. Between 1962 and 1965, the United States developed a strategy, labeled "Plan Lago," to help the Colombian military combat guerrillas. The military temporarily contained the insurgency, but guerrilla warfare would continue in Colombia into the 1990s. Political violence had such staying power in Colombia because it was rooted in the malignant feelings engendered by the bloody civil war between the Liberal and the Conservative Parties—*la violencia*—that began in 1948. By training the battalion that helped capture Ché Guevara, the United States could also claim success in Bolivia. But as one analyst speculated, U.S. aid might have been superfluous; Ché's movement "would certainly have collapsed of its own errors."[54] As the United States helped contain some insurgencies, new guerrilla movements appeared. In 1962 youthful Nicaraguan radicals, disgusted by the timid approach of the Moscow-aligned Nicaraguan Socialist Party, founded the Frente Sandinista de Liberación Nacional. The Sandinistas dedicated themselves to overthrowing the Somoza dynasty by force. They would not, however, gain widespread popular support or military success until the late 1970s. The Sandinistas encountered the formidable 5,000-man National Guard of Nicaragua, whose officers all trained at the School of the Americas. By the mid-1960s, U.S. officials assured Congress that "the chances of Communists gaining complete control of any Latin American country in the foreseeable future appear slight."[55]

★   Whereas the internal security policies of the Kennedy administration may have helped clear the region of Marxist-Leninists, they did not produce the other promised benefits for Latin Americans. President Kennedy's prediction to Venezuelan ambassador Mayobre that the new U.S. military policies would discourage Latin American officers from seeking political power turned out to be wrong. During the 1960s, sixteen extraconstitutional changes of government rocked Latin America. During the Kennedy years alone, military men overthrew six popularly elected Latin American presidents. The collapse of military dictatorships in the late 1950s had not proven to be "the twilight of the tyrants," ushering in a golden era of democracy and respect for basic human rights.[56] For two decades between the mid-1960s and mid-1980s, military governments dominated Latin America. These military rulers, whether in the larger South American nations of Argentina, Brazil, and Chile or in the smaller Central American countries of El Salvador and Guatemala, carried out vicious campaigns against their civilian opponents that evoked popular comparisons with the Nazi terror in Central Europe in the 1930s. The term *desaparecidos*, those who simply "disappeared," became commonplace to describe those Latin Americans who came under military custody.

The military men who seized power in Latin America during the 1960s had trained under U.S. direction. In Peru ten of the twelve officers in the military junta that took power after the overthrow of President

Prado received training from the U.S. military. In the Dominican Republic, U.S.-trained police helped overthrow Juan Bosch. Eighty percent of the core group of sixty Brazilian generals and military leaders who ousted João Goulart studied in the United States. The head of the U.S.-funded civic-action program in Bolivia, General René Barrientos, led the November 1964 military *golpe* against President Víctor Paz Estenssoro. So successful had U.S. officers become in fulfilling President Kennedy's dictum to "increase the intimacy" between themselves and their Latin American colleagues that the new military policies occasionally produced ironic results. Some left-wing guerrillas in Guatemala had previously served in the regular armed forces and received counterinsurgency indoctrination from U.S. instructors.[57]

Such results seemed to confirm Ambassador Mayobre's warning to President Kennedy that U.S. training for Latin American officers "would inevitably stimulate their interest in taking political power."[58] In retrospect, administration officials agreed with the ambassador. Presidential aide Arthur Schlesinger, who disliked the emphasis on internal security and argued for an unequivocal stand against military *golpes*, has subsequently been unsparing in his public criticism of the administration's military policies. Counterinsurgency was "the worst folly" of the Kennedy administration and contributed to a "militarist assault" on democracy that disfigured Latin America in the 1960s. The appalled Schlesinger further condemned Robert Kennedy for his direction of the Special Group and for his "most conspicuous folly," Operation Mongoose.[59] Near the end of his life, Robert Kennedy apparently agreed with Schlesinger, writing in his 1968 campaign treatise that counterinsurgency was "not a miracle detergent that whisks away Communists from any country." Kennedy called for a renewed emphasis on social reform in Latin America.[60] Secretary of State Rusk also had second thoughts about the impact of U.S. military aid in Latin America. In 1970 he confessed to an interviewer that "its very hard to draw a line between assisting a country to maintain its own internal security and supporting that country's government against its own people, and this was always a delicate line to draw and one that was not always successfully drawn."[61]

Scholars have debated whether the counterinsurgency doctrines and internal security programs had the "horrid impact" on Latin America that Schlesinger alleged. They have presented a mixed assessment. Military assaults on duly elected civilian leaders preceded the new emphasis on internal security. Two scholars calculated that between 1930 and 1965 Latin America experienced 105 illegal and unscheduled changes of heads of government, with Ecuador and Bolivia leading the way with eleven and ten *golpes* respectively.[62] Analysts also understood that military men did not strike solely because they received U.S. matériel. Reviewing the Honduran *golpe*, Ambassador Burrows concluded that Colonel López and his followers pursued their own conservative political agendas, although Burrows admitted that the "ease with which [the] military *golpe* [was] carried out testifies to improved discipline and ability to plan operations which [are] not unrelated to U.S. training."[63] Similarly, U.S. military assistance alone could not explain the overthrow of civilian leaders in Guatemala and Brazil. In both cases, the United States went beyond enhancing internal security and, in the name of anticommunism, actually encouraged Guatemalan and Brazilian officers to take power. But the United States did not control Latin American officers. Both the Kennedy and Johnson administrations found that the Peruvian military consistently defied the United States by overthrowing civilian governments. Such developments point to one negative finding. As one political scientist summarized, the "data do not support the contention that U.S. military training of Latin American officers inculcates apolitical professional values among the officers."[64] In fact, despite public pledges made to legislators, the United States did not try to teach democratic values to Latin American officers. In 1964 one State Department official, on a two-week tour of duty at the Defense Department, reviewed the courses available to Latin American officers at the Canal Zone schools and in the United States. He reported that courses "were strictly military"; none of the courses covered the subject of "the role of the military in a modern democratic society." He doubted that mere association with U.S. officers would transfer democratic values to Latin American military men.[65]

Just as the course of events in the 1960s demonstrated that the United States could not easily transfer the principle of military submission to civilian authority, they also demonstrated the shortcomings of social science theories on the role of the military in a modernizing society. When they took over governmental power, Latin American officers did not, as Professor Johnson, Pye, and others prophesied, fulfill the aspirations of civilian middle-sector groups. The social scientists correctly pointed out that the new Latin American military no longer came from the traditional oligarchy and favored administrative efficiency and technological progress. But military men primarily concerned themselves with protecting their institution. They judged criticism of military actions as illegal and imprisoned middle-sector groups—university students, journalists, lawyers—who questioned their policies. Military rulers falsely held that there could be apolitical solutions to problems of political and economic development. They also repressed organizations, like labor unions and peasant organizations, that called for thoroughgoing social reforms.[66] By the end of the 1960s, other scholars, who conducted case studies, discredited theories on the military and modernization. Commissioned by the U.S. Senate Foreign Relations Committee to study the military *golpes*, historian Edwin Lieuwen of the University of New Mexico found some common themes. Lieuwen defined the nine military takeovers that took place between 1962 and 1967 as "counter-revolutionary militarism." In every case, the military overthrew constitutional governments, adopted a conservative position on issues of social reform, and claimed they had forestalled the rise of communism. But military rulers indiscriminately equated populist policies, like land reform, with communism. Because they insisted upon social stability and abhorred social upheaval, the Latin American military rulers espoused a cautious, conservative philosophy that ran counter to the visions of the Alliance for Progress. As Lieuwen noted, "Without the restraining effect of the military, populist governments would probably be in power in most Latin American countries today (1967)."[67]

In prohibiting the elections of civilians who called for social change, Latin American officers acted to preserve their personal and institutional interests. But scholars now agree that the Kennedy administration's internal security policies in part provoked the two-decade-long "militarist assault" on constitutionalism. As one political scientist who focused on the issue of human rights argued, "Military aid inevitably increases the ability of military forces to coerce," and "an administration cannot increase access and influence without simultaneously increasing the coercive power of the military."[68] The new types of aid that the United States granted contributed to that coercive ability. A warship would perhaps not intimidate a labor organizer or a peasant leader, but gas grenades and shotguns could be used to terrorize social activists. To be sure, Latin American officers were capable of acting on their own anti-Communist convictions, but scholars believe that U.S. counterinsurgency and civic-action policies implicitly encouraged the Latin American military to enter the political arena by linking security and development and urging the military to become deeply involved in all stages of society in order to defeat or forestall guerrilla insurgencies.[69] The police assistance programs also added to the role of the military in Latin American life. U.S. officials wrongly assumed that the police and the military were distinct entities and that the police could serve as a useful check on the power of the military. But especially in Central America, military officers commanded police forces, transforming them into "militarized police units."[70]

Field reports sustained these scholarly judgments. Ambassador to El Salvador Murat Williams, a career officer, recalled that students and other middle-class groups would have been angered if they knew the extent of the U.S. role in police training. Officials from the Defense Department, CIA, and Attorney General's Office constantly showed up in San Salvador, checking on internal security. Agents from the Defense Department infiltrated Salvadoran universities to spy on politically active students. Williams not only "lamented" the U.S. cooperation with the Salvadoran police but also became "appalled" at the size of the military mission. The United States assigned more air attachés to the country than there were Salvadoran pilots. Two Special Forces teams taught counterinsurgency tactics. In Williams's opinion, the size of the mission left the impression that the United States controlled the destiny of the nation. Despite the Alliance for Progress, the United States had become identified in the popular mind with the guardians of the status quo, the police and security organizations. Salvadoran officers saw civic-action programs as an opportunity to collect money and to enhance their images. Most of the projects turned out to be frauds. The military built a health clinic that opened once every two weeks. The new internal security programs had predictably strengthened the military but had not improved El Salvador's "position as a republic."[71]

Department of Defense officials came to accept analyses like those of Ambassador Williams. In early 1965, the Office of International Security Affairs, under the direction of Assistant Secretary of Defense John T. McNaughton, called for the end of military assistance to Latin America. The remarkable recommendation apparently had the tacit support of Secretary McNamara. In a comprehensive study, the Defense Department charged that the United States had been wasting its money in Latin America, for "most Latin American armies are little more than professional officer and non-commissioned officer corps controlling masses of poorly trained conscripts." Latin American officers used their positions as sinecures. Sixty-four percent of military expenditures went for pay and allowances, whereas in the United States only 26 percent of military budgets went for personnel costs. The $500 million that had been dedicated to hemispheric defense in the 1950s had not increased continental security. Only Chile could make a "marked contribution" to hemispheric defense. The report also ridiculed the notion that U.S. military assistance had the effect of limiting arms expenditures. During the 1950s, Latin Americans had purchased $600 million in equipment, with two-thirds of those purchases made in Europe.

The United States now emphasized internal security, dedicating 55 percent of its military aid to that mission. Defense officials questioned whether the United States should persuade the armed forces of Latin America to accept this new task. Socioeconomic development and reform offered the best avenue to arrive at internal peace in the region. In any case, only 5,000 guerrillas operated throughout Latin America, 2,000 of them being Colombian "bandits." Police officers could handle the problem. The report opined that "military 'sweeps' through the area even with the most modern equipment may locate and eliminate a few guerrillas but are unlikely to yield any lasting result." Internal security programs also produced negative effects. If U.S. military advisors convinced the officer corps that internal security was its primary mission and main reason for existence, "they would have supplied the military with a powerful incentive not only to block the development of police programs but also to take over the reigns of a civil government which would not let them carry out their basic mission." Civil action programs might similarly encourage the "armed forces to play an even more influential societal role than they already do." The report conceded that the United States had accomplished its postwar goal of establishing predominant influence with the Latin American military. But it added that, "unless repressive military measures are an acceptable solution," it found no basis to believe that adding to the military capabilities of Latin Americans would appreciably increase internal security.[72]

Both the State Department and the Joint Chiefs of Staff flatly opposed the recommendation to end military assistance. They reiterated the arguments of the Truman, Eisenhower, and Kennedy administrations. The United States should continue to bar foreign influences from the region. The Joint Chiefs predicted that altering military assistance would have the effect of "degrading U.S. influence with Latin America." The State Department argued that the United States needed to keep Latin Americans prepared for "Castro-Communists" and a "growing internal security threat." And, in view of the fragmented, divisive nature of Latin American societies, the United States could not cut itself off from a key political actor that opposed extremism, served as a stabilizing force, and allegedly had become aware of the need for socioeconomic reform. Summarizing the bureaucratic debate, McNamara found irreconcilable differences, and in June 1965, he informed National Security Advisor Bundy that the Defense Department had withdrawn its bold recommendation to end military assistance. As McNamara interpreted it, the State Department feared "alienating the military forces on whom the Alliance for Progress must depend to maintain stability in the area."[73] Military assistance to Latin America, with an emphasis on internal security, continued through the 1960s and 1970s. But the U.S. Congress abolished the Office of Public Safety and police training programs in 1975, in response to public demands that the United States stop assisting organizations that violated basic human rights in Latin America and elsewhere.[74]

Kennedy administration officials set as their primary goal for Latin America the defeat of communism. They believed that their internal security policies contributed to that success. But they also preached that meaningful, lasting security could only be obtained through social reform within the framework of democratic institutions. Whether directly or indirectly, the administration had expanded the role of the military in Latin American life. The administration, at best, deluded itself when it professed that Latin American officers believed in the ideals of the Alliance for Progress. As one scholar who has written sympathetically about the U.S. mission in the world has observed, a key lesson of the Alliance for Progress was that "undemocratic means will not result in democratic ends; military governments rarely beget democratic orders. A censored press, a broken trade union movement, a terrorized peasantry are not the material from which a democratic order is easily assembled."[75] By the end of the 1960s, those officials who helped push counterinsurgency doctrines in Latin America—Dean Rusk, Robert McNamara, Robert Kennedy—seemed to accept that scholarly conclusion.

★   While many Kennedy administration officials eventually distanced themselves from counterinsurgency doctrines, they continued to believe in the Alliance for Progress. Much as the Truman administration had done in rebuilding Western Europe with the Marshall Plan, President Kennedy and his advisors hoped that they would leave their mark in history by building progressive, democratic Latin American nations. They always publicly proclaimed that the Alliance for Progress was the best cure for communism. President Kennedy wanted the economic aid and social reform program to be the centerpiece of his Latin American policy.

7 ✦ Alliance for Progress

The Kennedy administration devoted a remarkable amount of time and effort to inter-American relations. It intervened in the Dominican Republic and Haiti, attempting to create decent, democratic regimes. It confronted what it considered dangerous radicals in countries such as Brazil, British Guiana, Chile, and Guatemala. It changed regional military assistance programs from hemispheric defense to internal security. And it tried to overthrow the regime of Fidel Castro. Administration officials judged those efforts as emergency measures, aimed at countering the international Communist movement and protecting U.S. national security. Officials constantly professed that the United States would enjoy lasting security only when Latin Americans lived in prosperous, socially progressive, free societies. Once the economic growth and development engendered by the Alliance for Progress took hold, Latin America would no longer be "the most dangerous area in the world." The transformation of Latin America would justify U.S. global leadership and demonstrate the nation's ability to accomplish enlightened, anti-Communist policies. But the Kennedy administration found the challenge of nation building in Latin America far more daunting than it had envisioned. The Alliance for Progress proved a notable policy failure of the 1960s, superseded only by the U.S. debacle in Vietnam.

✦   The Alliance for Progress did not achieve the ninety-four enumerated goals set forth in the charter adopted at Punta del Este in August 1961. The fundamental goal was to achieve a real economic growth rate of "not less than 2.5 percent per capita per year." (Because Alliance planners expected Latin America's population to grow by 3 percent a year, they actually expected at least a 5.5 percent annual growth rate.) Economic growth was vital, for it would underwrite improvements in health, education, and welfare. Alliance planners considered the 2.5 percent goal a modest, readily attainable objective; most quietly expected an even better economic performance. Although analysts have offered slightly different data, all have concluded that Latin American economies performed poorly during the 1960s. Between 1961 and 1967, growth rates averaged less than 2 percent a year. Economic growth rates did not exceed those of the unprosperous 1950s. At less than 1 percent a year, economic growth during the Kennedy years was especially disappointing. Only smaller Central American nations, like Panama and Nicaragua, surpassed the 2.5 percent goal. Of the larger nations, Mexico enjoyed the best economic growth, but its economy had been expanding since 1940, and Mexico was not a major recipient of U.S. economic assistance.[1] Some analysts have subsequently suggested that the Alliance laid the foundation for future success. At the end of the decade, Brazil, under its military rulers, began to grow rapidly, and much of Latin America achieved some growth between 1968 and 1973. The rapid increase in petroleum prices that followed the Arab-Israeli War of 1973 and the ensuing Arab oil embargo halted that growth.[2] But at the time, administration officials found it hard to talk of progress. During his 1968 presidential campaign, Robert Kennedy emphasized the absence of growth and change in Latin America.[3] With slow economic growth, Latin American governments did not collect the new tax revenues that could be dedicated to reaching the Alliance's many goals, such as lowering infant mortality rates and reducing illiteracy.

Kennedy administration officials learned that their optimistic outlook, historical experiences, and theories on modernization and middle-class revolutions did not guarantee economic success in Latin America. In March 1961, when he announced the Alliance for Progress, President Kennedy and his advisors spoke enthusiastically about the U.S. ability to foster progressive change. In the past two decades, the United States had emerged from economic depression, defeated the Axis powers, rebuilt Western Europe and Japan, revivified international trade, and created a prosperous, middle-class consumer society at home. The United States was also on the brink of addressing a grievous social injustice, racial discrimination against African Americans. Teodoro Moscoso, the coordinator of the Alliance for Progress, displayed this sense of confidence and determination when he told U.S. senators in executive session that "the job is staggering. Within a decade, the direction and results of Latin American history is to be changed." The United States would undermine the status quo "of a society made up of the few who have much and the many who have little." To insure that all caught his purpose, Moscoso placed a sign behind his desk that directed: "Please be brief. We are 25 years late."[4]

In a short ten years, Moscoso expected to end privilege, abolish illiteracy, impart scientific training and technical expertise, and create political stability. Yet, he was speaking of a region where illiteracy rates were as high as 90 percent, life expectancy was as low as forty-five years, and as many as 11 percent of infants died. Moreover, the poorest of Latin Americans tended to be those of Amerindian and African heritage, people who had endured centuries of discrimination. Moscoso's naive optimism could perhaps be charitably labeled as persuasive discourse, designed to motivate citizens to enlist in a noble campaign. But Moscoso and other administration officials could not translate their exuberance into policies and programs that actually helped impoverished Latin Americans. President Kennedy admired Moscoso's spirit and vision but concluded that Moscoso could not administer the Alliance for Progress. In March 1962, after being presented with a "chaotic picture" of the Alliance, he ordered that a strong deputy for Moscoso be found "who could take over most of the administrative work." Personnel shifts changed little. In September 1963, presidential advisor Richard Goodwin informed Kennedy that a "generous estimate" was that the Alliance was "operating at about one-half effectiveness." Goodwin called for radical organization and personnel changes, for "it is a good idea to break up a losing ball club." Goodwin suggested replacing Moscoso with Sargent Shriver, the dynamic, skillful director of the Peace Corps program.[5]

Moscoso's administrative shortcomings pointed to the larger bureaucratic problems that constantly amazed and frustrated the president. In the early 1960s, Kennedy discovered the often ponderous, unresponsive nature of government that citizens would take as a commonplace during the 1980s and 1990s. Through his eloquence and spectacularly successful trips to Latin America, Kennedy had galvanized public and congressional support for the Alliance for Progress. With the money allocated, Kennedy took for granted that, given the foreign policy triumphs of the past, the United States could efficiently work wonders in Latin America. The president further presumed that the foreign policy bureaucracy would share his insight that Latin America deserved particular attention. On 16 February 1962, he assembled representatives from all agencies in the foreign policy bureaucracy and "indicated his strong view that the fate of the whole aid program rests on the success of the Alliance for Progress and that operations and activities connected with the Alliance for Progress should be given the highest priority."[6] A month later, he observed that officials responsible for U.S. relations with other areas of the world "would have to recognize the special position of Latin

America." Despite these presidential priorities, aid did not immediately flow to Latin America. Officials struggled with organizational problems such as defining clear lines of authority between the "political" side of the State Department and the Agency for International Development, which functioned under the auspices of the State Department. Determining where Moscoso's office fit in the organizational scheme became another distraction. Officials who had the authority to straighten out the bureaucratic disorder—Dean Rusk, George Ball, George McGhee —preferred to concentrate on Asian and European affairs. Economic officers, both in Latin America and in the United States, also struggled to put together coherent, sensible development plans. In October 1962, more than a year after his triumph at Punta del Este, Secretary of the Treasury Douglas Dillon publicly acknowledged the tardiness of the Alliance for Progress. In December 1962, President Kennedy privately conceded to Juscelino Kubitschek of Brazil and Alberto Lleras Camargo of Colombia, two former presidents, "that the general situation in Latin America had become worse over the last two years."[7]

Kennedy tried to shake the bureaucracy out of its torpor. Beyond grumbling to aides about the inertia of the State Department, he addressed foreign service officers in a closed session and chided them for not cooperating with other governmental agencies and for their lack of vigor, noting that "we move too slowly." He also took to demanding reports on the Alliance for Progress, actually sending handwritten inquiries to appropriate officials. For example, after his meeting in March 1963 in San José, Costa Rica, the president wanted to know if his government fulfilled the promises he made to Central American leaders.[8] In the end, he decided that the only way he could force the State Department to give Latin America the attention it deserved was to take up Adolf Berle's 1961 idea and create the position of "Under Secretary of State for Inter-American Affairs." Its occupant would have responsibility for both the Alliance for Progress and the State Department's Latin America section and would be the fourth-ranking official in the State Department. On 29 October 1963, Kennedy wrote to Rusk, informing him of his decision. He pointed out that top officers, "for good and sufficient reasons" were absorbed in the problems of Asia, Europe, and East-West relations. But Latin America "is the area of greatest danger to us." He added that he was familiar with the bureaucratic objections to his plan, such as "if we do this for Latin America, other geographical areas must receive equal treatment." The president wanted this time a "positive exploration" of the under secretaryship and hoped to announce the new position in early November to coincide with inter-American economic meetings to be held in São Paulo, Brazil.[9] As of 22 November 1963, Secretary Rusk had not formally responded to the president's direct request.

Although bureaucratic problems constantly bedeviled the Alliance for Progress, the United States gradually made good on Secretary Dillon's pledge to dedicate $10 billion in U.S. Treasury funds to Latin America during the 1960s. Nonetheless, even if President Kennedy had been able to spur the foreign policy bureaucracy to act in innovative, imaginative ways, the United States would have been unable to repeat the historical success of the Marshall Plan. Latin America was not Europe. Western European countries had been devastated by war, but they had financial and technical expertise, institutionalized political parties, skillful politicians, strong national identities, and, except for Germany, a democratic tradition. The United States had helped to rebuild countries whose social fabrics, political traditions, and economic institutions were notably similar to those of North Americans. On the other hand, the Iberian and Amerindian political heritage, characterized by planned economies, strong central governments, and the organization of society into corporate groups, was virtually nonexistent in the United States.[10] Beyond failing to account for these obvious cultural differences, the Kennedy administration compounded the Alliance's problems by adopting a program far more ambitious than the European recovery program. As historian Tony Smith has observed, the Alliance for Progress combined elements of the Marshall Plan and the U.S. civil rights movement. In the American South, for example, the Kennedy and Johnson administrations mandated political change but not a socioeconomic revolution. The United States had concentrated on economic recovery and growth in Europe. In Germany and Japan, where fundamental societal changes were ordered, the United States could make change through military occupation. The Kennedy and Johnson administrations similarly had to resort to armed force to end segregation and protect the voting rights of African Americans in the South. Although it repeatedly meddled and intervened covertly in Latin America, the Kennedy administration could not write new constitutions that sharply limited military expenditures or threaten governments with military invasion if they abused *campesinos*.[11] In any case, the history of the U.S. occupations of Central and Caribbean nations during the first third of the twentieth century suggested that the United States could not readily export U.S. values to Latin America.[12]

Administration officials quickly regretted their use of the Marshall Plan analogy. By August 1962, Ambassador to Brazil Lincoln Gordon, who helped design the Alliance, conceded that "development is a far more difficult undertaking than economic recovery." Latin America lacked Europe's administrative and socioeconomic infrastructure, and no Latin American version of Jean Monnet, who preached the virtues of European political and economic integration, had yet appeared. At a news conference, Kennedy admitted to being "depressed" about the "almost insuperable" nature of Latin America's problems.[13] On 18 November 1963, in his last address on inter-American affairs, the president asserted that the Alliance for Progress should not be compared to the Marshall Plan, for "then we helped to rebuild a shattered economy whose human and social foundation remained. Today we are trying to create a basic new foundation, capable of reshaping the centuries-old societies and economies of half of a hemisphere." Yet Kennedy assured his Miami audience that idealism, energy, and optimism would bridge the vast cultural gap and bring about the "modernization" of Latin America.[14]

Kennedy also regretfully informed Latin Americans in private that the United States "could not give aid to Latin American countries in the same way that it had helped to rebuild Europe with the Marshall Plan." In the immediate postwar period, the United States could concentrate its aid on one area. Kennedy pointed out that the United States now had global responsibilities and obligations to help such needy nations as India.[15] He also constantly worried about the persistent U.S. balance of payments deficit, which the nation had run since 1950 because of foreign aid, military assistance, and private investment abroad. The United States continued to enjoy a balance of trade surplus, but that surplus no longer covered foreign expenditures and investments. With a balance of payments deficit of over $3 billion in 1961, Kennedy feared that foreigners could destabilize the U.S. economy by suddenly redeeming their excess dollars for U.S. gold. Whenever a Latin American leader discussed the Alliance for Progress, Kennedy reminded him of his balance of payment concerns. His administration attacked the problem by encouraging foreigners to buy military equipment in the United States, limiting duty-free goods for U.S. tourists, and tying foreign aid to U.S. purchases. The administration succeeded in reducing the balance of payments deficit to $1.3 billion by 1965, but massive spending on the war in Vietnam by the Johnson and Nixon administrations undermined Kennedy's financial efforts.[16]

The constant anxiety about the U.S. standing in the international financial system meant that the Alliance for Progress would be less generous than the Marshall Plan. In 1962 Felipe Herrera, the president of the Inter-American Development Bank, estimated that Latin America would obtain only about 25 percent of the actual value of economic aid that Western Europe had received. Herrera calculated that 90 percent of Marshall Plan funds had been grants, whereas 70 percent of Alliance funds would be loans.[17] The United States also "hardened" the terms of loans during the 1960s. The Kennedy administration initially offered generous forty-year loans at a rate of 1.5 percent annual interest, with a ten-year grace period before requiring payment on the principal. The loan terms gradually hardened to twenty-five years at 2.5 percent annual interest, with only a five-year grace period. The United States further "tied" these loans, requiring loan recipients to purchase materials for construction projects in the United States. If the loan had not been tied to the U.S. market, Latin Americans often could have stretched their loan dollars by purchasing materials from a third party such as Japan. The United States insisted that these materials be shipped on U.S. bottoms. In addition, the bureaucratic procedures, or "red tape," involved in obtaining a loan become more elaborate during the 1960s. Worried about mounting balance of payment deficits, President Johnson insisted on personally approving project loans exceeding $10 million. Surveying what had transpired during the decade, David E. Bell, the administrator for the Agency for International Development, admitted that the value of U.S. foreign assistance had been dramatically reduced. An aid recipient might do as well to obtain a loan from the World Bank at a 6.5 percent annual rate of interest, because the loan was "untied" or "without strings." Bell's successor, William Gaud, agreed that the developments displeased poor nations, "but beggars can't be choosers."[18]

The "Marshall Plan for Latin America" can be subjected to additional statistical scrutiny. To be sure, President Kennedy had persuaded legislators and citizens that the United States had a vital national interest in promoting Latin America's economic development. During the 1960s, Latin America received 18 percent of U.S. foreign aid, whereas the Truman and Eisenhower administrations had sent only 3 and 9 percent respectively.[19] The United States also made good on its pledge to commit $10 billion to Latin America and to convince international organizations to commit another $10 billion. Many of these international entities—the Inter-American Bank, the International Monetary Fund, the World Bank—received a substantial portion of their funding from the United States. But bureaucratic snafus, poor planning, and balance of payment concerns reduced the amount of money actually disbursed to Latin America during the "decade of development." Latin America may have received only about 70–75 percent of the $20 billion authorized. Even then, the net capital flow to Latin America did not amount to $14–15 billion, because Latin Americans had to repay principal and interest on pre-1961 loans and on short-term loans made in the 1960s. One U.S. official, who helped planned the Alliance, calculated that between 1961 and 1968 the net capital flow to Latin America averaged $920 million a year. This meant that the annual net transfer of resources from the United States and international financial institutions amounted to about $4 per Latin American. By comparison, Marshall Plan money amounted to $109 a year in assistance for every man, woman, and child in the Netherlands.[20]

The Kennedy administration expected that Alliance for Progress funds would strengthen the political appeal of middle-class revolutionaries, who would accelerate the process of change from a traditional to a modern society. According to the prevailing development theories, rational, secular, literate societies that believed in free political expression and popular political participation would inevitably emerge from the economic growth that the United States would help finance. Middle-class leaders would displace selfish oligarchs and rectify deep-rooted social injustices, such as traditional landholding patterns. This straightforward, seemingly inevitable, theory on development had obvious appeal for a presidential administration that confidently believed it could build progressive, non-Communist nations. But modernization theories had been designed by generalists in government and academic life, not by specialists on Latin American thought, history, and culture. Kennedy administration officials again discovered that optimism, past successes, and idealistic theories might not be enough to overcome the complexities of Latin American life.

Administration officials began bravely, discussing papers prepared by Walt Rostow's Policy Planning Council on such subjects as "the usefulness of attempting to locate Latin American countries in one of four identifiable stages of modernization."[21] But debates quickly moved from the abstract to the concrete. Reporting on his travels to Latin America and his meetings with U.S. chiefs of missions, Under Secretary of State Chester Bowles warned that progress was not guaranteed and that "the obstacles to change vary from country to country but they are all deep-seated and each will be extremely difficult to remove." If the administration pursued its goal of economic and social revolution, "we will be subjected in country after country to powerful attacks by the local oligarchy which will equate every reform we propose with radicalism." Ruling elites in countries like El Salvador traditionally backed the U.S. global struggle against communism. U.S. ambassadors feared that Washington would temper its commitment to reform "in order to avoid the displeasure of politically friendly governments now in office." Bowles added that Latin Americans he had met doubted that the administration "would have the guts" to confront oligarchs and insist on change. Bowles remained hopeful but conceded that the Alliance for Progress was "far more complex" than the Marshall Plan, for "what we are asking is that the philosophy of Jefferson and the social reforms of F.D.R. be telescoped into a few years in Latin America."[22]

In a series of comprehensive studies, U.S. intelligence analysts, some of whom presumably had studied Latin American life, further questioned the theoretical underpinnings of the Alliance for Progress and modernization theory. They reiterated the point that the socioeconomic structure of Latin America could not be readily compared to that of Western Europe and the United States. Latin America's middle sectors pursued their own distinct agendas; they "emphasized national sovereignty, popular welfare, and industrial development rather than personal political and economic liberties." Moreover, they fretted little over issues like mixed government and constitutional checks and balances, believing national development goals could be best realized by a strong, centralized governmental authority. Alliance planners had also overestimated the power and wealth of middle-sector groups. In most Latin American societies, "the rank and file of the middle class, dependent salaried personnel and small business men," struggled to maintain a "decent subsistence level." They obviously could not be compared "to the moderate, propertied middle class of either Western European or US tradition." Analysts also wondered how middle-sector groups would respond to continued frustration, for their "loudest voices are chauvinistic, anti-capitalist, and resentful of a status quo that limits its horizons and seems to deny the possibility of rapid progress for the nation as a whole."[23] In February 1962, summarizing the studies, Secretary Rusk and his planners reached some sobering conclusions that ran counter to the initial, cheerful forecasts that had accompanied the adoption of the Alliance for Progress. Latin America no longer seemed "set for miracles." Oligarchic leaders opposed change, "a stable and responsible middle class" had not yet emerged, and the administration feared that, in promoting the Alliance, "we will so arouse mass impatience that we will release forces we cannot control." Ché Guevara allegedly expected the latter development. Rusk and his analysts also remembered that experience had already taught them that both the United States and Latin America lacked qualified people who could plan sound development projects and who possessed the necessary political skills to manage political and economic transitions.[24]

The course of the Alliance for Progress in the individual republics demonstrated shortcomings in theories of modernization and middle-class revolution. As two scholars pointed out, in jargon that social scientists could appreciate, political development specialists had emphasized "explanatory models over empirical studies," believing that "a theory was needed in order to approach the data." They had produced "rigid, non-compromising, deterministic" analyses.[25] To be sure, from the U.S. perspective, the Alliance for Progress worked reasonably well in Chile and Venezuela. Middle-sector politicians like Eduardo Frei and Rómulo Betancourt addressed social problems and preserved constitutionalism. Neither country came close, however, to achieving the 2.5 percent annual growth rate. As highlighted by President Kennedy's triumphant visit to San José, administration officials also thought their theories were validated by Costa Rica's development. The middle-sector leaders of the Central American nation maintained an open political system and spent money on education rather than on military hardware. Costa Rica also exceeded the Alliance's minimum growth rate, although it took on a heavy burden of debt. But in most of Latin America, middle-sector groups turned out to be faint-hearted revolutionaries, showing more interest in individual than in national goals. In 1962, for example, administration officials were perplexed when Lima's middle-sector groups did not rise up and protest the Peruvian military's annulment of Víctor Haya de la Torre's election. U.S. analysts had once feared that frustrated bank clerks and small businessmen would ally with peasants and workers and take their countries down unpredictable, perhaps radical, paths. In fact, urban middle-sector groups frequently aped the political and social tastes of elites, showed little interest in rural problems, and, in countries like Argentina, Brazil, and Ecuador, initially welcomed the stability and safety offered by military rule.[26]

Nicaragua's development further exposed the gap between the theory and the practice of the Alliance for Progress. The task force reports prepared by Adolf Berle had boldly called for the new administration to spurn tyrants like the Somozas who had turned Nicaragua into the family *hacienda*. The United States needed to act on principle and to undermine the appeal of Communists, for, as President Kennedy would later put it, "those who make peaceful revolution impossible will make violent revolution inevitable."[27] But the Somozas had been steadfast friends of the United States. Cuban exiles used Nicaragua as a staging ground for the Bay of Pigs invasion, and Nicaraguan diplomats always heartily approved of sanctions against Castro's Cuba. Nicaraguan officers dutifully attended counterinsurgency courses at the Canal Zone schools. Luis Somoza (1956–63) attended Louisiana State University and Anastasio Somoza Debayle (1967–79) graduated from the U.S. Military Academy at West Point. According to Assistant Secretary Edwin Martin, President Kennedy came away from his March 1963 meeting with President Luis Somoza impressed with the Nicaraguan. The Somoza brothers thereafter gave permission to Cuban exiles to launch attacks against Castro's Cuba from Nicaraguan bases.[28] To cut Nicaragua off from the Alliance for Progress would not only anger a Cold War ally but also jeopardize regional economic growth. The United States financially assisted the Central American Common Market, an Alliance success story; intraregional trade grew by over 700 percent during the 1960s. U.S. officials also reasoned that they could help the Nicaraguan poor. Apparently only the Peace Corps had second thoughts about working with the Somozas. Not wanting to tarnish the image of his agency, Sargent Shriver refused a Nicaraguan request for a Peace Corps program.[29]

Unlike the rest of Latin America, Nicaragua achieved during the decade an impressive annual per capita growth rate of approximately 4 percent. But economic growth did not produce the political and social benefits that Alliance planners and modernization theorists assumed would automatically follow a higher gross domestic product. The Somozas controlled national banks and development agencies, and they funneled Alliance funds into infrastructure projects, like roads and power plants, that enhanced Nicaragua's export capacity, particularly in the commercial agricultural fields of cotton production and cattle raising. Nicaragua, a small country, became the world's eleventh largest producer of cotton, and cattle production grew by 46 percent during the 1960s. U.S. development officials saw in this commercial development an opportunity for Nicaragua to increase its export income, resolve balance of payment problems, and develop new products for the growing Central American market. The Somoza family predictably profited from the economic growth. The family controlled the only two meat-processing plants licensed to export Nicaraguan beef. A family uncle, Luis Manuel Debayle, known popularly as "Tío Luz," or "Uncle Light," directed the national power and light company that sold power to the burgeoning cattle ranches and cotton farms. Short of moral suasion or the withholding of Alliance for Progress funds, U.S. officials had no mechanism either to insist on structural reform or to force the Somozas to share Nicaragua's bounty. The Somoza brothers pleased the United States by adopting an agrarian reform law but then ignored the statute; only 2,155 landless families received new land titles. In fact, conditions for rural Nicaraguans worsened during the 1960s. Cotton and cattle producers challenged land titles or bought out cash-poor *campesinos*. Small and medium-sized farms declined, while pasture land expanded by 31 percent. Food production for home consumption stagnated, and the demand for expensive, imported food rose. The landless poor, now 15–20 percent of the rural population, could either labor in the poorly paid agro-export industries or migrate to shantytowns that surrounded urban areas like Managua. Landholding patterns became even more concentrated than before the Alliance for Progress. By the early 1970s, 1.4 percent of landowners controlled 41 percent of the cultivated land.[30] The political explosions that rocked Nicaragua in the 1970s and 1980s provided ironic commentary on President Kennedy's aphorism on the relationship between peaceful and violent change.

Blame for the Alliance's problems could not, however, be placed solely on dictators. A lengthy staff study commissioned by the U.S. Senate Foreign Relations Committee found that the Alliance for Progress had brought neither economic growth nor social justice to Colombia. Between 1962 and 1967, the United States allocated $732 million to the South American republic. Foreign aid produced few tangible effects. Colombia's economy barely grew at 1.2 percent a year; its per capita income went from $276 to $295. Investigators found no real changes in landholding patterns, the tax structure, or the distribution of wealth and income. Colombia still had a social structure characterized by "close to two-thirds of the population not participating in the economic and political decision-making process."[31]

The staff study cited weaknesses within the Alliance for Progress. The hubris inherent in the vow to change Latin America's history within ten years led the United States to overemphasize its influence in Colombia. Real, meaningful change would take time. Eager to perform economic miracles, U.S. officials sponsored "high-impact, visible projects" that failed because of poor planning. The U.S. effort in Colombia also bore little resemblance to the Marshall Plan. The United States could not dedicate all of its aid to projects, like sewer construction, that would improve the quality of life for poor Colombians. The country was in such a desperate financial condition that almost half of the aid went to cover budgetary deficits and balance of payments problems. Investigators worried that Colombia was potentially assuming a new, crushing debt burden, because the interest rates on loans had risen from .75 percent to 2 percent. They further observed that, because of "additionality," Colombia was required to purchase expensive capital goods in the United States and to ship 50 percent of those goods on U.S. bottoms. With a guaranteed market, U.S. exporters could raise prices. The Alliance for Progress had "become a device for subsidizing specified U.S. exports."

The Kennedy administration also expected that the Alliance for Progress would shore up constitutional systems. It wanted to see a peaceful transfer of power in Colombia, and it fretted about Colombia's ongoing political violence and guerrilla warfare. The staff study concluded that Alliance money had helped facilitate power sharing between the Liberals and Conservatives, Colombia's ancient political enemies. But the easy relationship between political development, economic growth, and social reform assumed by theorists on modernization and middle-class revolution could not be found in Colombia. Because of concerns for security and stability, the United States exerted little pressure on leaders like President Guillermo León Valencia (1962–66) to enact reforms. Indeed, because he had budgetary assistance from Alliance funds, President Valencia took the safe political route and avoided the hazardous road of reform. In the Alliance for Progress, the desire for short-term stability always clashed with the need for far-reaching, permanent change. As the study noted, "The United States has genuinely been reluctant to attach strong conditions to aid for the same reasons which made aid necessary; that is, the tenuous position of the current government which undermined its ability to take strong reform measures." In view of this conundrum, the United States adopted policies similar to those it practiced in Nicaragua. It focused its agricultural loan program of $53 million on commercial farms and not on the 400,000–500,000 landless Colombian families. The value of exports of cattle, beef, and related products grew from $351,000 in 1961 to $11.7 million in 1965, helping ease Colombia's chronic trade problems. But as agricultural experts who surveyed the Alliance pointed out, technical modernization without structural reform would not resolve rural poverty and would add to urban problems by forcing people off the land.[32]

Even when the Alliance for Progress brought about change, the reform did not necessarily create progressive, democratic societies. In presenting their modernization theories and suggesting that Latin America needed to copy the institutions and values of the United States and Western Europe, Alliance planners implicitly disparaged Latin American culture. The region was "underdeveloped" and could only escape its status by discarding backward traditions in an evolutionary manner.[33] One legal scholar, in his study of lawyers and the Alliance for Progress, explored the ramifications of what happened when the United States tried to transfer models of development to Latin America. Like the social scientists who advised the Kennedy administration, U.S. lawyers "tended to perceive and attempted to change the world in their own glorified self-image." These "legal missionaries" also carried with them an "idealized image of American legal culture." They perceived lawyers as pragmatic problem solvers and social engineers who should be part of the "nation-building" process. They worked within the New Deal tradition that the state was a benign, positive agent of social change. Accordingly, U.S. lawyers, funded by the federal government and private foundations, worked on revising law school curriculums in Latin America. They taught a "rule-skeptical" approach to law; that is, "to look critically at formal rules and doctrines of law and to emphasize the social purposefulness and effect of law." They conversely argued against "legal-formalism" or the tradition that viewed law as a fixed and autonomous set of principles expressed in documents such as constitutions, codes, and statutes. But as happened with the agricultural modernization programs, this foreign aid had "unanticipated social consequences." Latin American legal scholars had traditionally seen lawyers as impediments to state power and guardians of the rule of law. Authoritarians, like the military dictators who governed Brazil after 1964, happily agreed that formal doctrinal law was antiquated and that, in the name of "development," legal rules and even the rule of law should be shelved. In the late 1970s, Brazilian jurists, who had adhered to "rule of law" concepts, helped rally Brazilians against violations of basic human rights.[34]

✦　　If U.S. officials had soberly analyzed Latin America's problems, displayed a healthy skepticism toward their models of development, showed respect for Latin America's traditions, and had the full resources of a Marshall Plan, they perhaps would have been more successful in helping the region generate and sustain a healthy rate of economic growth. They also needed the help of skilled technicians and development specialists and courageous, humane Latin American political leaders. But even if all officials had been wiser, braver, and richer, the Alliance for Progress would have been bedeviled by population, trade, and investment problems. Alliance enthusiasts could correctly and proudly count the numbers of low-cost homes, schools, and hospital beds that the United States provided during the 1960s. President Johnson enthusiastically read statistical reports of progress showing that more Latin Americans had access to potable water and that infant mortality rates had declined slightly. The Alliance for Progress did some good, yet because of population increase, the results seemed negligible. The number of unemployed Latin Americans rose from 18 million to 25 million. Alliance programs helped cut the percentage of children not attending school from 52 to 43 percent, but unfortunately, the actual number of children not attending school increased during the 1960s. The Inter-American Development Bank reported that Latin America added 151,670 hospital beds during the 1960s, but the number of hospital beds per 1,000 inhabitants fell from 3.2 to 3.0.[35]

With a 2.9 percent annual rate of increase, Latin America experienced the most rapid population growth in the world in the 1960s. Costa Rica, with the highest regional increase at 3.5 per cent a year, saw its population rise from 1.25 million to 1.75 million. Progressive Costa Rican governments went deeply into debt trying to educate these new children. El Salvador's population went from 2.45 million to 3.3 million. Living in a densely populated country of close to 400 people per square mile and losing out to commercial agriculture, Salvadorans migrated to Honduras looking for land and work. Hondurans increasingly resented the presence of foreigners, and the tension erupted into the so-called "Soccer War" of 1969 between El Salvador and Honduras. Although the war lasted only two weeks, it had a long-term negative effect on the Central American Common Market. Population pressures also hurt economic development in the larger South American nations. An increase in population from 15.6 million to 21 million added to Colombia's already substantial problems. Brazil's population increased by 25 million in the 1960s, from 70 to 95 million people. The largest population increases took place in impoverished areas such as the Brazilian Northeast.[36]

President Kennedy took no interest in population control, appar ently believing it to be politically and medically impractical and morally dubious. In an interview in late 1959, which was subsequently published in his campaign book, Kennedy disputed predictions that the world's population of 3 billion people would double in the next forty years. He noted that India and China had had little success controlling growth, politely noting that "the techniques are rather imperfect." To control population by legalizing medical abortions, as Japan allegedly did, "would be repugnant to all Americans." Kennedy, who came from an Irish American Catholic family of nine children, further observed that "most people consider their families to be their families, and that it is other people's families that provide the population explosion." Kennedy believed the solution to be economic development through foreign aid. He called on proponents and opponents of population control, including Roman Catholics, to support foreign aid. He warned against setting off a political firestorm by tying population control measures to foreign aid packages, for "what you'll end up with is not much foreign aid and no birth control."[37]

The charter of the Alliance for Progress did not make population control a hemispheric goal. No Latin American leader raised the issue with President Kennedy. In fact, President Luis Somoza told Kennedy that Nicaragua, with twenty-one people per square mile, needed to increase its population "by leaps and bounds."[38] Kennedy accepted the fact that Latin America would have to double its income between 1960 and 1990 just to stay even. Aides believed any direct pressure on Latin American nations "might have taken on poisonous racial overtones."[39] In 1961, Senator J. William Fulbright (D.-Ark.), the chairman of the Senate Foreign Relations Committee, questioned whether the Alliance could achieve its economic goals without population control. Secretary of the Treasury Dillon assured senators that "in Latin America the question of population control is not as serious as it may be in other areas of the world because there are substantial resources, substantial land, substantial availability for a growing, expanding population."[40]

By the end of the 1960s, U.S. officials no longer airily dismissed population issues. In 1964 Senator Fulbright attached an amendment to the Foreign Assistance Act that allowed the Agency for International Development to fund population control projects. In 1967 the agency spent $2.3 million in Latin America on fact gathering, although it did not promote family planning. In 1968 Robert Kennedy conceded that in Latin America "population growth threatens to eat up our gains as fast as they are made." He recognized that many Latin American nations remained suspicious of birth control. In that same year, the Vatican forbade Roman Catholics from using all methods of artificial contraception. Robert Kennedy responded, however, that Latin America would experience dreadful urban overcrowding if population growth continued unabated. In a noteworthy step for a man who fathered eleven children, he recommended U.S. support for birth control in those nations that wanted it and accelerated scientific research on population issues.[41] In fact, some ordinary Latin Americans were intensely interested in limiting the size of families. One U.S. official estimated that in Chile there were 150,000 illegal abortions as compared to 250,000 live births. In 1970 Mexican women underwent approximately 600,000 illegal abortions, and 32,000 women died. Mexico's population still soared from 22 million in 1945 to 87 million in 1990. The Mexico City metropolitan area grew from less than 3 million in 1950 to perhaps 20 million in 1990. In 1973 Mexican authorities permitted government-sponsored clinics to make birth control information available to those who requested it.[42]

Although U.S. officials became increasingly concerned about Latin America's population woes, they declined to address another key issue of Latin Americans—the terms of trade. Since the late 1940s, the Economic Commission on Latin America (ECLA), a United Nations agency, had been issuing studies that demonstrated that, for much of the twentieth century, the prices Latin Americans received for their exports of primary products had declined relative to the prices they paid for imports of finished goods. Led by Argentine economist Raúl Prebisch, ECLA developed theoretical models to explain this "unequal exchange" between the "center" and the "periphery." Whatever the merits of Prebisch's models, which perhaps had as many flaws as the modernization theories, the patterns of international trade worked against Latin America and the Alliance for Progress during the 1960s.[43] With poor domestic markets, Latin America absolutely depended on export earnings to generate the income necessary to underwrite economic development and social progress and to pay off foreign loans. During the decade, Latin America's export income steadily grew from $8 billion in 1960 to $10 billion in 1965 to $12 billion in 1968. The region also managed to maintain a balance of trade surplus. But global trade grew more rapidly than Latin America's trade in the prosperous 1960s; the value of U.S. exports, for example, more than doubled. Latin America did not reap its traditional share of the bounty. The region's share of international trade, which was over 10 percent in the 1950s, fell to barely 6 percent by the mid-1960s. Latin America also lost its position in lucrative markets. In 1960 Latin America supplied the United States with 24 percent of its imports. By the early 1970s, Latin America's market share was only 12 percent.[44]

Latin America faced new economic competitors in the 1960s. Western Europe and Japan had fully recovered from World War II, and the emerging Asian and African nations had entered the global marketplace. But Latin American political and economic leaders blamed their relative decline on the unpredictable but generally low prices they obtained for their exports. More than 90 percent of their exports continued to be primary products—tropical foods like coffee, sugar, bananas, and cacao and raw materials like copper, lead, zinc, and petroleum. In 1962 export prices, on average, were 9 percent below 1958 levels and 23 percent below the levels of 1951, a Korean War year. The price of coffee, Latin America's chief agricultural export, showed extreme volatility, ranging from 90 cents a pound in the 1950s to 36 cents a pound in late 1961. Whereas the prices of primary products fluctuated wildly, the prices of imported manufactured goods generally moved upward. ECLA calculated that in 1962 Latin America suffered a 22 percent decline in the terms of trade from the 1950–54 period.[45]

Latin American leaders gradually began to see "an immediate and progressive increase in export earnings" as the key to economic development rather than the promises of the Alliance for Progress.[46] At inter-American economic conferences, they wanted to talk about commodity price stabilization agreements and tariff preferences for the export of their manufactures. The Eisenhower administration had agreed to discuss stabilizing the price of coffee, and the Kennedy administration financed coffee marketing arrangements. But U.S. officials believed in the viability of the international capitalist system. The United States abstained on resolutions calling for compensatory pricing mechanisms for commodities such as meat and sugar. It also rejected Venezuela's efforts to set the price of petroleum through the Organization of Petroleum Exporting Countries (OPEC).[47] Latin Americans loudly complained about the decay in prices; President Raúl Leoni of Venezuela termed the price issue the "one black mark in our otherwise cordial relations."[48] Latin American nations also began to look outside the hemisphere for solutions. They took terms of trade issues to the U.N. Conferences on Trade and Development (1964, 1968). And Argentina, Brazil, and Chile tried to cultivate economic relations with the Soviet bloc. U.S. officials understood that poor export prices undercut the Alliance for Progress efforts. Those who continued to believe in the

Alliance called on the United States to show faith in free trade by lowering tariffs and abolishing quotas on imports of oil and sugar.[49]

The Alliance for Progress years witnessed not only Latin America's relative decline as a trading partner of the United States but also a relative reduction of U.S. direct investments in the region. In 1960 the U.S. business community had $8.4 billion in direct investments in Latin America, about 26 percent of U.S. international investments. By 1970, direct investments in Latin America rose to $12.3 billion but accounted for only about 16 percent of U.S. foreign investments.[50] Treasury secretary Dillon had set as a goal of the Alliance for Progress an annual increase of $300 million in U.S. direct investments in Latin America. Dillon argued that increased U.S. investment would raise the amount of capital available for the region's development. The $4 billion increase in direct investment represented one of the few Alliance goals met during the 1960s, although most new investments were made at the end of the decade. The composition of U.S. investments changed. U.S. businessmen traditionally invested in extractive industries like Venezuelan petroleum or Chilean copper or in public utilities like the Brazilian telephone system. In the late 1960s, they placed their money in the manufacturing sector, helping to diversify Latin America's future economy. Investments particularly grew in Argentina, Brazil, Mexico, and Central America. U.S. banks, like Chase Manhattan and First National City Bank, also established a presence in Latin America, opening branch banks. These banks would take over the funding role of the Alliance for Progress, lending Latin American governments hundreds of millions of dollars in the 1970s and early 1980s.[51]

U.S. businessmen initially objected to the Kennedy administration's foreign economic policies and the Alliance for Progress. In developing the Alliance, the administration largely ignored the business community, whereas the Truman administration worked closely with U.S. corporations on the Marshall Plan. Business people feared that the administration undermined private enterprise when it encouraged Latin American governments to draw up national development plans. One business advisory group, led by J. Peter Grace, who had extensive investments in South America, opposed the social aspects of the Alliance, including land reform. Businessmen also criticized the administration for not stoutly defending U.S. corporations when Latin American governments allegedly tampered with their properties.[52] In fact, in private conversations with Latin Americans, President Kennedy criticized "radical policies that pushed strongly in favor of the nationalization of capital and the expropriation of business investments." The administration pressed President Ramón Villeda Morales of Honduras to amend his agrarian reform law of 1962. The law, which Villeda Morales believed addressed the goals of the Alliance program, confiscated fallow land, including the holdings of Standard Fruit and United Fruit, both U.S.-owned companies. In retaliation, United Fruit halted its planting program. After speaking with President Kennedy and United Fruit representatives, Villeda Morales agreed to change the law.[53]

Clashes over U.S. companies, which evoked strong nationalist sentiments, soured Latin American economists and development specialists on foreign investments. During the 1960s, Latin Americans rarely called for new foreign investments, emphasizing instead equitable terms of trade. A new school of economic analysis, dependency theory, or *dependencia*, challenged the international capitalist system, modernization theory, and foreign assistance programs like the Alliance for Progress. Dependency theorists, like Fernando Henrique Cardoso, held that capitalism enriched the industrial world at the expense of nonindustrial regions like Latin America. They accepted the ECLA insight that the structure of foreign trade arrested economic growth and fostered political and social stagnation. But they went beyond Prebisch's views, charging that the United States consciously used foreign aid, private investments, trade agreements, and credit transactions to maintain its hegemony and Latin America's dependency and poverty. The triumph of socialism, both at home and abroad, would give Latin America its independence.[54] Like modernization theorists, the *dependencia* school favored explanatory models over empirical studies or practical experience, although the U.S. reaction to agrarian reform in Honduras probably offered the dependency theorists an excellent case study. But as happened to the social scientists who predicted that military rule would lead to the modernization and technological advance of Latin America, historical developments undermined grand theories. The Communist system collapsed in the Soviet Union and Eastern Europe, and after nearly four decades of revolution, most Cubans lived hard lives under Castro's dictatorship. Some dependency theorists, like Cardoso, who became president of Brazil in 1995, tacitly renounced their earlier analyses, espousing a "neo-liberal" faith in free trade and investment and, presumably, programs like the Alliance for Progress.

✦   As the dependency theorists claimed, the Kennedy administration used the Alliance for Progress to achieve its hemispheric goals. The administration may indeed have been more sensitive to the concerns of U.S. traders and investors than these capitalists realized. But the Cold War and frightening thoughts about the spread of Castro-style communism always remained uppermost in the minds of administration officials. Inadequate funding, bureaucratic turmoil, questionable theories, the population explosion, and low export prices all contributed to Latin America's dismal economic performance and the failure of the Alliance for Progress. At times, however, President Kennedy and his advisors undercut the Alliance by choosing security and stability over change and development.

President Kennedy frequently spoke about revolution and called for the redistribution of wealth and power. In mid-1962, while in Mexico City, he praised the Mexican Revolution and "the largest and the most impressive land reform program in the entire history of the hemisphere." He vowed that "the peaceful revolution of the Americas will not be complete" until *campesinos* owned the land they worked. In San José to meet with Central American presidents, Kennedy quoted Franklin Roosevelt, noting that "the test of our progress is not whether we add more to the abundance of those who have much; it is whether we provide enough for those who have too little." He followed up that speech by bluntly telling the Honduran president that Latin Americans needed to raise their tax revenues from the existing 8–10 percent of gross national product to a more acceptable 15 percent rate, still far short of the 26–27 percent tax rate in the United States.[55] Higher taxes could only come from the privileged of Latin America.

The president and his aides never fulfilled the promise of the lofty rhetoric of the Alliance for Progress. Far-reaching reform portended social instability, providing opportunities to dangerous radicals. The Kennedy administration took a timid approach toward agrarian reform. The Alliance could have succeeded only if it transformed socioeconomic conditions in the countryside, the locus of Latin America's poverty, underdevelopment, and population explosion. Forty-seven percent of Latin America's work force labored in the countryside, and another 10 percent provided services to the rural economy. In Peru, for example, 50 percent of the active population worked in agriculture, but the agricultural sector contributed only 22 percent to the national income. Ecuadorian agricultural laborers earned fifteen cents a day. Gross inequities in landholding, with 5–10 percent of the population owning 70–90 percent of the land, accounted for rural underdevelopment. OAS economists pointed out that there was more fallow land on these *lati-*

fundias than was in production on family farms. The great landholders enjoyed their social status and "accompanying control of labor" and declined to invest in their land or work force. They often paid their work force with food. They refused to tax themselves to build farm-to-market roads and other features of a modern rural infrastructure. They also ignored the educational and health needs of *campesinos*. As such, agricultural yields in Latin America of basic crops—corn, rye, oats, barley, potatoes—were below world averages. Food production barely kept up with population increase. By 1960, agricultural Latin America had become a net importer of wheat and feed grains.[56]

Mexico proved a notable exception to this stagnation. Between 1941 and 1960, agricultural productivity per capita had increased by 46 percent. In the aftermath of the Mexican Revolution, successive governments, especially the administration of President Lázaro Cárdenas (1934–40), had redistributed over 100 million acres, often in the form of communal holdings, or *ejidos*. This involved breaking up large estates and seizing unused land. President Kennedy celebrated this redistribution. In the approving view of Under Secretary Bowles, who also spoke in Mexico City, Mexico had baked a bigger economic pie and taken care to slice the pie fairly.[57] Despite this enthusiasm, neither the Kennedy nor the Johnson administrations recommended the Mexican model to the rest of Latin America. Sensitive to property rights, the United States refused to finance land expropriations. In the 1960s, many Latin American countries passed agrarian reform laws. But most laws made general, pious statements about reform and lacked a financing mechanism.[58] The Kennedy administration never made land redistribution a condition of any grant or loan, although it frequently tied aid packages to other conditions, such as monetary stabilization. During the 1960s, only Chile and Venezuela carried out anything more than token agrarian reform. Venezuela had begun its program before the enunciation of the Alliance for Progress.

Instead of advocating structural reform, the United States focused on technical modernization and the commercialization of Latin America's agricultural economy. This approach seemed intellectually defensible. Alliance planners worried about Latin America's balance of payments deficits and growing urban population. Latin America needed to produce and export more food. In any case, U.S. experts had more experience with mechanized, commercial agriculture than with land redistribution or *ejidos*. But this meant, in the judgment of scholars who studied agricultural issues and surveyed the Alliance's rural programs for the Senate Foreign Relations Committee, that the United States would "work with groups that have power and inevitably conservative agendas" and simultaneously cut itself off from meaningful contact with popular movements like peasant leagues and rural unions. These rural organizations admittedly often made anti-U.S. and anti–private enterprise statements. But commercialization would not solve rural income and employment issues. In fact, it would contribute to urban squalor by forcing subsistence farmers off the land.[59]

The Kennedy administration's agrarian reform efforts in Brazil underscored why it reneged on its commitment to long-range development and social change. The administration pledged to underwrite a concerted effort to develop the Brazilian Northeast, a nine-state region where one-third of Brazil's population lived. The region had the lowest per capita income in Latin America. In 1961 the president met in Washington with Celso Furtado, a Brazilian economist and director of the regional development agency, Superintendency for the Development of the Northeast (SUDENE). Kennedy promised to help, expressing "concern for the people of the area who suffer from a shortage of food, a high rate of infant mortality, and other symptoms of acute depression."[60] Furtado and his patron, President João Goulart, essentially accepted the arguments put forth in the task force reports prepared by Adolf Berle. The Brazilian Northeast was in a "pre-revolutionary" situation, not because of Communist agitators, "a small minority," but because of widespread poverty, illiteracy, hopelessness, and hunger. What was needed was to integrate the regional economy into the national one, produce more food, build roads and power stations, and attack antiquated land tenure patterns. In Furtado's opinion, it would be better to invest in those sectors that promised long-term economic growth and development than to siphon off money on expensive show projects, thinly spread over a vast region.[61]

Brazilian-American cooperation quickly broke down. The United States came to see the Brazilian Northeast as an international security problem. It thoroughly distrusted President Goulart. It worried about Brazilian peasant leagues that called for land redistribution; their leaders talked like Communists. Furtado suffered guilt by association. In 1963 the CIA labeled the respected economist and planner a former Communist who "still retains close associations with radical leftist and nationalist elements."[62] The administration, acting on direct orders from President Kennedy, decided to fund projects that would have immediate effects and undercut the appeal of agrarian radicals. In 1962 it allocated

$33 million for a "program primarily social in purpose and directed to the centers of greatest discontent in the northeast." The United States would build things like public fountains, which would carry "Alliance for Progress" markers. It aimed to complete the projects by October 1962, before the Brazilian congressional elections.[63] The administration bypassed SUDENE and worked through anti-Goulart, anti-Communist state governors, many of whom represented traditional oligarchic interests. These governors could boast that they had built new school and health centers. But because Brazil still lacked enough doctors and teachers, most of these facilities remained unoccupied. Only three of the fifty-nine new schools had teachers, furniture, and supplies. As one social scientist who carefully reviewed the U.S. effort in the Northeast concluded, the Kennedy administration failed to meet Brazil's basic needs for change and modernization, because it feared short-term conflict and disorder. The administration "chose a policy in the Northeast of cooperation with regional elites and justified the policy in terms of a communistic threat." The United States had "contributed to the retention of power by the traditional oligarchy" and "destroyed" a Brazilian program to modernize the political structure of the Northeast.[64]

The course of agrarian reform pointed to a tension between the administration's call for middle-class revolution and its search for an anti-Communist stability. As Assistant Secretary Martin once noted to Arthur Schlesinger, the Alliance for Progress contained "major flaws." Its "laudable social goals" encouraged political instability, yet their achievement demanded an 80 percent private investment, "which cannot be attracted amid political instability."[65] President Kennedy recognized the problem, observing, near the end of his administration, that the United States would have to learn to live in a "dangerous, untidy world."[66] To believe, however, that the administration would identify with future social revolutions would be to trust in hope over experience. As Chester Bowles harshly recalled, the president and his advisors never "had the real courage to face up to the implications" of the principles of the Alliance for Progress.[67]

✦   The Kennedy administration failed to perform miracles in Latin America. At a conference marking the twentieth-fifth anniversary of the Alliance for Progress, confreres seemed hard-pressed to cite enduring legacies of the program. Trying to be positive, one discussant weakly offered that the Alliance experience had taught Latin Americans how to prepare development plans. But none could claim that the

Alliance had built vibrant, progressive nations. Perhaps the best that could be said about the Alliance was that the infusion of money helped Latin America postpone the economic and financial disasters that hit the region in the 1980s.[68] Some Kennedy stalwarts continued, however, to believe in the promise of the Alliance for Progress. They blamed the Johnson administration for the Alliance's ultimate failure.

8 ★ Aftermath

Kennedy administration officials have conceded that they did not change the course and direction of Latin American history through the Alliance for Progress. But they continue to believe that President Kennedy adopted a bold program that could have succeeded. In their view, the United States ceased working for progressive change and development in Latin America after 22 November 1963. The Alliance for Progress died with the president. The new Lyndon Baines Johnson administration abandoned the U.S. commitment to democracy and social justice and focused instead on increasing U.S. private investment in the region. Johnson administration officials have predictably rejected those allegations. They claim that they upheld the Alliance for Progress and that continuity, not change, characterized U.S. efforts in Latin America during the 1960s.

★   Presidential aide and historian Arthur M. Schlesinger Jr. has persistently argued that the Alliance for Progress ended in 1963. President Johnson and his advisors removed the political and social components of the program, the "heart" of the Alliance. Within a month after the assassination of President Kennedy, Johnson had appointed veteran diplomat Thomas C. Mann to become both Assistant Secretary of State for Latin America and the Coordinator of the Alliance for Progress. Schlesinger considered Mann "a colonialist by mentality and a free enterprise zealot." He told his diary that the Mann appointment represented "a declaration of independence, even perhaps a declaration of aggression against the Kennedys." Johnson and Mann also removed from positions of influence those officials—Ralph Dungan, Richard Goodwin, Teodoro Moscoso, Arturo Morales-Carrión, and Schlesinger—who placed U.S. hopes in progressive Latin American democrats. Schlesinger alleged that Mann believed that "progressive democrats were either wishy-washy liberals or proto-Communists and that the hope for Latin America lay in the businessman and the armies." The administration's courting of bankers like David Rockefeller, its cordial relationship with the Brazilian generals, and its invasion of the Dominican Republic in 1965 sustained that harsh judgment. Unlike President Kennedy, Johnson did not constantly remind U.S. citizens of Latin America's needs. The Kennedy administration may have been long on rhetoric, but there are "moments when there is no substitute for eloquence." Schlesinger has readily admitted that the Alliance failed to meet its socioeconomic objectives, and that the president and his brother became foolishly infatuated with counterinsurgency doctrines. But the Kennedy administration simply needed more time and experience. As he opined, "The Alliance was never really tried. It lasted about a thousand days, not a sufficient test, and thereafter only the name remained." [1]

Robert Kennedy similarly alleged that the Johnson administration had forgotten the true meaning of the Alliance for Progress. Privately interviewed in 1964, he called Mann "a disaster." The new assistant secretary belittled Latin Americans, threatened to cut their foreign aid "if they misbehaved," and generally "sounded like Barry Goldwater making a speech at the Economic Club." [2] Kennedy subsequently complained about U.S. pressure on Peru over disputed oil contracts, economic assistance to the Brazilian generals, and the invasion of the Dominican Republic. If elected president in 1968, he pledged to renew the Alliance for Progress. What he observed during his 1965 tour of Latin America had reinforced his conviction that Latin America needed reform and democracy. Kennedy saw "tiny islands of enormous privilege in the midst of awful poverty." He wrote movingly of the people of the Brazilian coastal city of Recife "who live in shacks by the water in which they dump their refuse and garbage; the crabs that feed on that garbage are the staples of their diet." The presidential candidate called for a doubling of capital aid to Latin America; it would represent the cost of only "two weeks of war in Vietnam." The United States must insist, however, on structural reform. Reduction of tariff barriers, economic integration, and foreign investment, the measures the Johnson administration recommended, would spur economic growth. But the key to sustainable growth was creating large internal markets by breaking down class barriers. The United States should also should return to the policy of opposing military governments, as President Kennedy had when the Peruvian military annulled the 1962 presidential elections.

His encounters with the poor of Latin America and the growing popular disenchantment with the war in Vietnam had undoubtedly caused Senator Kennedy to do some hard thinking about his previous Cold War positions. He rejected the concept of a monolithic international Communist movement, noting that the Soviet Union, Cuba, and the People's Republic of China competed with one another in Latin America. He admitted that he had known of dubious CIA activities in Latin America and that he had placed too much faith in counterinsurgency programs. Reviewing the U.S. intervention in the Dominican Republic, he called for a renewed faith in the ideals of the Alliance for Progress. Kennedy warned that "our determination to stop Communist revolution in the hemisphere must not be construed as opposition to popular uprisings against injustice and oppression just because the targets of such popular uprisings say they are Communist-inspired or Communist led, or even because known Communists take part in them."[3] Like his brother, President Kennedy perhaps could have rethought his Cold War views and conscientiously pursued the principles inherent in his eloquent speeches, the task force reports, and the charter of the Alliance for Progress. The president had shown a capacity to grow, develop, and learn. However belatedly, he had embraced the domestic civil rights movement, and, in the aftermath of the Cuban Missile Crisis, he had negotiated a limited nuclear test ban treaty with the Soviet Union. But Arthur Schlesinger, Robert Kennedy, and other officials exaggerated the depth and certainty of President Kennedy's commitment to change and reform when they unfavorably compared President Johnson's Latin American policies to those of his predecessor.

In November 1963, President Kennedy understood that his Alliance for Progress was faring badly. The recent military *golpes* against constitutional governments in the Dominican Republic and Honduras distressed him. He could read the dismal economic numbers. He publicly admitted that the administration had underestimated the daunting nature of Latin America's socioeconomic problems and misled itself by using the Marshall Plan analogy. As his brother remarked in 1964, "The President thought we were moving in the right direction, thought it was the right concept, and was disappointed that it didn't work better." The attorney general emphasized that his brother had not given up and "thought that he could get it to work well."[4] But neither the president nor administration officials considered initiating a fundamental reassessment of U.S. policy or analyzing how Cold War security fears could be reconciled with calls for peaceful revolution in Latin America. U.S. officials seemed confused and uncertain, absurdly suggesting, for example, that the Alliance's problems arose from unfair press reports and poor public relations efforts. As a matter of "special, urgent responsibility," the State Department ordered U.S. diplomats to "provide maximum positive guidance to resident US correspondents as well as casuals passing through."⁵ President Kennedy thought in terms of bureaucratic reorganization and personnel shifts. He wanted Secretary Rusk to create a new position of under secretary of state for Latin American affairs.

In part, President Johnson's appointment of Mann in mid-December 1963 reflected Kennedy's thinking. On 29 October, Kennedy had demanded a single officer with full authority for Latin American affairs. He also wanted to see Alliance funds at work in Latin America and had lost confidence in Moscoso's administrative abilities. President Johnson undoubtedly wanted to put his own stamp on foreign and domestic policies. But Kennedy's men advised him to replace Moscoso and Assistant Secretary Martin. On 8 December 1963, National Security Advisor McGeorge Bundy recommended that Johnson create the position of under secretary of state for Latin America in order to give a "psychological boost" to the Alliance. The next day, he told the president that Martin "is just a little too fussy and detail-minded for the top job here."⁶ The State Department continued to oppose a special administrative slot for Latin America. Nonetheless, Secretary Rusk encouraged Johnson to make changes, and he spoke favorably of Johnson's desire, expressed during the first weeks of his presidency, for results rather than sloganeering in the area of foreign aid. According to Rusk, Johnson noted about the Alliance that "it's not rhetoric that counts, it's performance."⁷ In fact, the Johnson administration disbursed Alliance funds more rapidly than did the Kennedy administration.

President Kennedy would not have named Thomas Mann his "Mr. Latin America." Mann, a lawyer who had grown up bilingual in the Texas border town of Laredo, entered the foreign service in 1942. He spent most of his career in Latin America, where he developed a reputation for being a tough anti-Communist and stout defender of U.S. foreign investments. Although a political conservative, Mann did not oppose the idea of the United States being a catalyst for change in Latin America. During the last Eisenhower years, he served as assistant secretary of state for economic affairs and then assistant secretary of state for Latin America, and he favored the establishment of the Inter-American Development Bank and an agreement to stabilize the price of coffee. As Kennedy's first assistant secretary for Latin America, he supported the Alliance for Progress. He also opposed the Bay of Pigs invasion, believing it would damage the U.S. image in Latin America. In 1961 President Kennedy appointed him ambassador to Mexico, where he concentrated on resolving the Chamizal question, a long-standing boundary dispute near El Paso, Texas.[8] Mann's standing on Alliance issues was such that Adolf Berle heartily congratulated President Johnson on the new appointment, recalling that his task force had wanted Mann to be the first under secretary for Latin America.[9] By his own admission, however, Mann shifted his position on the Alliance during his years in Mexico City. He complained that White House officials espoused "revolution" without defining what they meant. Mann "thought we should favor orderly evolution and be careful of what we said and orient our program so that would be made clear." In a speech in Mexico in 1962, he subtly criticized the reform dimension of the Alliance, arguing that socioeconomic reform would be meaningful only if economic growth first occurred.[10] Although a native Texan, Mann was not a political crony of President Johnson, but Johnson approved of Mann's work on the Chamizal dispute.

Mann stayed a year as assistant secretary, became an ambassador-at-large in 1965, and retired from government in 1966. The turnover rate in the Latin American position was as rapid as during the Kennedy years. Johnson would appoint three more "Mr. Latin Americas." One of Mann's successors was Lincoln Gordon, who had helped design the Alliance, had served as Kennedy's ambassador to Brazil, and had once declined Kennedy's request to become assistant secretary. Gordon dubbed allegations that Johnson had abandoned the Alliance as "Camelot myth-making."[11] Covey Oliver, another bilingual lawyer from Laredo and former law professor and ambassador to Colombia, had the longest tenure, serving from mid-1967 to early 1969. Presuming reelection, Johnson promised the job to Oliver for four years. A self-described "New Deal, Great Society Democrat," Oliver tacitly rejected Mann's thesis, informing Johnson that he believed the Alliance needed to emphasize social and political change over economic growth. Johnson agreed, telling Oliver to maintain his idealism, press for reform, and not to let himself "be outflanked by the left rhetorically."[12]

Although Mann served briefly, Schlesinger and others believed that he destroyed the Alliance for Progress with a speech he gave in March 1964. In a confidential talk to the chiefs of mission stationed in Latin America, Mann presented what would be subsequently tagged the "Mann Doctrine." He listed four core principles of U.S. policy in Latin America: the promotion of economic growth; the protection of the $9 billion in U.S. direct investments; nonintervention in the internal affairs of Latin Americans; and anticommunism. The United States believed in democracy but would not try to impose it on Latin America and would no longer respond to military *golpes* by suspending U.S. economic and military assistance. Mann believed that the United States had been largely unsuccessful in unseating dictators and that, in any case, it should stay out of domestic political crises. He added that the nation should not identify with or give medals to dictators but then allegedly went on to say that he found it difficult to distinguish between President Adolfo López Mateos of Mexico or President Víctor Paz Estenssoro of Bolivia and Paraguayan strongman Alfredo Stroessner. According to attending diplomats, Mann never explicitly mentioned the Alliance for Progress. The talk was quickly "leaked" to *New York Times* correspondent Tad Szulc and became a front-page story with the title "U.S. May Abandon Effort to Deter Latin Dictators."[13] NSC officials confirmed that Szulc had written an accurate account of Mann's remarks.[14] Less than two weeks after Szulc's article appeared, Brazilian generals overthrew President João Goulart, and the Johnson administration immediately granted diplomatic recognition to the new government. It appeared that under the Mann Doctrine the United States now favored military dictators. In November 1964, the Bolivian military ousted Paz Estenssoro, the constitutional leader that Mann had belittled.

Mann continued to be remarkably indiscreet and insensitive during his time in Washington. In closed congressional hearings, he testified that Latin America generated irresponsible politicians and businessmen because of a "structural weakness of the cultural kind." He advised President Johnson not to tour Latin America, because Latin Americans had not learned "discipline, responsibility, simple Christian charity, respect for law, and dedication to the right values."[15] Mann's diatribes led editorial writers at prominent newspapers like the *New York Times* and the *Washington Post* to question the administration's commitment to Latin America. Mann also quarreled with Kennedy appointees like White House aide Ralph Dungan. Bundy recommended that President Johnson review Mann's speeches in order that "we will be in a good position to watch over drafts and make sure that they do the job Tom has in mind but with a minimum danger of a boomerang effect." Bundy also persuaded the president to appoint Dungan as ambassador to Chile and brought Robert Sayre, a friend of Mann's, into the White House. Bundy assigned Sayre the task of preventing Mann from committing further political indiscretions. At a June 1964 commencement ceremony at the University of Notre Dame, Mann, with Sayre's editorial help, gave a measured address on U.S. recognition policy.[16] Mann restated Thomas Jefferson's de facto recognition policy: the United States would conduct diplomatic relations with governments that fulfilled international obligations. The United States opposed military *golpes* and would encourage the rapid restoration of constitutional procedures. Mann also promised to consider withholding aid and diplomatic recognition based on a "case by case review" of each *golpe*.[17]

However abrasive and politically clumsy Mann was during his tenure as assistant secretary and ambassador-at-large, President Kennedy's admirers exaggerated when they charged Mann with fundamentally undermining U.S. policies. They seemingly forgot that Assistant Secretary Martin, with President Kennedy's explicit approval, had issued an October 1963 statement indicating that the administration would not necessarily shun unconstitutional military governments. The United States would only use force to prevent Communists from seizing power. Presidential advisor Theodore Sorensen confirmed that Kennedy judged some military rulers more competent and reliable than their civilian counterparts. Although disappointed by the *golpes* in late 1963 in the Dominican Republic and Honduras, Kennedy had decided to resume normal diplomatic relations with the military-dominated governments.[18] Whether President Kennedy would have ordered the U.S. military to prepare to assist the Brazilian generals in overthrowing President Goulart obviously cannot be determined. But Kennedy had directed a destabilization campaign against Goulart. Kennedy-era officials—Rusk, George Ball, Gordon, Bundy, Ralph Dungan, Robert McNamara—engaged in the 1964 conspiracy against Goulart. During his presidential campaign, Robert Kennedy lamented military rule in Brazil and implied that the Johnson administration bore responsibility for its continuation. Yet he declined to reveal to voters his role in undermining constitutionalism in Brazil, and he persisted in calling Goulart "ineffective and corrupt." Kennedy admitted, however, that he had voted in the U.S. Senate in favor of economic aid for authoritarian Brazil.[19]

President Kennedy surrounded himself with politically liberal supporters of the Alliance for Progress. Schlesinger, Goodwin, Moscoso, and others had easy access to the Oval Office. By comparison, Johnson did not meet frequently with those identified with the development of the Alliance, other than Walt Rostow, who became his national security advisor in 1966. But presidential access hardly guaranteed influence on critical policy issues; Kennedy usually rejected the advice of his liberal advisors. Schlesinger, for example, opposed the Bay of Pigs invasion, the recognition of the Argentine military in 1962, the resumption of military aid to the Peruvian junta, the uncompromising attitude toward

Cheddi Jagan, and Edwin Martin's statement on U.S. policy toward military governments. In October 1962, Schlesinger wrote an impassioned memorandum to the White House, decrying a renewed emphasis on orthodox monetary and investment policies. As Schlesinger summarized, "This apparent recrystalization of elements of the Eisenhower policy within the framework of the Alliance for Progress is troubling and, I believe, will get us nowhere."[20] Arturo Morales-Carrión, who served as deputy assistant secretary of state for inter-American affairs, similarly worried that Washington concentrated on economic and administrative problems and not on political and ideological goals like wedding the Alliance for Progress to Latin American nationalism.[21]

Liberals retained the power to criticize new directions in inter-American relations but gradually lost the power to change the course of policies. The president replaced Chester Bowles, who championed the concerns of Asians, Africans, and Latin Americans, with George Ball, who cared about Europe. Kennedy dispatched Goodwin to the State Department to shake up the bureaucracy and promote the Alliance. Goodwin blundered when, in early 1962, he and Moscoso decided on a loan for Chile without clearing the aid package with the responsible State Department officers. Goodwin suffered further embarrassment when the State Department, with President Kennedy's acquiescence, denied a visa to the distinguished Mexican novelist, Carlos Fuentes, because of an alleged Communist affiliation. Goodwin had planned to debate Fuentes on national television. A chagrined Goodwin left the State Department at the end of 1962.[22] In Schlesinger's view, the State Department "lost the imagination, drive, and purpose Goodwin had given so abundantly to the Alliance."[23] Goodwin's departure came, however, on Kennedy's, not Johnson's, watch.

Kennedy did not rely on U.S. businessmen for advice on inter-American affairs, and they decried their lack of influence. J. Peter Grace of the W. R. Grace Corporation wondered, for example, whether the Kennedy administration took seriously the goal of expanding foreign investments in Latin America by $300 million a year. In January 1964, bankers, traders, and investors formed the Business Advisory Group on Latin America, which subsequently joined the larger Council for Latin America. David Rockefeller of Chase Manhattan Bank headed both business groups, which included representatives from major corporations like Standard Oil of New Jersey and International Telephone and Telegraph. President Johnson and Vice President Hubert H. Humphrey met regularly with these business lobbies. The businessmen appreciated hearing Johnson talk about "property rights," and they applauded the appointment of Mann. In February 1966, the vice president informed Johnson that Rockefeller and his colleagues "believe that a substantial change in policy has occurred within the U.S. government within the last two years in regard to the question of private enterprise in Latin America." The Kennedy people had made economic growth secondary to social reform. Mann had reversed those priorities. The business community was now "most happy with U.S. policy."[24]

The Johnson administration pleased U.S. businessmen when it vociferously defended U.S. investments. Assistant Secretary Mann fulfilled his pledge to protect the $9 billion in direct investments. He insisted that the Argentine government of Arturo Illia reverse its decision to annul the contracts of U.S. oil companies. In Mann's judgment, lucrative oil investments in areas such as Venezuela and Saudi Arabia would be jeopardized if the United States did not defend the sanctity of contract in Argentina.[25] In Peru, in another dispute over the contractual rights of oil companies, Mann pressured the government of Fernando Belaúnde Terry by withholding U.S. economic assistance. Mann scolded President Belaúnde for confiscating U.S. property, a "bad" act.[26] Schlesinger and Robert Kennedy correctly charged that President Kennedy would not have approved such heavy-handed tactics. He preferred to negotiate solutions to contentious trade and investment issues. But too much can be made of Kennedy's relative inattention to the interests of the U.S. business community. While Cold War issues always attracted the president's interest, the tampering with U.S. investments was one of the Kennedy administration's justifications for destabilizing the Goulart government.

Whereas it mattered who advised the president, the decisions the president made and the priorities he attached to inter-American relations counted for more. During his five-year presidency, Lyndon Johnson showed only a fitful interest in Latin America. He apparently did not share President Kennedy's apocalyptic vision that the Cold War would be decided in Latin America. Johnson certainly talked about the significance of the region. Shortly after the assassination, with Mrs. Kennedy at his side, he appeared before Latin American ambassadors and pledged his wholehearted support to the Alliance for Progress. He remarked to Dean Rusk that "this hemisphere is our home. This is where we live. These people are our neighbors. If we can't make it work here, where we live, how can we expect to make it work anywhere else."[27] But in his 569-page memoir, Johnson devoted only four pages to the Alliance for

Progress. He blamed the Alliance's shortcomings on the congressional failure to allocate additional funds he requested in 1967.[28] Unlike Kennedy, Johnson did not keep the Oval Office open to influential Latin Americans; prior to 1967, he hosted only one Latin American president.[29] Johnson eventually met Latin American presidents at an OAS summit held at Punta del Este in April 1967. Unlike Kennedy, he never became close with Latin American democrats. Indeed, he admired the authoritarian Brazilian general Artur da Costa e Silva (1967–69) because, according to the testimony of presidential aides, Johnson judged the Brazilian a "barracks general" and "a tough personality who could be relied on to stand by his friends under fire."[30]

Johnson's relative inattention to inter-American affairs can be explained in several ways. An ambitious leader, Johnson naturally wanted to put his own mark on domestic and international policies. He obviously loved working on his domestic reform program, the Great Society. The Alliance for Progress would always be identified with Kennedy. Johnson further suspected that U.S. ambassadors in Latin America doubted that he could ever measure up to Kennedy. Ralph Dungan confirmed that suspicion. The ambassador to Chile suggested that, because he was a Texan, Johnson "had a kind of romantic, Tex-Mex view of Latin America" that "always really distorted his view of Latin American relations."[31] Whatever the merits of Dungan's condescending analysis, Johnson was not well served by his friends either. Neither Dean Rusk nor Walt Rostow advised him of problems or pushed for a vigorous approach to inter-American affairs. The fawning Rostow sent only happy, cheerful memorandums to Johnson, reassuring him "that the record will show that you have done more for Latin America than any of your predecessors—in terms of money and attentions."[32] Rostow should have known, however, that President Johnson spent his time and U.S. money on the war in Vietnam. In 1965 Robert Sayre pointed out that concerns about Vietnam prevented the NSC from addressing Latin American issues. In mid-1967, Assistant Secretary Gordon resigned, concluding that the Vietnam War would engulf U.S. foreign policy. Latin Americans similarly felt neglected. In 1966 David Rockefeller reported to Johnson and Humphrey that "many Latin Americans are concerned that the harsh exigencies of the war in Vietnam may again make Latin America a low priority area in U.S. policy." In 1967, the administration asked Mexico to take the lead on promoting the idea of a Latin American Common Market. Mexican foreign secretary Antonio Carrillo Flores demurred, observing that he believed "that the United

States could not give adequate attention and support to the common market as long as the Vietnamese war continued." [33]

Although overwhelmed by his war, Johnson had some accomplishments and talked about new approaches in inter-American relations. Reflecting his personal and political heritage, Johnson took seriously festering border issues—immigration, boundaries, water rights—between the United States and Mexico. In early 1965, the administration persuaded Mexico to drop plans to file charges in the World Court and sign a five-year agreement to negotiate various questions surrounding the salinity of the Colorado River. Mexico alleged that development in the United States had altered the quality of the Colorado's water. The agreement implied that the United States would provide a loan to rehabilitate the Mexicali Valley. In a demonstration of his legendary political skills, Johnson convinced governors of the seven Colorado basin states to support the agreement.[34] The Johnson administration also promoted hemispheric economic integration. In 1967 Johnson called for improvements in communication and transportation to facilitate regional trade and a Latin American Common Market. He spoke of obtaining an additional $2.5 billion from Congress over a five-year period to underwrite the program. Alarmed and angry over the crisis in Southeast Asia, Senator J. William Fulbright, chairman of the Senate Foreign Relations Committee, rebuffed Johnson; the president obtained only a $50 million annual increase in the U.S. contribution to the Inter-American Development Bank.[35] Robert Kennedy criticized Johnson's scheme because it did not address questions of social justice within countries. Notwithstanding Kennedy's critical point, Johnson's vision came to life in the 1990s when the southern cone countries of Argentina, Brazil, Paraguay, and Uruguay tied their economies together in a free-trade agreement known as Mercado Común del Sur (MERCOSUR), or "Common Market of the South." But Johnson knew he had failed the Alliance for Progress. On 6 March 1968, in the aftermath of the Tet offensive and just weeks before announcing his decision not to seek reelection, the president wistfully told aides that he hoped he would "have time to visit several Latin American countries to demonstrate our high-level interest in the area." In Rusk's words, Johnson left office in 1969 "disappointed that more was not accomplished for and with our Latin American neighbors." [36]

✦   Although President Johnson may have not lovingly embraced the Alliance for Progress, he faithfully pursued the Kennedy administration's other regional Cold War policies. Like Kennedy, he vowed to prevent another Cuba in the Western Hemisphere. Johnson made that explicit when he pronounced his Johnson Doctrine to justify the U.S. invasion of the Dominican Republic. A second Communist beachhead in the Western Hemisphere would pose a strategic threat to the United States and would generate a lethal political fallout for Johnson and the Democratic Party.[37] The Johnson administration also continued the policy of warning Latin Americans to avoid all political and economic contacts with Communists. In January 1965, Rusk repeated the arguments he made in his October 1963 circular to diplomatic posts in Latin America. The establishment of diplomatic and commercial relations "may lead to a considerable increase of Communist penetration, activity, and influence in this hemisphere." The Communists could be counted on to use diplomatic and consular posts for espionage and subversion. If the Soviets placed their personnel in Latin America, it "will only confirm their arrogant assumption that Free World governments are essentially gullible and lacking in toughness and determination." Rusk instructed U.S. diplomats to make the administration's views known to Latin Americans. He realized, however, that they would be greeted with "extreme skepticism," for Latin American officials "regard us as obsessed with communism."[38]

The fear of communism permeated the Johnson administration's approach toward Latin America. On 22 April 1964, Johnson issued NSAM No. 297, ordering that military aid to Latin America be oriented toward the "continued emphasis on civic action and internal security missions."[39] Despite doubts expressed by Defense Department officials, Johnson maintained counterinsurgency and police training programs that had been devised by President Kennedy and his brother. Indeed, in May 1964 U.S. military officers, seconded by National Security Advisor Bundy, suggested that Attorney General Kennedy attend a "Strategic Intelligence Seminar" in the Canal Zone as a way of enticing Chilean military officers to enroll in the course. The Chilean military had resisted counterinsurgency training on the grounds that Communist guerrillas did not threaten their peaceful country.[40] In mid-1965, the administration helped Peru purchase three transport planes that would carry men and equipment into remote areas to combat guerrillas. The administration found the necessary $10 million in military aid, even as it withheld economic assistance over the disputed contracts of U.S. oil companies.[41] CIA agents also continued to cultivate contacts with Latin American security officers.[42] Johnson resisted congressional efforts to limit military aid, telling aides in 1967 that "it would be a wise course to get out some of these old Cuba speeches and show the Congress what could happen if we weren't able to help these countries."[43] As Johnson indicated, his administration accepted the Kennedy thesis that the Latin American military could be both a source of anti-Communist stability and an agent of modernization. Thomas Mann noted to U.S. diplomats that the relationship with the military was "a delicate and important one." Latin American officers could be politically irresponsible, but sometimes they intervened "out of the ultimate necessity to prevent internal chaos and extremism, as in the recent case of Brazil."[44]

Like its predecessor, the Johnson administration preferred working with anti-Communist democrats. In Chile the administration covertly carried out the massive spending campaign to elect as president the Christian Democratic reformer, Eduardo Frei. It also quietly conducted numerous public opinion polls to measure the Chilean electorate's sentiments. As Gordon Chase of the NSC told Bundy, U.S. officials must "simply do what we can to get people to back Frei," for a President Salvador Allende supposedly would nationalize the U.S.-owned copper mines, end the Alliance, and turn to the Soviet bloc.[45] The administration appointed Ralph Dungan to the ambassadorship in Chile. Sending Dungan to Santiago ended the feuding between him and Mann. But Bundy recommended to Johnson a man "who is fundamentally sympathetic to the cause of democratic reform." Mann could be relied on to look out for the copper companies in Chile, "so Dean Rusk and I believe that a progressive and imaginative Ambassador will be needed as a counterweight."[46] The administration took delight in aiding President Frei, because it undercut the criticism of Kennedy people that it favored Brazilian generals over decent democrats.[47]

The Johnson administration also shared the Kennedy administration's dislike of *golpes* against anti-Communist, constitutional leaders. It tried to stop the military *golpe* against President Arturo Illia of Argentina. In late 1965, Secretary Rusk ruled that the United States should resume the Alliance for Progress in Argentina; the Illia government had made satisfactory progress toward resolving contractual disputes with the oil companies. The United States had also grown to respect the efforts of President Illia to reform the Argentine economy and restrain the wage demands of the Peronist unions. Argentina now followed the U.S. lead on Cuba, and Rusk hoped to have the support of the Argentine foreign ministry in the future.[48] But on 1 June 1966, CIA officers in Argentina predicted that the military would overthrow President Illia in July. Several days later, the CIA moved up the predicted *golpe* date to

June. Argentine generals repeated the arguments that they had used to justify the overthrew of President Arturo Frondizi in March 1962. Illia presided over political and economic chaos and was soft on communism. The generals further feared that the Peronists would win the national elections scheduled for March 1967. Edwin Martin, now the U.S. ambassador in Buenos Aires, immediately expressed his opposition to the military plans. Assistant Secretary Lincoln Gordon backed Martin, instructing him "to make absolutely clear" to the *golpistas* "that we would not repeat not be able easily to cooperate with a de facto government that had ousted constitutional Illia administration." Martin could remind the generals that the United States had authorized $42 million in military assistance and $167 million in loans and credits for economic development. The administration also had a U.S. general meet with an Argentine general and reiterate U.S. opposition to the overthrow of Illia.[49] The Argentine military, led by Lieutenant General Juan Carlos Onganía, ignored U.S. entreaties and, on 28 June 1966, ejected President Illia from office. National Security Advisor Rostow reported to President Johnson that "this unjustified military coup is a serious setback to our efforts to promote constitutional government and representative democracy in the hemisphere. It will be necessary to re-examine our whole policy toward Argentina."[50]

Ambassador Martin had previously explained why the Argentine military would ignore U.S. pressure and why the United States would not punish Argentina. In June 1965, Martin commented on CIA reports that some generals, although not Onganía, wanted to strike immediately. Argentine officers had convinced themselves that if they ousted Illia they would be performing the same role as the Brazilian military in removing Goulart and that "they would be acting with [the] identical spirit of renovation, of anti-communism, anti-corruption, and of unreserved support for pro-Western foreign policy." Argentine officers followed closely U.S. economic assistance to the government of General Humberto Castello Branco, and they believed that U.S. investors had become enthusiastic about the new regime in Brazil. If the United States publicly opposed the Argentine military, the diplomatic pressure would be "met with incredulity and the historic feeling that the US favors Brazil over Argentina."[51] Martin proved prescient. The Johnson administration acted much like the Kennedy administration did in March 1962, when the Argentine military overthrew President Arturo Frondizi. Security concerns and economic interests outweighed the U.S. commitment to democracy. Despite the internal blustering, the Johnson administration decided a day after General Onganía seized power to accept the *golpe*. It did not even require the Onganía regime to issue a statement on human rights or a pledge to restore constitutionalism. Such demands might appear "unduly vindictive" to Argentine officers. As Under Secretary Ball advised the president, the Argentine generals would protect U.S. trade and investment and would provide "strong" support in international forums in "the struggle against communism."[52]

✦   Two crises marked inter-American relations during the Johnson years: violent, anti-American demonstrations in Panama in January 1964 and the U.S. invasion of the Dominican Republic in the spring of 1965. In both cases, the Johnson administration pursued policies consistent with those of its predecessor. Less than two months after taking office, President Johnson faced what President Kennedy had tried to forestall. On 9 January 1964, a confrontation between Panamanian university students and U.S. residents of the Canal Zone erupted into four days of fighting. The clash began over the largely symbolic issue of where in the Canal Zone Panamanians could fly their national flag. The riots left over 300 casualties, including twenty-four Panamanians and four U.S. soldiers dead. The violence represented a failure of President Kennedy's Panamanian policy.

Panamanians cared about more than where they could fly their flag. Led by President Roberto Francisco Chiari (1960–64), they demanded a fundamental renegotiation of the 1903 treaty, the Hay-Bunau-Varilla Convention, that sanctioned the U.S. presence in the Canal Zone. In particular, they wanted their nation's sovereignty over both the canal and the accompanying zone unequivocally established, and they demanded an end to the "in perpetuity" clause, calling on the United States to set a date when it would transfer operation of the canal to Panama. Panamanians also considered the annual U.S. payment of $1.93 million as insufficient. President Kennedy found merit in the Panamanian position, although he declined to say so publicly or in private correspondence with President Chiari. Kennedy could focus on the issue of nationalism, because the Cold War did not intrude into U.S.-Panamanian relations. Panama faithfully backed the anti-Castro crusade, and President Chiari and the National Guard easily controlled Panama's small contingent of radicals. In the disapproving view of Assistant Secretary Martin, the president had a "guilt complex" about Panama, hoped to erase a "black mark" in history, and wished to make Panama "happy."[53] Kennedy also accepted the argument that the United

States paid too little rent for the control of the canal. The president's position reflected his anticolonial sentiments, as expressed in his famous speech in the U.S. Senate denouncing France's domination of Algeria, and his genuine desire to improve the welfare of Latin Americans. Ambassador to Panama Joseph Farland and Dr. Carl Kaysen, an academic from Harvard who worked on Panamanian issues for the NSC, similarly believed that the United States needed to accommodate Panama. They understood that there was "a deep and continuing nationalistic drive which impels articulate leaders of Panama to press for their objectives regarding the Zone and the Canal."[54]

Most U.S. public officials and private citizens opposed any major change in the status of the Panama Canal. The State Department did not accept the argument that nationalism underlay President Chiari's insistence on change. The department judged President Chiari an unprincipled oligarch interested in obtaining additional tolls and revenues so he could spend freely. It could point out that Chiari's family had long dominated Panama's economic and political life; the family monopolized milk distribution in Panama City and held substantial interests in sugar, and Chiari's father, Rudolfo, had been president in the 1920s. The department argued against any substantive changes in U.S. relations with Panama. It recommended, in Martin's words, making "small concessions, dragged out over a period of time"—just "enough to keep the pot from boiling over."[55] Secretary Rusk put his under secretary, George Ball, in charge of negotiations with Panama; Ball skillfully parried President Chiari's incessant requests for a new relationship.[56] Defense Department officials also called for delay. U.S. officials dreamed of opening, sometime between 1980 and 2000, a new sea-level canal wide enough to allow the largest ships, such as aircraft carriers and oil tankers, to pass through. A sea-level canal, free of locks, might also be less vulnerable to various types of enemy attacks. Engineers would need years to study the feasibility of this new canal, because excavation involved using nuclear explosions. What dangers in the form of radioactive fallout these explosions posed for nearby populations remained uncertain. Officials also could not say where in Central or Middle America this sea-level canal might be built.[57]

Legislators also opposed renegotiating the treaty of 1903. They understood that their constituents saw the canal as a testament to U.S. ingenuity and enterprise. President Kennedy doubted that he could convince two-thirds of the U.S. Senate to ratify a new treaty or even persuade a majority of House members to support a higher rent payment to Panama. Leonor Sullivan (D.-Mo.), the chair of the House committee with oversight responsibilities for the canal, distrusted Panamanians. Representative Daniel Flood (D.-Penn.) constantly reminded colleagues that they would besmirch the reputation of Theodore Roosevelt if they permitted alterations to the 1903 treaty. Only a few legislators, like Mike Mansfield (D.-Mont.), argued that the U.S. interest was in an open, trouble-free passage through the canal and "not an outdated position of privilege." The civilian residents of the Canal Zone led the popular opposition to change. They operated the canal's intricate lock system and disparaged the abilities of Panamanians to keep the canal working. They also wanted to protect their high salaries and privileged lives in the zone.[58]

Despite this formidable opposition, President Kennedy took Panamanian nationalism seriously. He accepted the recommendation of a special NSC working group headed by Ball that the United States needed at least five years to study the feasibility of a sea-level canal. In the meantime, the United States should "contain" Panama by accelerating Alliance for Progress aid and by addressing a variety of symbolic grievances, such as whether Panamanian postage stamps should be used in the Canal Zone postal system. Between 1961 and 1964, the United States allocated $78 million to Panama, which made Panama the highest recipient, on a per capita basis, of Alliance for Progress funds. The president also encouraged Chiari to inform him of vexatious issues. But in accepting the NSC recommendation, as expressed in NSAM No. 152, Kennedy reminded aides that "we would probably be forced to renegotiate the treaty in the not too distant future regardless of any delaying action we might conduct."[59]

Kennedy's keen insight into nationalist pressures became apparent when he hosted President Chiari in Washington on 12 June 1962. The main meeting was lengthy and contentious. The memorandum of conversation noted that Chiari "became frustrated and petulant in his speech" and that Kennedy warned that the United States would not take action "at the point of a mob." The Panamanian wanted to discuss not details but the basic sovereignty and perpetuity issues. He called for an explicit recognition of Panama's sovereignty over the canal and a term limit set for the end of U.S. control, suggesting "something like 50 years." He further noted Panamanians had grown weary waiting for the United States to complete its studies. President Kennedy acknowledged historical injustices but tried patiently to explain U.S. political realities. An aide to Chiari shot back that "in Panama there was also a

problem of national sentiment that it was difficult to control and postpone." Kennedy held his position that "1964, 1965, or 1966 would be a
better time to go about a 'basic document.'" Kennedy would then be
in his second and last presidential term and presumably could afford to
pay the political price of a treaty ratification fight. In the meantime,
Kennedy promised a "liberal" interpretation of the existing treaty. On
15 June, he issued NSAM No. 164, appointing a commission to address
legitimate Panamanian complaints. The president expected "an appropriate flow of concrete results in order to contain Panamanian pressures
for immediate and radical treaty revision."[60]

Although he had been unyielding with Chiari on the renegotiation
issue, Kennedy continued to show sensitivity to the Panamanian leader's
political position. Talks on minor issues did not produce immediate
agreements. In November 1962, in a handwritten letter, Chiari reiterated that Panama could not wait five years, and "he emphasized the
urgency of prompt action, asserting that his people cannot remain patient much longer." In March 1963, during his time in San José for the
meeting of Central American presidents, Kennedy agreed to meet alone
with Chiari. After the meeting the president ordered Rusk to give particular attention to Panama and Ambassador Farland to consult with
U.S. legislators. In May, Kennedy met with Farland, and notably not
with other senior State Department officers. The president told the ambassador that "the $1.93 million we paid every year for the Canal was
not enough." He inquired what Panama wanted in a new treaty. Farland opined that Panama would accept what Theodore Roosevelt had
originally offered Colombia in the Hay-Herrán Treaty (1903)—a recognition of Colombian sovereignty and an agreement that Colombia
would take control of the canal in the early twenty-first century. Farland also thought that the United States should begin negotiating basic
issues in late 1964 or early 1965. Kennedy concluded the meeting by
telling Farland that "we do not want an explosion in Panama, we must
keep the lid on the next couple of years the best way we can." In July,
Kennedy provided Panama with $3 million in special assistance funds.
Although he politely implied in a letter to Chiari that the money could
be considered part of the Alliance for Progress, Kennedy meant that
the United States should pay a higher rent.[61] The president decided,
however, not to risk political capital and ask Congress to appropriate a
higher annuity. During the last months of Kennedy's life, U.S. policy
toward Panama drifted. The Defense Department insisted on studying every issue. Ambassador Farland resigned, apparently believing that

the State Department disapproved of his conciliatory approach. And the new nuclear testing agreement with the Soviet Union jeopardized a sea-level canal; the agreement permitted underground testing, but it banned cratering technology.[62]

President Johnson eventually accepted Kennedy's wisdom that the United States would have to renegotiate the Hay-Bunau-Varilla Convention. The governor of the Canal Zone, Robert Fleming, blamed his citizens for precipitating the crisis. The Johnson administration initially saw, however, only political opportunism, not nationalist fervor, in the January 1964 riots. Assistant Secretary Mann offered that "the crisis was largely inspired by the government for domestic political purposes in the hope that the United States would become frightened and cave under that kind of pressure." Secretary Rusk continued his agency's denigration of the Panamanian political milieu, alleging that Panamanians "have changes of government simply to pass around the perquisites of benefiting from the canal in different hands."[63] But by December 1964, President Johnson announced that the United States would negotiate "an entirely new treaty" with Panama. His special representative to Panama, former secretary of the treasury Robert Anderson, told him that Panamanians would not be satisfied with cosmetic changes to the 1903 treaty. Anderson, a close friend of President Eisenhower, had come to the same conclusion that Kennedy and Farland had reached. Johnson had some political freedom to act, because he had won a huge electoral mandate, and President Chiari had left office in mid-1964, after the election of his cousin, Marco Robles. In mid-1967, the United States and Panama reached agreements on three treaties that established Panamanian sovereignty over the canal, returned the canal and the zone to Panama in 1999, arranged for the United States to operate a sea-level canal until 2067, and gave the United States the exclusive right to defend both canals. Neither U.S. nor Panamanian legislators voted to ratify the treaties. The now politically weakened President Johnson decided to defer a ratification fight until after the 1968 election, and Panamanian nationalists feared that the treaties still left the United States dominant in their country.[64] Nonetheless, the Johnson administration had adopted the considerate approach to Panamanian nationalism first established by President Kennedy.

President Johnson's decision in 1965 to order over 20,000 U.S. troops to invade and occupy the Dominican Republic seemed a distinct break from past policies. By intervening, Johnson broke the nonintervention pledges associated with the Good Neighbor policy and violated the charter of the OAS. The Dominican intervention also betrayed the spirit of inter-American cooperation inherent in the Alliance for Progress. Although they initially muted their criticism, Kennedy-era officials eventually castigated Johnson for his action. The Johnson administration had falsely labeled as "Communist" a democratic movement to restore Juan Bosch to the presidency. Schlesinger saw "hysteria" in the cable traffic between the embassy in Santo Domingo and Washington. Robert Kennedy alleged that the administration had intervened to put down a popular uprising against injustice and oppression.[65] The intervention dismayed Latin American democrats, like the Venezuelans, and garnered support only from despots, like the Brazilian generals. Scholars have subsequently agreed with contemporary critics, such as Senator J. William Fulbright of the Foreign Relations Committee, that Johnson and his aides badly overreacted; the uprising in the Dominican Republic did not pose a threat to the security of the United States.[66]

President Johnson publicly defended the intervention by asserting that "the American nations cannot, must not, and will not permit the establishment of another Communist government in the Western Hemisphere." Johnson falsely implied that he had acted after multilateral consultations. The invasion was a unilateral action; the administration justified its intervention to the OAS after military action had begun. The president's assertion that his Johnson Doctrine superseded the Good Neighbor policy and the OAS charter did not represent a radical departure in U.S. foreign policy. Both Presidents Eisenhower and Kennedy had developed their own doctrines for Latin America. In his last address on inter-American affairs, Kennedy had declared that the United States would act unilaterally to prevent the establishment of another Cuba in the hemisphere.

President Johnson did not refer to the Kennedy Doctrine when he defended his unilateral intervention. But he subsequently pointed to Kennedy's determination to act boldly by citing a 4 October 1963 memorandum. Writing shortly after the overthrow of Juan Bosch, Kennedy noted to Secretary of Defense McNamara that "the events of the past few days in the Dominican Republic and Honduras show that the situation could develop in the Caribbean which would require active United States military intervention." He asked, "How many troops could we get into the Dominican Republic in a 12-24-36-48 hour period?"[67] Johnson might have also noted that Kennedy officials, like Rusk and Bundy, counseled him on the intervention. Indeed, in preparing President Johnson for his first NSC meeting, Bundy advised him that, whereas the United States had to live in the same world as the Soviet Union, "we do not have to accept Communist subversion in this hemisphere" and "we should let no day pass without asking what more we can do against Communist subversion and against the Castro government in particular." John Bartlow Martin, who served as Kennedy's ambassador to the Dominican Republic, exclaimed that Johnson had averted "the danger of Communists capturing the April revolution." Adolf Berle effusively congratulated Johnson on his Cold War decision.[68]

The Kennedy administration's use of gunboat diplomacy in the Dominican Republic involved every diplomatic pressure short of the actual landing of troops. The president's admirers might argue that he had acted against the Trujillo family and in favor of progressive democrats like Bosch. Johnson, Rusk, and Mann belittled Bosch's administrative abilities and questioned his courage. The Dominican, fearing for his security, declined to campaign actively in the 1966 election supervised by the United States. In any case, the Johnson administration barely disguised its preference for the authoritarian Joaquín Balaguer.[69] President Balaguer subsequently dominated Dominican political life for the next three decades. In the post-1963 period, a Kennedy administration would have perhaps not succumbed to anti-Communist hysteria and perhaps would have been able to find the decent democrats in the Dominican political milieu. But the historical record does not provide much support to that speculation. The administration, with Ambassador Martin acting as its point man, badgered President Bosch to prove his anti-Communist credentials. The Kennedy administration's actions in countries such as Brazil, British Guiana, and Guatemala also suggest that it did not readily distinguish between political radicals loyal to Moscow and Havana and nationalist reformers.

✦   Although Kennedy and Johnson administration officials debated who bore responsibility for the Alliance for Progress's shortcomings, they did not dispute the contention that the Alliance had failed to live up to expectations. The quality of life had not markedly improved for most Latin Americans, and authoritarian military officers increasingly dominated the region's political life. The sense of promise and hope that had characterized inter-American relations at Punta del Este in August 1961 had dissipated. By the end of the 1960s, Republicans, with obvious delight, accused the Democrats of a familiar foreign policy failing. Kennedy and Johnson had allowed the "special relation-ship" that the United States had "historically maintained with the other nations of the Western Hemisphere to deteriorate badly."[70] Despite its pledge to do better, however, the new Richard M. Nixon administration would not achieve beloved status in Latin America.

⟡ Conclusion

Close, critical studies of the foreign policies of President John F. Kennedy are unlikely to diminish the admiration, respect, and even reverence that citizens in the United States and Latin America maintain for their fallen leader. They recall his eloquence, grace, and wit, and they grieve over his tragic death. His multitudinous admirers, including my Costa Rican friend, probably will always ignore uncomfortable questions about whether President Kennedy steadfastly pursued the lofty ideals that he articulated to the people of the Western Hemisphere. Although scholarly analyses may not alter popular feelings about Kennedy, they can help determine what substance underlay the president's compelling style. They can also highlight a critical period in the history both of inter-American relations and of the Cold War.

The Kennedy administration attached more significance to inter-American relations than any other presidential administration in the post–World War II period. Other than perhaps Jimmy Carter, who took time to study Spanish in the White House, addressed the Mexican legislature in Spanish, and promoted his human rights policy throughout the region, no other president cultivated relations with Latin American nations with as much vigor as did Kennedy. His Latin American policies provide a clear case of presidential leadership. Although he lacked a background in Latin American studies, Kennedy worked hard to educate himself. He read his briefing books, consulted with aides, and hosted an amazing number of Latin American visitors. The documentary record reveals an informed, intelligent leader who treated Latin Americans with dignity and could skillfully discuss the key political and economic issues in the individual Latin American countries. U.S. diplomats, like Ambassador to Chile Charles Cole and Ambassador to Costa Rica Raymond Telles, testified to the president's remarkable knowledge about both regional and bilateral concerns. The documentary record further demonstrates that the president devoted an extraordinary amount of time and energy to promoting economic development and social welfare in countries such as Chile, Costa Rica, and Venezuela. Kennedy's commitment to Latin America flowed from two sources. He perceived the region as a momentous Cold War battleground. He also genuinely wanted to help the poor of Latin America and confidently assumed that, unlike its efforts in other regions of the world, such as Southeast Asia, the United States could accomplish its goals in Latin America.

The administration notably failed, however, to build prosperous, socially just, democratic societies. Any number of reasons can be offered to explain why the Alliance for Progress lost its way. Alliance planners placed too much faith in their development theories and misapplied the lessons of history. Taking for granted that the interests of the United States and Latin America were compatible, they believed that U.S. institutions and values could be readily transferred to their hemispheric neighbors. The Kennedy administration encountered formidable obstacles in its attempt to modernize Latin American societies, however. To President Kennedy's surprise, the U.S. foreign aid bureaucracy often proved slow, ponderous, and inefficient. The population explosion in Latin America undercut improvements in health, education, and welfare. Administration officials also discovered that Latin American elites resisted change and that middle-class groups did not always favor a fundamental reordering of the social structure. The United States could hardly force them to act like decent democrats. The administration particularly realized the limits to U.S. power in the Dominican Republic and Haiti. Despite employing substantial military power, reminiscent of the gunboat diplomacy of the early twentieth century, the administration ultimately failed to prevent despotism in the two Caribbean nations. It learned that democracy and social justice could not be easily imparted to poor countries with turbulent political pasts.

The Kennedy administration gradually realized that Latin America was not set for miracles. But it also undermined the Alliance for Progress with its Cold War initiatives. That the Alliance was a Cold War policy was never a subject of dispute. But, in Arthur Schlesinger's words, "answering Castro was a byproduct, not the purpose of the Alliance." What presumably distinguished the Latin American policy of President Kennedy was the belief that the key to stability and anticommunism was democracy, economic growth and development, and social change. The Alliance for Progress, as one observer put it, was "enlightened anticommunism."[1] An examination of the course of inter-American relations between 1961 and 1963 demonstrates, however, the need to separate the president's words from his decisions and his administration's deeds. Through its recognition policy, internal security initiatives, and military and economic aid programs, the administration demonstrably bolstered regimes and groups that were undemocratic, conservative, and frequently repressive. Its destabilization campaigns in Argentina, Brazil, British Guiana, and Guatemala had ironic results. Arturo Frondizi, João Goulart, Cheddi Jagan, and Juan José Arévalo respected constitutional processes and praised the Alliance for Progress, while their authoritarian, anti-Communist successors opposed free elections and disdained the idea of social reform. The president's oft-quoted remark about the descending order of possibilities in the post-Trujillo Dominican Republic proved to be a reliable guide to what choices the administration would make. The administration would not trust any progressive leader or group deemed suspect on the issues of Castro and international communism. Administration officials never reconciled their security fears with their calls for peaceful revolution in Latin America. They constantly violated their core belief that violence, extremism, and even revolution would ensue if the United States bolstered regimes that resisted social progress. Like Dwight Eisenhower and John Foster Dulles, the president and his advisors opted for the short-term security that anti-Communist elites, especially military officers, could provide over the benefits of long-term political and social democracy.

Although President Kennedy continually expressed frustration at the slow pace of economic progress in the region, he might have taken satisfaction in his Latin American policy. He seemingly won a major Cold War battle in what he considered the most dangerous area in the world. During the 1960s, neither the Soviet Union nor Cuba measurably expanded its influence in the hemisphere. Guerrilla insurgents in countries such as Venezuela largely retreated from their mountain hideouts, although, by the end of the 1960s, radical insurgent movements began to strengthen in Central American nations like Nicaragua. Scholars have subsequently questioned whether the Soviet Union judged Latin America a target of opportunity or whether other Latin American nations were ripe for a Cuban-style revolution. In part, they base their skepticism on contemporary analyses produced by U.S. intelligence officers that outlined the complex nature of Latin America's political milieu. Their new research in the archives of the former Soviet Union further suggests that Soviet leaders restricted their objectives in Latin America.[2] Nevertheless, Kennedy administration officials believed that their counterinsurgency doctrines, military aid packages, and police training programs helped Latin American security forces clear the region of Marxist-Leninists. Officials like Dean Rusk, Robert

McNamara, and Robert Kennedy later admitted, however, that they regretted arming personnel who assaulted constitutional leaders and violated the basic human rights of Latin Americans.

President Kennedy might have also concluded that containing Castro and other political leftists enhanced the credibility of the United States in the international arena. Kennedy administration officials constantly suggested that they could not exercise U.S. power in areas of the world such as West Berlin if the United States did not reign supreme in the hemisphere. Kennedy's anti-Communist triumph further included removing the issue of communism in the Americas from the domestic political agenda. Kennedy was absolutely determined not to allow political opponents to charge him with losing a neighbor to communism. The president made that goal explicit in his lecture to Prime Minister Harold Macmillan on the subject of British Guiana. The ouster of Goulart and Jagan in 1964 helped insure the reelection of a Democrat to the presidency that year.

Although John Kennedy gave a special emphasis to relations with Latin America, his policy can be interpreted as being firmly within the context of the history of twentieth-century inter-American relations. Scholars have long held that the United States has pursued consistent objectives in the region. U.S. officials have sought to exclude extracontinental powers from the Western Hemisphere and have attempted to establish the dominant political and economic presence of the United States in the region. To secure those objectives, the United States has needed stable Latin American regimes that acquiesced in U.S. foreign policy goals.[3] Whereas the objectives have remained constant, presidential administrations have varied their tactics. As a presidential candidate, Kennedy lambasted the Eisenhower administration for foolishly trying to win the friendship and support of Latin Americans by relying on military dictators like Colonel Marcos Pérez Jiménez. Kennedy's task forces on Latin America argued that the only way to win the Cold War in Latin America was for the United States to assist democratic reformers. In office, however, Kennedy tempered his commitment to constitutionalism, unequivocally backing only those leaders like Rómulo Betancourt who were ferocious anti-Communists. Like his predecessors including Franklin Delano Roosevelt, Kennedy had few qualms about dealing with unsavory sycophants. Both Roosevelt and Kennedy appreciated that the Somoza family of Nicaragua deferred to U.S. leadership.

During his brief tenure, President Kennedy may have authorized more covert interventions in Latin America than any other postwar president—including Ronald Reagan, who fomented wars in Central America. Kennedy's campaigns against Castro, Goulart, and Jagan set no precedent in the history of inter-American relations, however. The Truman administration plotted against Jacobo Arbenz Guzmán of Guatemala, and the Eisenhower administration toppled him. Kennedy completed his predecessor's work by insisting that Arbenz's associate, former president Arévalo, not be permitted to contest again for the Guatemalan presidency. Kennedy's use of gunboat diplomacy against the Dominican Republic and Haiti recalled the thirty-five armed interventions that the United States carried out in the circum-Caribbean region during the first part of the twentieth century. Like Woodrow Wilson, Kennedy proved unable to restructure the political and social order of the Dominican Republic and Haiti. And like Theodore Roosevelt, Kennedy pronounced his own doctrine for the region. In his last speech on inter-American affairs, Kennedy made it clear that the United States would not hesitate to exercise international police power to prevent the installation of a Communist regime in the Western Hemisphere. In the previous thirty-four months, the president had already given substance to those words. Although the Kennedy Doctrine may have been rooted in the same assumptions inherent in the Roosevelt Corollary to the Monroe Doctrine, the president extended the U.S. patrol area. During most of the twentieth century, the United States confined its armed interventions and covert activities to the Caribbean Basin, reflecting geopolitical interests and the special U.S. concern for the Panama Canal. But by undermining constitutional governments in Argentina, Brazil, and British Guiana, and by intervening massively in the Chilean electoral process, the Kennedy administration signaled that U.S. vital interests included South America. From the Kennedy administration's perspective, the Cold War had global dimensions.

President John F. Kennedy brought high ideals and noble purposes to his Latin American policy. Ironically, however, his unwavering determination to wage Cold War in "the most dangerous area in the world" led him and his administration ultimately to compromise and even mutilate those grand goals for the Western Hemisphere.

Notes

Abbreviations

DDEL   Dwight D. Eisenhower Library
DSB   U.S. Department of State, *Department of State Bulletin*
ECLA   U.N. Economic Commission for Latin America
FRUS   U.S. Department of State, *Papers Relating to the Foreign Relations of the United States*
JFKL   John F. Kennedy Library
LBJL   Lyndon Baines Johnson Library
NSAM   National Security Action Memorandum
NSF   National Security File
NSFCO   National Security File: Country File
OAS   Organization of American States
OH   Oral History
POFCO   President's Office File: Country File
PPP   U.S. General Services Administration, *Public Papers of the President*
SCFR   U.S. Senate Committee on Foreign Relations
WHCF   White House Central File

Introduction

1. Kennedy quoted in Goodwin, *Remembering America*, 221.
2. Martin, *Kennedy and Latin America*, 464–65.
3. *DSB* 44 (3 April 1961): 471–74.
4. Dillon's speech in *DSB* 45 (28 August 1961): 356–60. See also Levinson and de Onís, *Alliance That Lost Its Way*, 59–73.
5. *DSB* 44 (1 May 1961): 617–21.
6. Levinson and de Onís, *Alliance That Lost Its Way*, 5–13, 23; OAS, *Analysis*, 2:1–94.
7. Tulchin, "Promise of Progress," 218. See also Hellmann, *Kennedy Obsession*.
8. *New York Times*, "Week in Review," 18 August 1996, 2. See also Brogan, *Kennedy*, 214–24.
9. Murray and Blessing, "Presidential Performance Study," 535–55; Schlesinger, "Ultimate Approval Rating," 46–51.
10. Schlesinger, *Thousand Days*, 1030. See also Hilsman, *To Move a Nation*; Sorensen, *Kennedy*; Kennedy, *Thirteen Days*. New scholarly praise for Kennedy's management of the missile crisis can be found in May and Zelikow, *Kennedy Tapes*, 692–96.
11. Halberstam, *Best and the Brightest*.
12. Walton, *Cold War and Counterrevolution*, 10.

13. Divine, "Education of John F. Kennedy," 317, 338–39.

14. Kaufman, "John F. Kennedy as World Leader," 447–69.

15. Paterson, *Kennedy's Quest for Victory*, 22–23.

16. Giglio, *Presidency of John F. Kennedy*, 282–87.

17. Schlesinger, *Thousand Days*, 172–90, 766–69.

18. Sorensen, *Kennedy*, 535–36.

19. Schlesinger, "Alliance for Progress," 83; Schlesinger, *Robert Kennedy*, 454–67; Scheman, *Alliance for Progress*, 67–72.

20. Scheman, *Alliance for Progress*, 54.

21. Hanson, *Five Years*, 10–11.

22. Levinson and de Onís, *Alliance That Lost Its Way*, 140.

23. Smetherman and Smetherman, "Alliance for Progress," 79–86.

24. Gordon OH, pp. 31–32, JFKL; Scheman, *Alliance for Progress*, 78.

25. Lowenthal, "United States Policy toward Latin America," 3–25.

26. Gil, "Kennedy-Johnson Years," 3–27; Tulchin, "United States and Latin America in the 1960s," 1–36; Tulchin, "Promise of Progress," 211–43; Walker, "Mixing the Sweet with the Sour," 42–79.

27. Schlesinger, *Robert Kennedy*, xii.

28. Herring, "My Years with the CIA," 5–6.

29. *New York Times*, 29 May 1997, A11.

Chapter One

1. *DSB* 44 (3 April 1961): 471–74.

2. Ibid., 474–78.

3. Kennedy to President Víctor Paz Estenssoro of Bolivia, *DSB* 44 (12 June 1961): 920–21.

4. Rabe, *Eisenhower and Latin America*, 101–16.

5. Ibid., 134–73.

6. SCFR, *Executive Sessions, 1959*, 11:606–26.

7. Speech at Democratic Party dinner, San Juan, Puerto Rico, 15 December 1958, Speech File, Pre-Presidential Papers, JFKL; Kennedy, *Strategy of Peace*, 134–41. See also Wofford, *Of Kennedys and Kings*, 342–43.

8. Kennedy, *Strategy of Peace*, 66–80. See also Rostow, *Eisenhower, Kennedy, and Foreign Aid*, 3–12, 57–72.

9. Speech at Democratic Party dinner, San Juan, Puerto Rico, 15 December 1958, Speech File, Pre-Presidential Papers, JFKL.

10. Kennedy quoted in Walton, *Cold War and Counterrevolution*, 9, 36–38. See also Beck, "Necessary Lies, Hidden Truths," 37–59; Hersh, *Dark Side of Camelot*, 170, 175–78.

11. Berle, *Navigating the Rapids*, 713.

12. Berle, "The Cuban Crisis," 40–55.

13. Speech in Tampa, Florida, 18 October 1960, Campaign Speech File, Pre-Presidential Papers, JFKL.

14. Giglio, *Presidency of John F. Kennedy*, 29–33; "Preface," *FRUS, 1961–1963*, vol. 12, *American Republics*, vii–viii; Morrison, *Latin American Mission*, 112–13.

15. Martin, *Kennedy and Latin America*, 47.

16. Schaffer, *Chester Bowles*, 203-7.

17. Martin, *Kennedy and Latin America*, 2, 73.

18. Kennedy to Rusk, 29 October 1963, *FRUS, 1961–1963*, 12:158–59.

19. Martin, *Kennedy and Latin America*, 30; Rostow, *Diffusion of Power*, 217.

20. Memorandum of conversation between Kubitschek and Kennedy, 13 December 1962, *FRUS, 1961–1963*, 12:117-25; memorandum of conversation between Chiari and Kennedy, 12 June 1962, ibid., 831-38.

21. Kennedy quoted in Goodwin, *Remembering America*, 147; and memorandum of conversation between Kennedy and President João Goulart of Brazil, 4 April 1962, *FRUS, 1961–1963*, 12:464-67. See also Martin OH, p. 20, JFKL; Salinger, *With Kennedy*, 123; Ambassador to Costa Rica Raymond Telles OH, pp. 66-74, JFKL; and State Department memorandum, 25 March 1962, *FRUS, 1961–63*, 12:143-44.

22. Memorandum of conversation with Ambassador Roberto de Oliveira Campos of Brazil, 26 December 1962, *FRUS, 1961–1963*, 12:486-87; Martin, *Kennedy and Latin America*, 126-29. For trade and investment figures, see Dietz and Street, *Latin America's Economic Development*, 163; Stallings, *Banker to the Third World*, 116, 125, 323-47; U.S. Department of Commerce, *Business Statistics, 1961*, 106-13.

23. Memorandum of conversation between Kennedy and Alvaro Alsogaray, Argentine Minister of Economy, 27 July 1962, *FRUS, 1961–1963*, 12:398-99. See also Cobbs, *Rich Neighbor Policy*, 11-14; Goodwin, *Remembering America*, 147.

24. Memorandum of conversation between Chiari and Kennedy, 12 June 1962, *FRUS, 1961–1963*, 12:831-38; memorandum of conversation between Kennedy and Farland, 7 May 1963, ibid., 846-49; letter, Kennedy to Chiari, 23 July 1963, ibid., 849-51.

25. Memorandum of conversation between Macmillan and Kennedy, 30 June 1963, ibid., 607-9.

26. Schlesinger, *Thousand Days*, 773.

27. Kennedy quoted in Goodwin, *Remembering America*, 147; memorandum of conversation between Aramburu and Kennedy, 6 November 1962, POFCO: Argentina, box 111, Argentine Security, 1961-63, folder, JFKL; memorandum of conversation between Macmillan and Kennedy, 30 June 1963, *FRUS, 1961–1963*, 12:608; Kennedy to Rusk, 29 October 1963, ibid., 158-59; memorandum of conversation between López Mateos and Kennedy, 29 June 1962, ibid., 312-14. See also memorandum of conversation between José Ramón Villeda Morales, president of Honduras, and Kennedy, 30 November 1962, ibid., 331-33.

28. Hersh, *Dark Side of Camelot*, 220.

29. Notes on cabinet meeting, 20 April 1961, *FRUS, 1961–1963*, vol. 10, *Cuba, 1961–1962*, 304-6; notes on 478th meeting of NSC, 22 April 1961, ibid., 313-14.

30. Hersh, *Dark Side of Camelot*, 268-70, 278; Paterson, *Kennedy's Quest for Victory*, 123.

31. May and Zelikow, *Kennedy Tapes*.

32. Attorney General Kennedy to president, 19 April 1961, *FRUS, 1961–1963*, 10:302–4.

33. Beschloss, *Crisis Years*, 60–61; Blaufarb, *Counterinsurgency Era*, 54; Schlesinger, *Robert Kennedy*, 423.

34. Rostow, "Guerrilla Warfare," 108–16; Gordon, "US-Brazilian Reprise," 168; Kennedy quoted in *PPP, 1961*, 441–45.

35. Rusk to U.S. Embassy in Santiago, Chile, on president's talks with Khrushchev, 26 June 1961, NSFCO: Chile, box 20, JFKL; Rusk testimony, 16 June 1961, in SCFR, *Executive Sessions, 1961*, 13:185; memorandum of conversation between Dr. Oscar H. Camilión, Argentine Under Secretary of Foreign Affairs, and Rusk, 18 January 1962, *FRUS, 1961–1963*, 12:292–94.

36. Rostow, *Diffusion of Power*, 218.

37. Berle, *Navigating the Rapids*, 729; Report from the Task Force on Immediate Latin American Problems to President-elect Kennedy, 4 January 1961, *FRUS, 1961–1963*, 12:2–4; Berle to Goodwin, "Summary of Recommendations of Task Force on Latin America," 9 January 1961, Task Force on Latin America file, box 94, Berle Papers, Roosevelt Library.

38. Furtado, *Economic Development of Latin America*, 46–48, 54–55; OAS, *Latin America*, 227; Perloff, *Alliance for Progress*, 24–26; Scheman, *Alliance for Progress*, 24, 34–37.

39. Martin, *Kennedy and Latin America*, 73; Ball quoted in *DSB* 44 (5 June 1961): 864–68; Schlesinger to Kennedy, 10 March 1961, *FRUS, 1961–1963*, 12:10; Dillon quoted in Stebbins, *United States in World Affairs, 1961*, 326. See also Gutiérrez Olivos, *Subdesarrollo*, 43–44.

40. Berle to Goodwin, "Summary of Recommendations of Task Force on Latin America," 9 January 1961, Task Force on Latin America file, box 94, Berle Papers, Roosevelt Library; Berle to Kennedy, "Report of the President's Task Force on Latin America," 7 July 1961, *FRUS, 1961–1963*, 12:38–43.

41. Schlesinger to Kennedy, 10 March 1961, ibid., 10–18; Berle to Goodwin, "Summary of Recommendations of Task Force on Latin America," 9 January 1961, Task Force on Latin America file, box 94, Berle Papers, Roosevelt Library.

42. Schlesinger, *Thousand Days*, 201; Berle to Kennedy, 25 April 1961, *FRUS, 1961–1963*, 12:23–25. See also Schoultz, *National Security*, 11–33,

43. Berle to Kennedy, "Psychological Offensive in Latin America," 29 June 1961, Task Force on Latin America file, box 94, Berle Papers, Roosevelt Library.

44. Millikan and Blackmer, *Emerging Nations*, ix. See also Hughes and Mijeski, "Contemporary Paradigms," 19–43; Klarén and Bossert, *Promise of Development*, 3–35; Packenham, *Liberal America*, 4–62.

45. Almond and Coleman, *Politics of the Developing Areas*, 12–64; Johnson, *Political Change in Latin America*, 1–14; Silvert, "Politics of Social and Economic Change in Latin America," 76–87; Lipset and Solari, *Elites in Latin America*, 3–60; Whitaker, *Western Hemisphere Idea*.

46. Millikan and Blackmer, *Emerging Nations*, x, 101–56; Rostow, "Guerrilla Warfare," 109–10; Millikan and Rostow, *A Proposal*; Rostow, *Stages of Economic Growth*, 4–36; Gordon OH, p. 15, JFKL.

47. Memorandum, Rostow to Kennedy, 2 March 1961, in Rostow, *Diffusion of Power*, 647.

48. Gordon to Goodwin, 6 March 1961, *FRUS, 1961–1963*, 12:6–8.

49. Mann OH, pp. 7–15, JFKL.

50. Gordon, *New Deal for Latin America*, 9–46; Rostow, "Guerrilla Warfare," 113.

51. Rabe, *Eisenhower and Latin America*, 102–10.

52. Berle to Goodwin, "Summary of Recommendations of Task Force on Latin America," 9 January 1961, Task Force on Latin America file, box 94, Berle Papers, Roosevelt Library; Caldera quoted in Manger, *Alliance for Progress*, 23–38. See also remarks by Figueres in Dreier, *Alliance for Progress*, 66–88.

53. Stevenson to Kennedy, 27 June 1961, *FRUS, 1961–1963*, 12:30–32.

54. Baer, "Economics of Prebisch and ECLA," 203–18; Love, "Raúl Prebisch and the Origins of Unequal Exchange," 45–72; Dietz and Street, *Latin America's Economic Development*, 76–78; remarks by Prebisch in Dreier, *Alliance for Progress*, 24–65.

55. Dillon to Kennedy, 1 August 1961 and 16 August 1961, *FRUS, 1961–1963*, 12:46–47, 59–60.

56. Ruíz, *Cuba*, 6–17, 143–69.

57. Remarks by Schlesinger in Scheman, *Alliance for Progress*, 71–72; Gordon, "US-Brazilian Reprise," 168.

58. Remarks by Howard J. Wiarda in Scheman, *Alliance for Progress*, 95–118.

59. Smith, *America's Mission*, 18, 217–35; Packenham, *Liberal America*, 34–35.

60. Park, *Latin American Underdevelopment*, 198–203; Pike, *United States and the Andean Republics*, 305–7.

61. Ball, *Past Has Another Pattern*, 183.

62. Goodwin, *Remembering America*, 148.

63. Ibid., 190.

64. Dillon to Kennedy, 1 August 1961, *FRUS, 1961–1963*, 12:46–47; Dillon speech in *DSB* 45 (8 August 1961): 356–60.

65. For text of the charter, see *DSB* 45 (11 September 1961): 462–69. See also Ortega Aranda, *La Carta de Punta del Este*, 45–64.

66. *New York Times*, 9 August 1961, 1, 4, and 16 August 1961, 3; Anderson, *Che Guevara*, 509–23; Morrison, *Latin American Mission*, 83–92; Dillon to State Department, 9 August 1961, *FRUS, 1961–1963*, 12:50–51. For Guevara's account of Punta del Este, see "Cuba and the 'Kennedy Plan,'" 33–39. See also Ruelas Crespo, *Alianza para el Progreso*, 53–57, 91–94.

67. Dillon to State Department, 11 August 1961, and State Department to Dillon, 12 August 1961, *FRUS, 1961–1963*, 12:53–56; *New York Times*, 17 August 1961, 1, 8.

68. *New York Times*, 15 August 1961, 14, and 16 August 1961, 3; Dillon to State Department, 16 August 1961, *FRUS, 1961–1963*, 12:59–60.

69. Goodwin to President Kennedy on conversation with Guevara, 22 August 1961, *FRUS, 1961–1963*, 10:642–45; Goodwin, *Remembering America*, 194–208.

Chapter Two

1. Rabe, *Eisenhower and Latin America*, 171–73.
2. Ibid., 153–54.
3. Ibid., 154–61.
4. Rabe, "Caribbean Triangle," 64–66.
5. Ibid., 69; Senate Select Committee to Study Governmental Operations with Respect to Intelligence Activities (hereafter Church Committee), *Alleged Assassination Plots*, 196–201.
6. Cuban Task Force of NSC to Bundy, 15 May 1961, *FRUS, 1961–1963*, 12:629–30; Dearborn to State Department, 22 March 1961, ibid., 621–23.
7. *DSB* 44 (3 April 1961): 471–74.
8. Richard Bissell, Deputy Director of CIA, to Bundy, "Briefing Paper on Dominican Republic," 17 February 1961, and CIA study, "Situation in Dominican Republic," 8 May 1961, NSFCO: Dominican Republic, box 66, General, 1–6/61, folder, JFKL.
9. Church Committee, *Alleged Assassination Plots*, 202–4; Rusk to Kennedy, 15 February 1961, *FRUS, 1961–1963*, 12:616–18.
10. Church Committee, *Alleged Assassination Plots*, 202–14; Goodwin, *Remembering America*, 210; Schlesinger, *Robert Kennedy*, 491–92; Guthman and Shulman, *Robert Kennedy*, 325–26.
11. Dearborn to State Department, 22 March 1961, *FRUS, 1961–1963*, 12:621–23.
12. Church Committee, *Alleged Assassination Plots*, 210; Schlesinger, *Robert Kennedy*, 488.
13. Church Committee, *Alleged Assassination Plots*, 201–5, 215. See also Agee, *Inside the Company*, 425.
14. Bundy to Kennedy with attachment from Murphy, 2 May 1961, *FRUS, 1961–1963*, 12:625–28; Balaguer, *Two Essays on Dominican History*, 22. For Balaguer's defense of his Trujillo-era activities, see his *Memorias de un cortesano*, 259–61. Attorney General Kennedy subsequently prosecuted Cassini for being an unregistered agent of a foreign government. See Guthman and Shulman, *Robert Kennedy*, 358.
15. Church Committee, *Alleged Assassination Plots*, 205–13; notes of the 483d meeting of NSC, 5 May 1961, *FRUS, 1961–1963*, 10:479–81; memorandum from Cuban Task Force of NSC to Bundy, 15 May 1961, and covering memorandum from State Department officer Theodore C. Achilles to Rusk, 26 May 1961, ibid., 12:629–33. On military preparations to invade Dominican Republic, see General Earle Wheeler of Joint Chiefs of Staff to General C. V. Clifton, 5 May 1961, NSFCO: Dominican Republic, box 66, General, 1–6/61, folder, JFKL.
16. Church Committee, *Alleged Assassination Plots*, 213–15; Grimaldi, *Estados Unidos en el derrocamiento de Trujillo*.
17. Salinger, *With Kennedy*, 172–73.

18. Dearborn's telegram in Clifton to Bundy for Kennedy in Paris, 31 May 1961, POFCO: Dominican Republic, box 115A, Security, 2/61–9/63, folder, JFKL; Church Committee, *Alleged Assassination Plots*, 214–15.

19. Memorandum for record by Bowles, 3 June 1961, *FRUS, 1961–1963*, 12:635–41; Schaffer, *Chester Bowles*, 220; Goodwin, *Remembering America*, 187. Robert Kennedy also repeatedly spoke about staging or provoking an incident at the U.S. base at Guantánamo Bay in order to justify an attack on Castro's Cuba. See, for examples, Attorney General Kennedy to president, 19 April 1961, *FRUS, 1961–1963*, 10:302–4; CIA Director John McCone's memorandum for file, 21 August 1962, ibid., 947–49; May and Zelikow, *Kennedy Tapes*, 100–101.

20. Berle, *Navigating the Rapids*, 747.

21. Goodwin to Bundy on 7 June meeting at White House Mansion, 8 June 1961, *FRUS, 1961–1963*, 12:642–44; Dearborn's recommendation in Clifton to Bundy for Kennedy in Vienna, 5 June 1961, POFCO: Dominican Republic, box 115A, Security, 2/61–9/63, folder, JFKL.

22. Schlesinger, *Thousand Days*, 769.

23. Memorandum of conversation between Assistant Secretary Robert F. Woodward and Kennedy, 10 July 1961; State Department paper, "Courses of Action in the Dominican Republic," 17 July 1961; Rusk to Kennedy on instructions to Hill, 19 July 1961, all in *FRUS, 1961–1963*, 12:644–55. See also Hill to Rusk, 1 August 1961, NSFCO: Dominican Republic, box 66, General, 7–8/61, folder, JFKL; and Hill to Rusk, 12 August 1961, NSFCO: Dominican Republic, box 67, Cables, 8–9/61, folder, JFKL.

24. Special National Intelligence Estimate, "The Dominican Situation," 25 July 1961, *FRUS, 1961–1963*, 12:656–59.

25. Kennedy quoted in Schlesinger, *Thousand Days*, 770–71; Kennedy to Woodward, 10 July 1961, *FRUS, 1961–1963*, 12:646; Morrison, *Latin American Mission*, 113–14.

26. Rusk to Kennedy, 27 July 1961, NSFCO: Dominican Republic, box 66, Subjects, Murphy Trips, 5–7/61, folder, JFKL; Rusk to Kennedy with editorial note, 24 August 1961, *FRUS, 1961–1963*, 12:661–64.

27. Roger Hilsman, Director of Bureau of Intelligence and Research, to Bowles, 20 September 1961, ibid., 665–66; Martin report on Dominican Republic, n.d. (but September 1961), POFCO: Dominican Republic, box 115A, folder 9, JFKL. See also Martin, *Overtaken by Events*, 64–83.

28. McGhee's instructions in State Department to Consulate General, 13 October 1961, *FRUS, 1961–1963*, 12:674–76; U.S. military moves in Hill to State Department, 19 November 1961, ibid., 682; Rusk's warning in *DSB* 45 (4 December 1961): 931. See also Vega, *Kennedy y los Trujillo*, 275–392; and Balaguer, *Memorias de un cortesano*, 167–68, 313–14.

29. Ambassador Lincoln Gordon to State Department on conversation with Brazilian Foreign Minister Francisco Clementino San Tiago Dantas, 24 November 1961, NSF: Trips, boxes 244–45, folder 5/8/61–2/21/62, JFKL.

30. White House to State Department for Hill, 16 December 1961, and State Department from Hill to Kennedy, 16 December 1961, both in *FRUS*,

1961–1963, 12:683–89; Hill to Rusk, 19 December 1961, NSFCO: Dominican Republic, box 66, 9–12/61 folder, JFKL.

31. State Department to Embassy in Dominican Republic, 17 January 1962, and Hill to State Department, 4 March 1962, *FRUS, 1961–1963*, 12:694–98.

32. State Department Policy Directive, "Dominican Republic: Plan of Action from Present to February 1963," 15 May 1962, ibid., 704–9; Third Report on Policy Directive on Dominican Republic, September 1962, NSF: Meetings and Memoranda, box 336, NSAM No. 153 folder, JFKL; State Department memorandum on Dominican Republic, 30 April 1962, NSFCO: Dominican Republic, box 66, 5/62 folder, JFKL.

33. Editorial note on White House meeting, 1 May 1962, *FRUS, 1961–1963*, 12: 704; Third Report on Policy Directive on Dominican Republic, September 1962, NSF: Meetings and Memoranda, box 336, NSAM No. 153 folder, JFKL.

34. Memorandum of conversation between Kennedy and Bosch, 10 January 1963, NSFCO: Dominican Republic, box 66, General, 1–6/63, folder, JFKL; Bosch OH, pp. 3–6, JFKL. See also "Status of Alliance for Progress in Dominican Republic," 6 April 1962, POFCO: Dominican Republic, box 115A, Security, 1961–63, folder, JFKL.

35. Ball, *Past Has Another Pattern*, 327; Rusk, *As I Saw It*, 369; Johnson, *Vantage Point*, 188–89.

36. Director of Bureau of Intelligence and Research Hilsman to Assistant Secretary Martin, 19 December 1962, *FRUS, 1961–1963*, 12:126. See also Gleijeses, *Dominican Crisis*, 86–106.

37. Martin to State Department, 22 September 1963, *FRUS, 1961–1963*, 12:733–38. See also testimony of Ambassador Martin and Assistant Secretary Martin, 26 September and 3 October 1963, SCFR, *Executive Sessions, 1963*, 15: 600–29, 644–78.

38. Martin to State Department, 13 January 1963, *FRUS, 1961–1963*, 12:726–29.

39. Martin to State Department, "Bosch's First Two Months," 28 April 1963, and State Department Executive Director William H. Brubeck to Bundy, 4 June 1963, both in NSFCO: Dominican Republic, box 66, General, 1–6/63, folder, JFKL.

40. CIA memorandum, "President Bosch and Internal Security in the Dominican Republic," 14 June 1963, NSFCO: Dominican Republic, box 66, 6/14–7/31/63 folder, JFKL.

41. Martin to State Department, 27 September 1963, NSFCO: Dominican Republic, box 67, Cables, 9/26–9/27/63, folder, JFKL.

42. Thomas L. Hughes, Director of Intelligence and Research, to Acting Secretary of State, 25 September 1963, NSFCO: Dominican Republic, box 67, Cables, 9/25/63, folder, JFKL.

43. Kennedy to McNamara, 4 October 1963; State Department to Embassy in Dominican Republic, 4 October 1963; and State Department to Embassy in Dominican Republic, 17 October, 1963, all in *FRUS, 1961–1963*, 12:739–46.

44. Memorandum of presidential meeting on Honduras and Dominican Republic, 1 November 1963, ibid., 746–47; Martin, *Kennedy and Latin America*,

179, n. 41; Rusk, *As I Saw It*, 370; Schlesinger, *Thousand Days*, 773; appendices for 4 October 1963 meeting on Dominican Republic, POFCO: Dominican Republic, box 115A, Security, 1961–63, folder, JFKL.

45. State Department to Embassy in Venezuela, 13 December 1963, *FRUS*, *1961–1963*, 12:747–48.

46. Martin to State Department, 22 September 1963, POFCO: Dominican Republic, box 115A, Security, 2/61–11/63, folder, JFKL; Martin to State Department, 13 January 1963, *FRUS*, *1961–1963*, 12:726–29.

47. Embassy in Dominican Republic to State Department, 23 September 1963, NSFCO: Dominican Republic, box 67, Cables, 9/21–9/24/63, folder, JFKL; briefing memorandum, "Principal Problems Confronting Dr. Bosch," 2 January 1963, POFCO: Dominican Republic, box 115A, Security, 1961–63, folder, JFKL; Klare, *War without End*, 248.

48. Hughes to Rusk on new Dominican leaders, 30 October 1963, NSFCO: Dominican Republic, box 66, 10/18–11/28/63 folder, JFKL.

49. Plummer, *Haiti and the United States*, 166–68.

50. Ambassador Gerald A. Drew to State Department, 11 June 1958, *FRUS*, *1958–1960*, vol. 5, *American Republics, Microfiche Supplement*, HA-4.

51. Special National Intelligence Estimate, "Situation and Prospects in Haiti," 27 September 1960, ibid., HA-26; Heinl and Heinl, *Written in Blood*, 615.

52. Berle, *Navigating the Rapids*, 737, 745; State Department memorandum on United States–Haitian Relations, 23 March 1961, and Acting Assistant Secretary of State Wimberly Coerr to Rusk, 23 May 1961, both in *FRUS*, *1961–1963*, 12:750–54.

53. Rusk to State Department, 2 June 1961, ibid., 757–58.

54. Special National Intelligence Estimate, "Short-Term Prospects in Haiti," 7 June 1961, ibid., 758–60; testimony of Under Secretary Ball, 13 May 1963, SCFR, *Executive Sessions, 1963*, 15:285–318.

55. Colonel Robert Heinl quoted in Heinl and Heinl, *Written in Blood*, 620–21.

56. Ibid., 617; Rusk quoted in Thurston OH, p. 21, JFKL; Morrison, *Latin American Mission*, 191–94.

57. Kennedy quoted in Martin, *Kennedy and Latin America*, 230–43; memorandum from State Department Executive Secretary Brubeck to Bundy, 8 August 1962, and Martin to Thurston, 11 August 1962, both in *FRUS* *1961–1963*, 12:766–73.

58. Thurston OH, p. 35, JFKL.

59. Ibid., p. 27.

60. Martin, *Kennedy and Latin America*, 243.

61. Ibid., 243–45; State Department memorandum, "Haiti Situation and United States Policy," 21 January 1963, and State Department paper, "Haiti Plan of Action from February 15 to September 15, 1963," both in *FRUS*, *1961–1963*, 12:773–78.

62. Record of 509th NSC meeting, 13 March 1963, ibid., 780–81.

63. Thurston to State Department, 2 May 1963, ibid., 781–83; Martin, *Kennedy and Latin America*, 245–46.

64. SCFR, *Executive Sessions, 1963*, 15:285–318.

65. Rusk to Embassy in Haiti, 14 May 1963, *FRUS, 1961–1963*, 12:785–87.
66. Martin, *Kennedy and Latin America*, 247–48.
67. Memorandum of conversation between Kennedy and Thurston, 18 June 1963, *FRUS, 1961–1963*, 12:800–802; memorandum of conversation between Kennedy and Dominican Ambassador del Rosario, 1 June 1963, ibid., 796.
68. Roorda, "Genocide Next Door," 301–6.
69. State Department Executive Secretary Benjamin Read to Bundy on "Abortive Invasion of Haiti," 14 August 1963, *FRUS, 1961–1963*, 12:802–4.
70. "Proposed Plan of Action," 13 November 1963, ibid., 804–6.
71. Plummer, *Haiti and the United States*, 187; Heinl and Heinl, *Written in Blood*, 655.
72. Rusk quoted in Heinl and Heinl, *Written in Blood*, 622.
73. Timmons quoted in Plummer, *Haiti and the United States*, 188–89.

Chapter Three

1. Martin, *Kennedy and Latin America*, 265–67.
2. Frondizi letter in *DSB* 44 (29 May 1961): 815–17; State Department to Embassy in Argentina, 27 September 1961, *FRUS, 1961–1963*, 12:357–59.
3. Potash, *Army and Politics in Argentina*, 338–39.
4. Martin, *Kennedy and Latin America*, 196.
5. Frondizi quoted in Potash, *Army and Politics in Argentina*, 343.
6. Blasier, *Giant's Rival*, 21, 30; Miller, *Soviet Relations*, 222. For the U.S. position on Latin American nations having diplomatic relations with Communist nations, see Secretary of State Rusk's circular to all embassies in Latin America, 31 August 1963, NSF, box 216, Latin America (II) folder, JFKL; and Rusk to all embassies in Latin America, 18 January 1965, NSFCO: Latin America, box 2, LBJL.
7. Memorandum of conversation between Frondizi and Kennedy, 24 December 1961, *FRUS, 1961–1963*, 12:359–62.
8. Memorandum of conversation between Kennedy and Ambassador Julio César Turbay of Colombia, 25 September 1961, ibid., 258–59.
9. Memorandum of conversation between Frondizi and Kennedy, 27 September 1961, ibid., 357–59; Tulchin, *Argentina and the United States*, 121; Potash, *Army and Politics in Argentina*, 335.
10. State Department to Embassy in Argentina, 26 December 1961, *FRUS, 1961–1963*, 12:278–79.
11. Kennedy quoted in Martin, *Kennedy and Latin America*, 269–70; Kennedy letter in State Department to Embassy in Argentina, 11 January 1962, *FRUS, 1961–1963*, 12:288–90. See also memorandum of conversation between Kennedy and Frondizi, 26 September 1961, ibid., 10:657–58.
12. Memorandum of conversation between Rusk and Argentine diplomats, 18 January 1962, ibid., 12:292–94.
13. Rusk to State Department, 31 January 1962, ibid., 307–8; Morrison, *Latin American Mission*, 192–94.
14. Rostow quoted in memorandum of NSC meeting, 6 February 1962, *FRUS, 1961–1963*, 12:308–9.

15. Rusk to Embassy in Argentina, 10 February 1962, ibid., 362–63; Fowler Hamilton, Director of the Agency for International Development, to Kennedy, 6 April 1962, ibid., 373–75.

16. Martin to Acting Secretary Ball, 26 March 1962, ibid., 366–68; McClintock to State Department, 28 March 1962, POFCO: Argentina, box 111, Security, 1961–63, folder, JFKL; Martin, *Kennedy and Latin America*, 272–73; Potash, *Army and Politics in Argentina*, 368.

17. Schlesinger to Kennedy, 30 March 1962, *FRUS, 1961–1963*, 12:368–69; editorial note, 2 April 1962, ibid., 373. See also Rusk statement on *golpe* in *DSB* 46 (14 May 1962): 800.

18. SCFR, *Executive Sessions, 1962*, 14:691, 760.

19. Martin, *Kennedy and Latin America*, 273, 333; Agee, *Inside the Company*, 222–30.

20. McClintock to Martin, 31 May 1962, *FRUS, 1961–1963*, 12:385–88. For economic aid figures see memorandum of conversation between Kennedy and Argentine Foreign Minister Carlos Manuel Muniz, 22 January 1963, ibid., 406–10; Perloff, *Alliance for Progress*, 55; and Tulchin, *Argentina and the United States*, 112.

21. Memorandum of conversation between Kennedy and Aramburu, 6 November 1962, *FRUS, 1961–1963*, 12:402–3.

22. McClintock to State Department, 22 November 1963, NSFCO: Argentina, box 6, Cables, 11/63–8/64, folder, LBJL.

23. Tulchin, *Argentina and the United States*, 121.

24. State Department paper, "Guidelines of U.S. Policy and Operations, Brazil," 7 February 1963, *FRUS, 1961–1963*, 12:488–90; State Department to Embassy in Brazil on Kennedy conversation with Brazilian Foreign Minister Francisco Clementino San Tiago Dantas, 13 March 1963, ibid., 500–503.

25. McCann, "Brazil, the United States, and World War II," 59–76.

26. Quadros, "Brazil's New Foreign Policy," 19–27; memorandum of conversation between Rusk and Foreign Minister Dantas, 12 April 1962, *FRUS, 1961–1963*, 12:471–72; Black, *United States Penetration of Brazil*, 38.

27. Blasier, *Giant's Rival*, 34–35; Miller, *Soviet Relations*, 173, 222.

28. Rusk to State Department, 25 January 1962, *FRUS, 1961–1963*, 12:299–301; memorandum of conversation between Rusk and Foreign Minister Dantas, 12 March 1963, ibid., 334–37; Gordon to State Department on conversation with President Goulart, 21 October 1961, ibid., 448–50.

29. Rusk to Kennedy on Brazilian loan, n.d. (but February 1961), NSF: Meetings and Memoranda, National Security Action Memorandum No. 14, box 328, JFKL; Cabot to State Department on Berle meeting with Quadros, 3 March 1961, *FRUS, 1961–1963*, 12:426–27; Cabot OH, pp. 4–5, JFKL.

30. Memorandum of conversation between Kennedy and Mariani, 15 May 1961, *FRUS, 1961–1963*, 12:435–36.

31. Editorial note on Quadros resignation, ibid., 444; Niles Woodbridge Bond, Embassy in Brazil, to State Department, 1 September 1961, NSFCO: Brazil, box 12, JFKL; Bond to State Department, 7 September 1961, ibid.; Embassy quoted in CIA, Office of Current Intelligence, "Communism in Brazil,"

27 March 1961, ibid. See also memorandum for record by General Andrew Goodpaster of President Eisenhower's dinner with President Kubitschek and Vice President Goulart, 23 February 1960, Records of the Office of the Staff Secretary, International Series, box 2, Brazil (2) folder, DDEL.

32. Gordon quoted in Weis, *Cold Warriors and Coups d'Etat*, 149–66; State Department paper, "Proposed Short Term Policy—Brazil," 30 September 1963, *FRUS, 1961–1963*, 12:507–12.

33. Memorandum of conversation between Kennedy and Kubitschek, 15 September 1961, NSFCO: Brazil, box 12, JFKL; memorandum of conversation between Kennedy and Kubitschek, 13 December 1962, *FRUS, 1961–1963*, 12:117–25; memoranda of conversations between Kennedy and Goulart, 3 and 4 April 1962, ibid., 460–67; Martin, *Kennedy and Latin America*, 294–300.

34. Special National Intelligence Estimate, "The Character of the Goulart Regime in Brazil," 27 February 1963, *FRUS, 1961–1963*, 12:490–93; Leacock, *Requiem for Revolution*, 149–71; Skidmore, *Politics in Brazil*, 205–93.

35. Martin, *Kennedy and Latin America*, 306–11.

36. Memorandum of conversation between Kennedy and Kubitschek, 13 December 1962, *FRUS, 1961–1963*, 12:117–25.

37. Black, *United States Penetration of Brazil*; Leacock, *Requiem for Revolution*; Parker, *Brazil and the Quiet Intervention*; Weis, *Cold Warriors and Coups d'Etat*.

38. Report from the Inter-Departmental Survey Team on Brazil to President Kennedy, 3 November 1962, *FRUS, 1961–1963*, 12:472–78; State Department paper, "Proposed Short Term Policy—Brazil," 30 September 1963, ibid., 507–12.

39. NSC memorandum, "U.S. Short-Term Policy toward Brazil," 11 December 1962, ibid., 481–85; Guthman and Shulman, *Robert Kennedy*, 348; Weis, *Cold Warriors and Coups d'Etat*, 158–59.

40. Weis, *Cold Warriors and Coups d'Etat*, 156; Leacock, *Requiem for Revolution*, 135; Agee, *Inside the Company*, 254; Thomas, *Very Best Men*, 323–24; Martin, *Kennedy and Latin America*, 306–11, 376, n. 71; Martin to Deputy Under Secretary of State U. Alexis Johnson, 27 June 1962, *FRUS, 1961–1963*, 10:833–34; Roett, *Politics of Foreign Aid*, x, 116, 170.

41. SCFR, *Survey of the Alliance for Progress*, 577–615; Romualdi, *Presidents and Peons*, 287–90, 415–33; Spalding, "Two Latin American Foreign Policies," 423–30; Spalding, "U.S. Labour Intervention," 263–70.

42. Walters quoted in Parker, *Brazil and the Quiet Intervention*, 62–63.

43. Ibid., 99.

44. Guthman and Shulman, *Robert Kennedy*, 366.

45. Bundy to President Johnson on Salinger, 26 May 1964, NSF: Memorandums, box 1, folder 4, LBJL.

46. Gordon OH, pp. 23–27, LBJL; Mann to Horace Busby of White House Staff, 17 August 1964, NSFCO: Latin America, box 1, 11/63–6/64 (I) folder, LBJL; Perloff, *Alliance for Progress*, 55. See also Beschloss, *Taking Charge*, 306, 318.

47. Schlesinger, *Robert Kennedy*, 694.

48. Gordon, "US-Brazilian Reprise," 169.

49. Hildebrand, "Latin-American Economic Development," 357–58.

50. Memorandum of conversation between Nixon and Ydígoras, 24 February 1958, *FRUS, 1958–1960, 5: Microfiche Supplement,* GT-3.

51. Muccio OH, p. 7, JFKL; Martin, *Kennedy and Latin America,* 8, n. 4; Perloff, *Alliance for Progress,* 55.

52. Ydígoras to Kennedy, 28 February 1961, NSFCO: Guatemala, box 101, General, 2/61–3/62, folder, JFKL; memorandum of conversation between Kennedy and Foreign Minister Daniel Oduber of Costa Rica, 7 February 1963, *FRUS, 1961–1963,* 12:129–31; Rusk to State Department, 25 January 1962, ibid., 299–301; Morrison, *Latin American Mission,* 68, 90, 156–57.

53. Eisenhower to Ydígoras, 12 September 1960, *FRUS, 1958–1960, 5: Microfiche Supplement,* GT-31; Muccio to State Department, 13 November 1960, ibid., GT-34; Muccio to State Department, 14 November 1960, ibid., GT-35; Muccio OH, pp. 1–6, JFKL.

54. Martin, *Kennedy and Latin America,* 117–18; Ambassador John O. Bell to State Department, 15 March 1962, NSFCO: Guatemala, box 101, General, 2/61–3/62, folder, JFKL.

55. Ambassador Lester D. Mallory to State Department, 11 November 1959, *FRUS, 1958–1960, 5: Microfiche Supplement,* GT-24; Martin, *Kennedy and Latin America,* 119, 365.

56. CIA, Office of National Estimates, "Guatemala's Dilemma," 18 January 1966, NSFCO: Guatemala, box 54, Memorandums (II) folder, LBJL.

57. Ambassador Bell to State Department, 11 February 1963, and Bell to State Department, 4 March 1963, both in NSFCO: Guatemala, box 101, General, 1–3/63, folder, JFKL.

58. Bell's cables to State Department of 4 March 1963, 12 March 1963, and 13 March 1963, all in ibid.

59. Bell to State Department, 25 March 1963, State Department to Embassy in Guatemala City, 27 March 1963, and Bell to State Department, 4 March 1963, all in ibid.

60. Ambassador to Mexico Thomas C. Mann to State Department, 27 March 1963, and CIA Information Report, "Arévalo's Return to Guatemala," 29 March 1963, both in ibid.

61. CIA Information Report, "Possible Attempt to Overthrow the Guatemalan Government," 30 March 1963, ibid.; Martin to Embassy in Guatemala City, 31 March 1963, ibid.; Bell to State Department, 1 April 1963, NSFCO: Guatemala, box 101, General, 4–7/63, folder, JFKL; Defense Department to President Kennedy, "Capability of the Guatemalan Government to Control Riots," 11 April 1963, ibid.; Bell to State Department, 15 April 1963, ibid. In his memoirs, Martin claims that the administration deplored the *golpe. Kennedy and Latin America,* 122.

62. Undersecretary Bowles to Kennedy on military aid, 29 March 1961, *FRUS, 1961–1963,* 12:187–90; Adams, "Development of the Guatemalan Military," 103.

63. Defense Department to President Kennedy, "Capability of the Guatemalan Government to Control Riots," 11 April 1963, NSFCO: Guatemala, box 101, General, 4–7/63, folder, JFKL; Holden, "Real Diplomacy of Violence," 305–6.

64. Bell to State Department, 23 May 1963, NSFCO: Guatemala, box 101, General, 4–7/63, folder, JFKL; Martin, *Kennedy and Latin America*, 125.

65. Bell to State Department, 9 March 1964, NSFCO: Guatemala, box 54, Cables, 3/64–1/66, folder, LBJL; CIA, Office of National Estimates, "Guatemala's Dilemma," 18 January 1966, NSFCO: Guatemala, box 54, Memorandums (II) folder, LBJL; SCFR, *Survey of Alliance for Progress*, 225.

66. Thomas Hughes, State Department's Intelligence and Research Bureau, to Rusk, 23 October 1967, NSFCO: Guatemala, box 54, Cables (II) folder, LBJL; CIA, Director of Intelligence, "Guatemala after Military Shakeup," 13 May 1968, ibid.; White House Situation Room to Tom Johnson at President Johnson's ranch on assassination of Ambassador Mein, 29 August 1968, ibid.

Chapter Four

1. Memorandum of conversation between Kennedy and Macmillan, 30 June 1963, *FRUS, 1961–1963*, 12:607–9.

2. Schlesinger, *Thousand Days*, 773.

3. David, *Economic Development of Guyana*, 44–45, 53; Singh, *Guyana*, 3–10.

4. David, *Economic Development of Guyana*, 4–5, 240–41; Special National Intelligence Estimate, "The Situation and Prospects in British Guiana," 11 April 1962, *FRUS, 1961–1963*, 12:567, n. 2.

5. Hintzen, *Cost of Regime Survival*, 33–34; Singh, *Guyana*, 16–19.

6. Singh, *Guyana*, 24; Despres, *Cultural Pluralism*, 179.

7. Despres, *Cultural Pluralism*, 210–16; Hintzen, *Cost of Regime Survival*, 48; Singh, *Guyana*, 25–27.

8. Singh, *Guyana*, 29.

9. Guthman and Shulman, *Robert Kennedy*, 295.

10. Johnson quoted in memorandum of conversation between U.S. and Colonial Office officials, 17 March 1962, *FRUS, 1961–1963*, 12:558–64; Rusk to Embassy in United Kingdom, 11 August 1961, ibid., 519–20.

11. Memorandum of conversation between Kennedy and Villeda Morales, 30 November 1962, ibid., 331–33.

12. Lucius D. Battle, Executive Secretary of Department of State, to Bundy on NSC meeting of 5 May 1961, 19 May 1961, ibid., 517–18; Ball to Rusk, 5 August 1961, ibid., 519.

13. Rusk to Embassy in United Kingdom, 11 August 1961, ibid., 519–20; Foreign Secretary Home to Rusk, 18 August 1961, ibid., 521–22.

14. Rusk to Embassy in United Kingdom, 26 August 1961, ibid., 522–23. See also Jagan, *West on Trial*, 255.

15. Special National Intelligence Estimate, 21 March 1961, "Prospects for British Guiana," *FRUS, 1961–1963*, 12:514–17; Special National Intelligence Es-

timate, "The Situation and Prospects in British Guiana," 11 April 1962, ibid., 564–69.

16. State Department paper, "Possible Courses of Action in British Guiana," 15 March 1962, ibid., 555–58; Stevenson to Rusk, 26 February 1962, ibid., 545–46.

17. Schlesinger to Kennedy, 30 August 1961, ibid., 524–25; Schlesinger to Deputy Under Secretary of State Johnson, 7 September 1961, ibid., 531; Schlesinger, *Thousand Days*, 774–79.

18. Memorandum of conversation between U.S. Consul Everett K. Melby and Governor Grey, 16 February 1961, *FRUS, 1961–1963*, 12:513.

19. Foreign Secretary Home to Rusk, 26 February 1962, ibid., 546–48; Schlesinger to David Bruce, U.S. Ambassador to United Kingdom, on conversation with Maulding, 1 March 1962, ibid., 530–31; MacLeod quoted in Jagan, *West on Trial*, 258.

20. Home to Rusk, 18 August 1961, *FRUS, 1961–1963*, 12:521–22; Schlesinger to Ambassador Bruce on conversation with MacLeod, 27 February 1962, ibid., 549; Ball to Kennedy on visit to White House of Colonial Office officials, 15 March 1962, ibid., 554. See also Singh, *Guyana*, 49.

21. Schlesinger, *Thousand Days*, 778; Schlesinger to Ambassador Bruce on conversation with MacLeod, 27 February 1962, *FRUS, 1961–1963*, 12:549.

22. Schlesinger to Kennedy, 30 August 1961, ibid., 524–25.

23. Rusk (Johnson) to Bruce, 4 September 1961, ibid., 528–29; Rusk (Johnson) to Bruce, 5 September 1961, ibid., 530; Hilsman to Johnson, 17 October 1961, ibid., 534–36.

24. Rabe, *Eisenhower and Latin America*, 123–24.

25. Memorandum of conversation between Kennedy and Jagan, 25 October 1961, *FRUS, 1961–1963*, 12:536–38; memorandum of conversation between Jagan, United Kingdom officials, and U.S. officials, 26 October 1961, ibid., 538–40; Schlesinger, *Thousand Days*, 776–78.

26. Schlesinger to Kennedy, 12 January 1962, *FRUS, 1961–1963*, 12:540–41; Kennedy to Hamilton, 12 January 1962, ibid., 542.

27. Draft transcript of Kennedy's remarks to State Department employees, 30 March 1962, NSF: Departments and Agencies, box 285, JFKL.

28. Schlesinger, *Thousand Days*, 777.

29. Kennedy to Hamilton, 12 January 1962, *FRUS, 1961–1963*, 12:542; State Department paper, "Possible Courses of Action in British Guiana," 15 March 1962, ibid., 555–58; remarks of Smathers in SCFR, *Executive Sessions, 1963*, 15:842.

30. Romualdi, *Presidents and Peons*, 346.

31. Guthman and Shulman, *Robert Kennedy*, 294.

32. Rusk to Embassy in United Kingdom, 19 February 1962, *FRUS, 1961–1963*, 12:544–45.

33. Schlesinger to Ambassador Bruce on conversation with MacLeod, 27 February 1962, ibid., 549. See also Singh, *Guyana*, 31.

34. *New York Times*, 29 May 1997, A11; editorial preface, *FRUS, 1961–1963*, 12:ix–x.

35. Blum, CIA, 117-23; Radosh, *American Labor*, 393-405; Agee, *Inside the Company*, 293-94, 406; Jagan, *West on Trial*, 251; Romualdi, *Presidents and Peons*, 346-52; Smith, *Portrait of a Cold Warrior*, 357-58; "How the CIA Got Rid of Jagan," *Sunday Times* (London), 16 April 1967, 1, 3; *New York Times*, 22 February 1967, 1, 17; ibid., 30 October 1994, 10.

36. NSAM No. 135, 8 March 1962, *FRUS, 1961-1963*, 12:551-52.

37. Schlesinger to Kennedy, 21 June 1962, ibid., 572-73; Schlesinger to Ralph Dungan, 19 July 1962, ibid., 578; Schlesinger, *Thousand Days*, 778.

38. State Department to Embassy in United Kingdom with copy of Macmillan letter of 30 May 1962, 7 June 1962, *FRUS, 1961-1963*, 12:569-71; memorandum of conversation between U.S. and Colonial Office officials, 17 March 1962, ibid., 558-64.

39. Rusk to Kennedy, 12 July 1962, ibid., 575-76; Bundy to Kennedy, 13 July 1962, ibid., 577.

40. Draft State Department telegram on Kennedy meeting with Ambassador Ormsby Gore, n.d. (but July 1962), ibid., 579.

41. Bundy to Helms, 6 August 1962, ibid., 581; Executive Secretary of State Department William Brubeck to Bundy, 8 August 1962, ibid., 581-82.

42. Blum, CIA, 120-22; Despres, *Cultural Pluralism*, 264; Singh, *Guyana*, 32-33; Jagan, *West on Trial*, 249; Romualdi, *Presidents and Peons*, 352; *Sunday Times* (London), 16 April 1967, 1, 3; ibid., 23 April 1967, 3; *New York Times*, 22 February 1967, 1, 17.

43. Hintzen, *Costs of Regime Survival*, 54; David, *Economic Development of Guyana*, 4-5.

44. Melby to State Department, 14 March 1963, *FRUS, 1961-1963*, 12:584-94.

45. Rusk to Embassy in United Kingdom, 21 June 1963, ibid., 605-6.

46. Memorandum of conversation between Kennedy and Macmillan, 30 June 1963, ibid., 607-9.

47. Singh, *Guyana*, 34-35; Blum, CIA, 122.

48. Jagan to Kennedy, 16 April 1963, *FRUS, 1961-1963*, 12:595-603.

49. Melby to State Department, 5 September 1963, ibid., 610-11; Rusk to Consulate General in Georgetown, 7 September 1963, ibid., 613.

50. Singh, *Guyana*, 34-35.

51. Wilson quoted in Jagan, *West on Trial*, 320-21.

52. *New York Times*, 31 October 1964, 7; ibid., 1 November 1964, 21.

53. Singh, *Guyana*, 120; Prendas, "Guyana," 136.

54. Schlesinger, *Thousand Days*, 779.

55. Singh, *Guyana*, 36.

56. "Tale of Two Books," 763-64.

57. Singh, *Guyana*, 40-51; Prendas, "Guyana," 133-64.

58. *New York Times*, 30 October 1994, 10.

59. Documents on the Truman administration's covert intervention in Guatemala were released in 1997. See *New York Times*, 28 May 1997, A5.

60. Rabe, "Johnson (Eisenhower?) Doctrine," 95-100.

61. Bundy to Kennedy, 25 May 1963, *FRUS, 1961-1963*, 12:348-49; Summary

Record of the 10th Meeting of the Standing Group of the NSC, 16 July 1963, *FRUS, 1961–1963*, vol. 11, *Cuban Missile Crisis and Aftermath*, 850–53.

62. Gordon Chase of NSC to Bundy on Kennedy Doctrine, 6 June 1963, *FRUS, 1961–1963*, 12:350–51.

63. *DSB* 49 (9 December 1963): 900–904.

64. Bundy to Robert Kennedy, 21 February 1964, *FRUS, 1961–1963*, 12:351, n. 3.

65. Memorandum of meeting between president and U.S. national security officials on Cuban issues, 19 December 1963, *FRUS, 1961–1963*, 11:904–9.

Chapter Five

1. *PPP, 1963*, 184–86.

2. Memorandum of conversation between Eisenhower and national security advisors, 29 November 1960, *FRUS, 1958–1960*, vol. 6, *Cuba*, 1126–31.

3. Martin, *Kennedy and Latin America*, 359; Bundy to President Johnson, 21 April 1964, NSF: Memorandums, box 1, folder 3, LBJL.

4. Betancourt quoted in Rabe, *Road to* OPEC, 144.

5. Goodwin, *Remembering America*, 214; Martin, *Kennedy and Latin America*, 360; Salinger, *With Kennedy*, 167.

6. Betancourt to Kennedy, 25 October 1961, and Betancourt to Kennedy, 29 March 1962, both in POFCO: Venezuela, box 128, 1961–63 folder, JFKL; Kennedy to Betancourt, 20 August 1962, NSFCO: Venezuela, box 192, 7/1–8/19/62 folder, JFKL; Kennedy to Betancourt, 16 August 1963, NSFCO: Venezuela, box 192, 8/63 folder, JFKL.

7. Rabe, *Road to* OPEC, 139–54.

8. Ibid., 154–67.

9. Schlesinger to Kennedy, 10 March 1961, *FRUS, 1961–1963*, 12:10–18; Berle to Goodwin, "Summary of Recommendations of Task Force on Latin America," 9 January 1961, Task Force on Latin America file, box 94, Berle Papers, Roosevelt Library.

10. Gott, *Guerrilla Movements*, 133; Blasier, *Giant's Rival*, 83.

11. Memorandum for President-elect Kennedy from Berle, 13 December 1960, and Berle to Goodwin, "Summary of Recommendations of Task Force on Latin America," 9 January 1961, both in Task Force on Latin America file, box 94, Berle Papers, Roosevelt Library; Sherman Kent, CIA Office of National Estimates, "Cuba—A Year Hence," 22 April 1963, NSF: Meetings and Memoranda, box 315, Standing Group Meetings folder, JFKL; Rabe, *Road to* OPEC, 154.

12. Rabe, "Caribbean Triangle," 63–64.

13. U.S. Foreign Broadcast Information Service, "Report on Cuban Propaganda—No. 5: Venezuelan President Betancourt's Trip," 15 March 1963, NSFCO: Venezuela, box 193, Betancourt Trip folder, JFKL.

14. Memorandum of conversation between Betancourt and Kennedy, 16 December 1961, *FRUS, 1961–1963*, 12:271–74; Ambassador C. Allan Stewart to State Department, 22 October 1962, NSFCO: Venezuela, box 192, 9/20–10/31/62 folder, JFKL; Levinson and de Onís, *Alliance That Lost Its Way*, 60.

15. Martin, *Kennedy and Latin America*, 255, n. 10. For another assassination plot against Castro that Betancourt allegedly supported, see Fursenko and Naftali, *"One Hell of a Gamble,"* 135-37.

16. Fursenko and Naftali, *"One Hell of a Gamble,"* 363; Betancourt to Kennedy, 25 October 1961, POFCO: Venezuela, box 128, 1961-63 folder, JFKL.

17. William Brubeck of NSC to Ralph Dungan of White House, "Background Papers on Dr. Rafael Caldera," 27 June 1962, NSFCO: Venezuela, box 192, 6/62 folder, JFKL; memorandum of meeting between Kennedy and Briceño Linares, 30 August 1962, NSFCO: Venezuela, box 192, 8/20-8/31/62 folder, JFKL; Stewart to State Department, 4 June 1962, NSFCO: Venezuela, box 192, 6/62 folder, JFKL; Stewart to State Department, 13 June 1962, ibid. See also *DSB* 46 (25 June 1962): 1023.

18. Stewart to State Department on Kennedy-Betancourt correspondence, 10 May 1962, NSFCO: Venezuela, box 192, 5/62 folder, JFKL; Rabe, *Road to* OPEC, 145; Martin, *Kennedy and Latin America*, 359.

19. Memorandum of conversation between Kennedy and Mayobre, 11 April 1962, NSFCO: Venezuela, box 192, 4/62 folder, JFKL.

20. Memorandum of conversation between Kennedy and Briceño Linares, 30 August 1962, NSFCO: Venezuela, box 192, 8/20-8/31/62 folder, JFKL; Stewart to State Department, 14 August 1962, NSFCO: Venezuela, box 192, 7/1-8/19/62 folder, JFKL.

21. Brubeck of NSC to Kenneth O'Donnell of White House, 28 August 1962, NSFCO: Venezuela, box 192, 8/20-8/31/62 folder, JFKL; Stewart to State Department, 15 June 1962, NSFCO: Venezuela, box 192, 6/62 folder, JFKL; Martin, *Kennedy and Latin America*, 369; Rabe, *Road to* OPEC, 146.

22. Rusk to Stewart, 17 August 1962, NSFCO: Venezuela, box 192, 7/1-8/17/62 folder, JFKL.

23. Rusk to Embassy in Caracas on Betancourt-Kennedy conversations, 28 December 1961, NSFCO: Venezuela, box 192, 12/62 folder, JFKL.

24. Blasier, *Giant's Rival*, 87; Gott, *Guerrilla Movements*, 19-35, 166-67; Jackson, *Castro*, 17-22, 45-46; Miller, *Soviet Relations*, 53. See also statement of Assistant Secretary of State Thomas C. Mann, 9 February 1965, in House Committee on Foreign Affairs, *Hearings on "Communism in Latin America,"* 119-21.

25. Special Memorandum No. 31-65 by Sherman Kent, CIA Office of National Estimates, "Some Thoughts about the Latin American Left," 29 December 1965, NSFCO: Latin America, box 2, LBJL.

26. Betancourt speech to National Press Club, 20 February 1963, POFCO: Venezuela, box 128, 1963 folder, JFKL.

27. Kennedy to McCone, 19 February 1963, NSFCO: Venezuela, box 192, 1-2/63 folder, JFKL.

28. Beschloss, *Crisis Years*, 666-67.

29. CIA to Director, "Current Thinking of Cuban Government Leaders," 5 March 1964, NSF: Memorandums, box 1, vol. 2 folder, LBJL. See also Thomas L. Hughes of Bureau of Intelligence and Research to Rusk, 29 November 1963, NSFCO: Latin America, box 1, folder 1, LBJL; and Benjamin

Read of State Department to Bundy, 13 February 1964, NSFCO: Cuba, box 24, OAS Resolution—Arms Cache (I), Cuba, Memorandums—Vol. II folder, LBJL.

30. Smith, *Portrait of a Cold Warrior*, 381–84; Agee, *Inside the Company*, 322, 364–65; Beschloss, *Crisis Years*, 692.

31. Bundy quoted in memorandum of record of Cuba meeting of 19 February 1964 submitted by NSC officer Gordon Chase, 22 February 1964, NSFCO: Cuba, box 24, OAS Resolution—Arms Cache (I), Cuba, Memorandums— Vol. II folder, LBJL; McCone quoted in editorial note on 30 November 1963 meeting between McCone and Johnson, *FRUS, 1961–1963*, vol. 11, *Cuban Missile Crisis and Aftermath*, 896. See also Rusk to President Johnson, 27 November 1963, and Rusk to U.S. Posts in American Republics, 4 December 1963, in *FRUS, 1961–1963*, 12:352–54. See also Beschloss, *Taking Charge*, 87, 234,

32. Guthman and Shulman, *Robert Kennedy*, 256.

33. Scheman, *Alliance for Progress*, 15, 26–28, 34–37; Rabe, *Road to* OPEC, 165–67.

34. Furtado, *Economic Development*, 43–149; Sigmund, *United States and Democracy in Chile*, xi, 17.

35. Dulles to Eisenhower on Chilean election, 20 October 1958, Whitman File: International Series, box 7, folder 5, DDEL; Ambassador to Chile Fisher Howe to State Department, 18 January 1960, *FRUS, 1958–1960*, 5: *Microfiche Supplement*, CI-27.

36. William Brubeck of NSC to Bundy of NSC and Ralph Dungan of White House on Alessandri visit, 1 August 1962, NSF: Brubeck Series, box 384, Chile folder, JFKL; Martin, *Kennedy and Latin America*, 317.

37. Allende quoted in Sater, *Chile and the United States*, 133.

38. Ibid., 134–35; Rusk to State Department, 31 January 1962, *FRUS, 1961–1963*, 12:307–8; memorandum of conversation between Ambassador Howe and Alessandri, 17 May 1960, *FRUS, 1958–1960*, 5: *Microfiche Supplement*, CI-36; Martin, *Kennedy and Latin America*, 318.

39. Perloff, *Alliance for Progress*, 55.

40. State Department, American Republic Affairs, "Review of U.S. Policy toward Chile in Regard to 1964 Election and Copper Companies," 10 January 1963, NSF: Brubeck Series, box 384, Chile folder, JFKL. See also Taylor Belcher of State Department to Assistant Secretary Martin, 16 August 1962, ibid.

41. Cole OH, p. 33, JFKL.

42. Belcher to Martin on Cole dispatch of 13 November 1962, 8 January 1963, NSF: Brubeck Series, box 384, Chile folder, JFKL; Martin, *Kennedy and Latin America*, 320.

43. Kennedy quoted in Martin, *Kennedy and Latin America*, 317, 320, 366.

44. Ibid., 313; memorandum of conversation between Kennedy, Martin, and Cole, 3 August 1962, NSF: Brubeck Series, box 384, Chile folder, JFKL.

45. Sater, *Chile and the United States*, 137–38; Sigmund, *United States and Democracy in Chile*, 17; Martin, *Kennedy and Latin America*, 314, 321.

46. Martin, *Kennedy and Latin America*, 317.

47. State Department, American Republic Affairs, "Review of U.S. Policy toward Chile in Regard to 1964 Election and Copper Companies," 10 January 1963, NSF: Brubeck Series, box 384, Chile folder, JFKL.

48. Church Committee, *Covert Action in Chile*, 14–19, 57–58; Agee, *Inside the Company*, 371–72, 382, 389; Thomas, *Very Best Men*, 324.

49. Belcher to Martin on Cole dispatch of 13 November 1962, 8 January 1963, NSF: Brubeck Series, box 384, Chile folder, JFKL.

50. Sigmund, *United States and Democracy in Chile*, 47.

51. Church Committee, *Covert Action in Chile*, 15–16.

52. William S. Gaud, Administrator of Agency for International Development, to President Johnson, 16 November 1966, NSFCO: Chile, box 13, Memorandums, 10/65–7/67, folder, LBJL. See also Sigmund, *United States and Democracy in Chile*, 25–43.

53. Church Committee, *Covert Action in Chile*, 17–19.

54. Frei Montalva, "The Alliance That Lost Its Way," 437–48.

55. Scheman, *Alliance for Progress*, 55; Sigmund, *United States and Democracy in Chile*, 31.

56. *DSB* 47 (6 August 1962): 213–14; Schlesinger, *Thousand Days*, 787–88.

57. Martin, *Kennedy and Latin America*, 342.

58. Memorandum of conversation between Rusk and Beltrán, 4 April 1961, *FRUS, 1961–1963*, 12:852–54; Assistant Secretary Woodward to Rusk on talks between Kennedy and Prado, 20 September 1961, ibid., 854–56; Rusk to State Department, 28 January 1962, ibid., 301–2.

59. *DSB* 45 (23 October 1961): 676–77.

60. Humphrey quoted in Van Cleve, "Latin American Policy," 40.

61. Martin, *Kennedy and Latin America*, 345; Hughes, Director of Intelligence and Research, to Woodward, "Creating Allies for Socio-Economic Progress with Political Stability in Latin America," 19 January 1962, *FRUS, 1961–1963*, 12:86–91.

62. Martin OH, pp. 2–3, JFKL.

63. State Department to Embassy in Peru, 24 March 1962, *FRUS, 1961–1963*, 12:858; Martin, *Kennedy and Latin America*, 346–49.

64. Martin, *Kennedy and Latin America*, 350; State Department to Embassy in Peru, 29 May 1962, *FRUS, 1961–1963*, 12:859–60.

65. State Department to Embassy in Peru, 12 July 1962, ibid., 863; Martin, *Kennedy and Latin America*, 351.

66. Ambassador Stewart's memorandum of conversation with Venezuelan Foreign Minister Marcos Falcón-Briceño, 31 July 1962, NSFCO: Venezuela, box 192, 7/1–8/19/62 folder, JFKL; Carey, *Peru and the United States*, 217.

67. Martin OH, pp. 43–45, JFKL.

68. Morrison, *Latin American Mission*, 267.

69. Ball to Kennedy, 27 July 1962, *FRUS, 1961–1963*, 12:864–67; State Department to Embassy in Peru, 30 July 1962, ibid., 869–70.

70. Memorandum of conversation between Kennedy and Falcón-Briceño, 2 August 1962, ibid., 872–75; Kennedy to Betancourt, 16 August 1963, NSFCO: Venezuela, box 192, 6–9/63 folder, JFKL.

71. Martin to Ball on military assistance to Peru, with accompanying footnotes, 3 October 1962, *FRUS, 1961–1963*, 12:876–79.
72. Sharp, *U.S. Foreign Policy and Peru*, 57–124, 164–98, 246–52.
73. National Intelligence Estimate, "Political Prospects in Peru," 1 May 1963, *FRUS, 1961–1963*, 12:880–81.
74. Memorandum of conversation between Kennedy and Ambassador Jones, 25 January 1963, ibid., 879–80.
75. Lieuwen, *Generals vs. Presidents*, 116–18.
76. Martin, *Kennedy and Latin America*, 125–41; SCFR, *Executive Sessions, 1963*, 15:679–83.
77. Burrows OH, pp. 33–37, JFKL.
78. Martin's statement was reprinted in *DSB* 49 (4 November 1963): 698–700.
79. Schlesinger to Kennedy, 8 October 1963, *FRUS, 1961–1963*, 12:150–52; *PPP, 1963*, 767–75.
80. Martin OH, pp. 101–8, JFKL; editorial note, *FRUS, 1961–1963*, 12:149.
81. Sorensen, *Kennedy*, 535–36.
82. Lieuwen, *Generals vs. Presidents*, 118; Agee, *Inside the Company*, 294–97; Martin, *Kennedy and Latin America*, 337–41; editorial note, *FRUS, 1961–1963*, 12:149.

Chapter Six

1. Rabe, *Eisenhower and Latin America*, 21–23, 34–36, 88–90, 106–9; Francis, "Military Aid to Latin America," 389–404.
2. Rabe, *Eisenhower and Latin America*, 146–48.
3. Kennedy quoted in Blaufarb, *Counterinsurgency Era*, 54. For a different view of Kennedy's motives, see Dean, "Masculinity as Ideology," 29–62.
4. Memorandum by Joint Chiefs of conference with Kennedy, 23 February 1961, *FRUS, 1961–1963*, vol. 8, *National Security Policy*, 48–54. See also Record of Action of 475th Meeting of NSC, 1 February 1961, ibid., 20–23; and Schlesinger, *Robert Kennedy*, 461–62.
5. NSAM No. 88, 5 September 1961, *FRUS, 1961–1963*, 12:180; NSAM No. 124, 18 January 1962, ibid., 8:236–38; NSAM No. 163 (Inter-Departmental Seminar), 14 June 1962, NSF: Meetings and Memoranda, box 337, JFKL; Schlesinger, *Robert Kennedy*, 462–65.
6. Johnson, *Military and Society*, 261; Pye, "Armies in the Process of Political Modernization," 69–89; Millikan and Blackmer, *Emerging Nations*, 113; Huntington, *Soldier and the State*, 80–97.
7. Rostow, "Guerrilla Warfare," 116.
8. Lucius D. Battle, Executive Secretary of State Department, to Bundy of NSC, transmitting State/Defense report on NSAM No. 118, 2 February 1962, *FRUS, 1961–1963*, 12:214–17. See also Shafer, *Deadly Paradigms*, 79–83, 112–16.
9. Joint Chiefs to Kennedy, 30 November 1961, *FRUS, 1961–1963*, 12:197–202; Bundy to Rusk and McNamara on NSAM No. 118, 5 December 1961, ibid., 214, n. 1.
10. Defense Department draft paper, "U.S. Policy for the Security of Latin

America in the Sixties," 19 May 1961, ibid., 173–76; Attorney General Kennedy to president, 11 September 1961, ibid., 182; "Report and Recommendations of the Washington Assessment Team on the Internal Security Situation in South America," 10 January 1962, ibid., 202–9.

11. Schoultz, *Human Rights*, 214; Barber and Ronning, *Internal Security*, 236; Klare, *War without End*, 270–310.

12. Bowles to Kennedy on presidential waiver for military assistance to Central America, 29 September 1961, *FRUS, 1961–1963*, 12:187–90; editorial note on presidential waiver for South America, 28 February 1962, ibid., 223. See also Barber and Ronning, *Internal Security*, 30.

13. Lemnitzer to Kennedy, "Training of Police and Armed Forces of Latin America," 19 May 1961, POFCO: Countries, box 121A, Latin American Security, 1960–63, folder, JFKL.

14. Barber and Ronning, *Internal Security*, 145–49; Klare, *War without End*, 297–309; Schoultz, *Human Rights*, 230–33.

15. Stepan, *Military in Politics*, 178, n. 20.

16. Agee, *Inside the Company*, 63–64, 81.

17. Attorney General Kennedy to president, 11 September 1961, *FRUS, 1961–1963*, 12:182; "Report and Recommendations of the Washington Assessment Team on the Internal Security Situation in South America," 10 January 1962, ibid., 202–9.

18. NSAM No. 177, 7 August 1962, NSF: Meetings and Memoranda, box 338, JFKL. See also Schoultz, *Human Rights*, 179–83.

19. Klare and Arnson, *Supplying Repression*, 20; Klare, *War without End*, 247, 382–83.

20. Bowles to Kennedy, transmitting report on police training, 30 September 1961, NSF: Meetings and Memoranda, box 331, NSAM No. 88 folder, JFKL.

21. Klare, *War without End*, 249.

22. NSAM No. 206, 4 December 1962, *FRUS, 1961–1963*, 12:235–37.

23. Bundy to Rusk and McNamara on NSAM No. 119 (Civic Action), 18 December 1961, *FRUS, 1961–1963*, 8:231–32; Klare, *War without End*, 247.

24. Kennedy quoted in Barber and Ronning, *Internal Security*, 73.

25. McNamara quoted in SCFR, *Foreign Assistance Act of 1962*, 60.

26. McNamara quoted in ibid., 76, and in Klare, *War without End*, 296; memorandum of conversation between Kennedy and Venezuelan Ambassador Mayobre, 11 April 1962, *FRUS, 1961–1963*, 12:224–25; Enemark quoted in SCFR, *Executive Sessions, 1962*, 14:433; Rusk to Morse, 15 September 1962, *FRUS, 1961–1963*, 12:230–32.

27. McNamara's testimony to Morse in SCFR, *Foreign Assistance Act of 1963*, 206–8; McNamara quoted in Klare, *War without End*, 287.

28. Bowles to Kennedy, 30 September 1961, NSF: Meetings and Memoranda, box 331, NSAM No. 88 folder, JFKL; Bowles to Jeffrey C. Kitchen, Deputy Assistant Secretary of State for Politico-Military Affairs, 29 September 1961, *FRUS, 1961–1963*, 12:190–91.

29. International Cooperation Administration memorandum between Dennis

A. Fitzgerald, Deputy Director, to Seymour J. Rubin, General Counsel, 21 August 1961, ibid., 179; Kenneth R. Hansen, Assistant Director of Bureau of Budget, to Bowles, 28 September 1961, ibid., 185–87.

30. State Department to all posts in American Republics, 18 April 1962, ibid., 226–27; Schlesinger, *Robert Kennedy*, 466–67.

31. Stepan, *Military in Politics*, 174–86.

32. Barber and Ronning, *Internal Security*, 205, 223.

33. Burrows OH, p. 45, JFKL.

34. NSAM No. 206, 4 December 1962, *FRUS, 1961–1963*, 12:235–37.

35. Embassy in Honduras to State Department, 23 July 1961, ibid., 178; Special National Intelligence Estimate, "The Threat to US Security Interests in the Caribbean Area," 17 January 1962, ibid., 209–13; Bowles to embassies in South America, 4 November 1961, NSFCO: Cuba, box 40, Cables, 1/61–11/61, folder, JFKL.

36. "Summary of Communist-Directed Indoctrination and Training of Latin Americans," 7 May 1962, POFCO: Latin America, box 121A, Latin America Security, 1960–63, folder, JFKL.

37. Rusk to all posts in American Republics, 31 August 1963, NSF, box 216, Latin America, Vol. II, folder, JFKL.

38. Blasier, *Giant's Rival*, 75.

39. Miller, *Soviet Relations*, 2–5, 219–225.

40. Blasier, *Giant's Rival*, 83–92, 169–78; Blaufarb, *Counterinsurgency Era*, 13–16; Fursenko and Naftali, "*One Hell of a Gamble*," 138, 330; Gott, *Guerrilla Movements*, 19–35, 426–40; Jackson, *Castro, the Kremlin, and Communism*, 20–21; Miller, *Soviet Relations*, 51–53.

41. Castro quoted in Naftali and Fursenko, "*One Hell of a Gamble*," 141.

42. CIA memorandum for record, "Meeting at the White House concerning Proposed Covert Policy and Integrated Program of Action towards Cuba," 19 June 1963, *FRUS, 1961–1963*, 11:837–38; CIA memorandum for record, "Meeting on Policy Relating to Cuba," 12 November 1963, ibid., 883–85; memorandum for record of Special Group Meeting No. 105, "Cuban Operations," 12 November 1963, ibid., 885–89. See also Schlesinger, *Robert Kennedy*, 492–543.

43. House Foreign Affairs Committee, *Hearings on Communist Activities in Latin America, 1967*, 22.

44. National Intelligence Estimate, "Situation and Prospects in Cuba," 1 August 1962, *FRUS, 1961–1963*, 10:893–94; National Intelligence Estimate, "Situation and Prospects in Cuba," ibid., 11:834–36; Jackson, *Castro, the Kremlin, and Communism*, 22–36, 83; Anderson, *Che Guevara*, 701–39; Gott, *Guerrilla Movements*, 426–40.

45. Testimony of Robert M. Sayre, Acting Assistant Secretary of State for Inter-American Affairs, in House Foreign Affairs Committee, *Hearings on Communist Activities in Latin America, 1967*, 79.

46. Jackson, *Castro, the Kremlin, and Communism*, 93; Miller, *Soviet Relations*, 23, 46–49.

47. Special National Intelligence Estimate, "The Threat to US Security Inter-

ests in the Caribbean Area," 17 January 1962, *FRUS, 1961–1963*, 12:209–13; Special National Intelligence Estimate, "Castro's Subversive Capabilities in Latin America," 9 November 1962, ibid., 234–35; Charles W. Maechling Jr., Director of Internal Defense in the Office of Politico-Military Affairs, to W. Averell Harriman, Under Secretary of State for Political Affairs, 29 July 1963, ibid., 8:494–97.

48. Hughes to Rusk, 29 November 1963, NSFCO: Latin America, box 1, vol. 1 folder, LBJL.

49. CIA to Director, 5 March 1964, NSF: Memorandums, box 1, vol. 2 folder, LBJL.

50. Hughes to Rusk, 20 October 1964 and 18 November 1964, both in NSFCO: Latin America, box 2, vol. 2, 9–12/64, folder, LBJL; Sherman Kent, Chairman, Office of National Estimates, CIA, "Some Thoughts about the Latin American Left," 29 December 1965, NSFCO: Latin America, box 2, LBJL.

51. Kennedy's remarks at the 496th meeting of the NSC, 18 January 1962, *FRUS, 1961–1963*, 8:238–42; oral statement of Ambassador Thompson to Khrushchev, 13 September 1963, *FRUS, 1961–1963*, vol. 6, *Kennedy-Khrushchev Exchanges*, 307–9.

52. Guthman and Shulman, *Robert F. Kennedy*, 255–57. For the Special Group's comprehensive reports, see Taylor to Kennedy, 30 July 1962, *FRUS, 1961–1963*, 8:352–55, and U. Alexis Johnson, Deputy Undersecretary of State for Political Affairs, 15 July 1963, ibid., 464–67. See also editorial note on President Kennedy's July 1963 desire to dispatch Special Forces to the underdeveloped world, ibid., 484–85.

53. Circular by Secretary Mann to ambassadors in Latin America on military assistance program, 2 January 1965, NSFCO: Latin America, box 2, 1–6/65 folder, LBJL; memorandum of meeting to consider internal security in Latin America, recorded by William Bowdler, 5 July 1967, NSFCO: Latin America, box 3, vol. 6, 6–9/67, folder, LBJL; Rostow to Johnson, transmitting memorandum by Assistant Secretary Covey Oliver, 7 September 1964, ibid.

54. Blaufarb, *Counterinsurgency Era*, 284–86; Randall, *Colombia and the United States*, 249.

55. Testimony of Alva R. Fitch, Deputy Director of Defense Intelligence Agency, in House Committee on Foreign Affairs, *Hearings on "Communism in Latin America,"* 8.

56. Szulc, *Twilight of the Tyrants*.

57. Lieuwen, *Generals vs. Presidents*, 127; Levinson and de Onís, *Alliance That Lost Its Way*, 93–94; Barber and Ronning, *Internal Security*, 208, 218; Adams, "Development of the Guatemalan Military," 93.

58. Memorandum of conversation between Kennedy and Mayobre, 11 April 1962, *FRUS, 1961–1963*, 12:224–25.

59. Schlesinger, "Alliance," 74; Schelsinger quoted in Scheman, *Alliance for Progress*, 70–71; Schlesinger, *Robert Kennedy*, 534.

60. Kennedy, *To Seek a Newer World*, 113.

61. Rusk OH, Interview No. 3, pp. 9–11, LBJL.

62. Barber and Ronning, *Internal Security*, 4.

63. Burrows to State Department, 28 February 1964, NSFCO: Latin America, box 1, folder 1, LBJL.

64. Stepan, *Military in Politics*, 247.

65. Robert M. Sayre to Bundy, 8 October 1964, NSFCO: Latin America, box 2, 9–12/64 folder, LBJL.

66. Stepan, *Military in Politics*, 31–52.

67. SCFR, *Survey of the Alliance for Progress*, 85–128.

68. Schoultz, *Human Rights*, 247.

69. Stepan, *Military in Politics*, 127–28; Adams, "Development of the Guatemalan Military," 103; Barber and Ronning, *Internal Security*, 223.

70. Holden, "Real Diplomacy of Violence," 306.

71. Williams OH, pp. 7–8, 32–34, JFKL. See also Coatsworth, *Central America*, 103–4.

72. Office of Assistant Secretary of Defense, International Security Affairs, "U.S. Policies toward Latin American Military Forces," 25 February 1965, NSFCO: Latin America, box 2, 1–6/65 folder, LBJL.

73. Jack H. Vaughan, Assistant Secretary of State, to McNaughton, 29 March 1965, ibid.; Extract of Views of Joint Chiefs of Staff on a Study, "U.S. Policy toward Latin American Military Forces," n.d., ibid.; McNamara to Bundy, 11 June 1965, ibid.

74. Schoultz, *Human Rights*, 177–83.

75. Smith, *America's Mission*, 235.

Chapter Seven

1. Levinson and de Onís, *Alliance That Lost Its Way*, 5–16; Perloff, *Alliance for Progress*, 67; OAS, *Analysis*, 2:1–94.

2. Scheman, *Alliance for Progress*, 12–15, 73–79; Inter-American Development Bank, *Socio-Economic Progress in Latin America, 1971*, 3–4.

3. Kennedy, *To Seek a Newer World*, 60–121.

4. SCFR, *Executive Sessions, 1962*, 14:429; Rogers, *Twilight Struggle*, 224.

5. State Department memorandum of conversation with Kennedy on aid matters, 9 March 1962, *FRUS, 1961–1963*, 12:97–98; Goodwin to Kennedy, 10 September 1963, ibid., 146–48.

6. State Department memorandum of conversation with Kennedy on Alliance for Progress, 16 February 1962, ibid., 94–97; State Department memorandum of conversation with Kennedy on aid matters, 9 March 1962, ibid., 97–98.

7. Editorial note, ibid., 110–11; memorandum of conversation between Kennedy and Kubitschek and Lleras Camargo, 13 December 1962, ibid., 117–25. See also Perloff, *Alliance for Progress*, 29–67.

8. Draft transcript of Kennedy talk to State Department officers, 30 March 1962, NSF: Departments and Agencies, box 285, JFKL; State Department memorandum, "Implementation of Agreements Reached at San José," 25 March 1963, *FRUS, 1961–1963*, 12:143–44.

9. Kennedy to Rusk, 29 October 1963, ibid., 158–59.

10. Packenham, *Liberal America*, 34-35, 59-75, 111-60.

11. Smith, *America's Mission*, 18, 217-27.

12. An excellent analysis of this issue can be found in Calder, *Impact of Intervention*.

13. Gordon, *New Deal*, 101-2; Kennedy quoted in Sorensen, *Kennedy*, 535.

14. *DSB* 49 (9 December 1963): 900-904.

15. Memorandum of conversation between Kennedy and Presidents Kubitschek and Lleras Camargo, 13 December 1962, *FRUS, 1961-1963*, 12:117-25.

16. Treasury Secretary Dillon to Kennedy, 2 March 1962, *FRUS, 1961-1963*, vol. 9, *Foreign Economic Policy*, 15-18; Dillon to Kennedy, 9 October 1962, ibid., 35-43; Dillon to President Johnson, 2 December 1963, ibid., 101-4; Collins, "Economic Crisis of 1968," 396-422.

17. Manger, *Alliance for Progress*, 43-66.

18. Rusk and Dillon to Kennedy, 9 April 1962, *FRUS, 1961-1963*, 9:19-21; Bell OH, pp. 15-33, LBJL; Gaud OH, pp. 2-20, LBJL.

19. Smith, *Talons of the Eagle*, 151.

20. Hanson, *Five Years*, 4-7; Levinson and de Onís, *Alliance That Lost Its Way*, 132-40; Perloff, *Alliance for Progress*, 48-53; Stallings, *Banker to the Third World*, 87, 323-40; *New York Times*, 29 May 1997, A5.

21. First meeting of Working Group on Problems of the Alliance for Progress, 16 January 1962, *FRUS, 1961-1963*, 12:75-78.

22. Bowles in Mexico City to State Department, 19 October 1962, ibid., 66-70; minutes of meeting of under secretaries on foreign economic policy, 29 November 1961, ibid., 70-74.

23. Bureau of Intelligence and Research, "Latin American Political Stability and the Alliance for Progress," 17 January 1962, ibid., 79-85; Thomas Hughes, Director of Bureau of Intelligence and Research, to Assistant Secretary Robert Woodward, 19 January 1962, ibid., 86-91. See also Agudelo Villa, *La Alianza para el Progreso*, 63-64.

24. Discussion at Secretary of State's Policy Planning Committee meeting, 13 February 1962, *FRUS, 1961-1963*, 12:91-93.

25. Hughes and Mijeski, "Contemporary Paradigms," 34-40.

26. Alba, *Alliance without Allies*, 205; Scheman, *Alliance for Progress*, 105-6; Schoultz, *Human Rights*, 5-16.

27. Kennedy quoted in Schlesinger, *Thousand Days*, 789.

28. Martin, *Kennedy and Latin America*, 176, n. 15; Desmond Fitzgerald of CIA to Bundy on "Luis Somoza's Involvement in Cuban Exile Operations," 9 August 1963, *FRUS, 1961-1963*, 11:853-55.

29. Martin, *Kennedy and Latin America*, 110. See also Cobbs, "Decolonization," 81.

30. Booth, "Socioeconomic and Political Roots," 36-43; Dosal, "Accelerating Dependent Development and Revolution," 75-96; Enríquez, *Harvesting Change*, 34-49.

31. SCFR, *Survey of Alliance for Progress*, 665-69.

32. Ibid., 179, 665-865. See also Gonzalez, "Failure of the Alliance for Progress," 87-96; Randall, *Colombia and the United States*, 232-37.

33. Park, *Latin American Underdevelopment*, 203.

34. Gardner, *Legal Imperialism*, 4–109.

35. Levinson and de Onís, *Alliance That Lost Its Way*, 10; OAS, *Alliance for Progress and Latin American Development Prospects*, 191–95; Scheman, *Alliance for Progress*, 28–37; Gordon OH, pp. 28–31, LBJL; Inter-American Development Bank, *Socio-Economic Progress in Latin America, 1971*, 95–99.

36. SCFR, *Survey of Alliance for Progress*, 513.

37. Kennedy, *Strategy of Peace*, 224–26.

38. Martin, *Kennedy and Latin America*, 110.

39. Rogers, *Twilight Struggle*, 77.

40. SCFR, *Executive Sessions, 1961*, 13:432–40.

41. Rogers, *Twilight Struggle*, 77–78; Kennedy, *To Seek a Newer World*, 100–102.

42. Rogers, *Twilight Struggle*, 79; Meyer and Sherman, *Course of Mexican History*, 700–707.

43. Baer, "Economics of Prebisch," 203–18; Love, "Raúl Prebisch," 45–72.

44. Levinson and de Onís, *Alliance That Lost Its Way*, 162–84; OAS, *Alliance for Progress and Latin American Development Prospects*, 60–69, 146; Perloff, *Alliance*, 76–77.

45. ECLA, *Development Problems*, 243–56.

46. Ibid., 253.

47. State Department to all posts on inter-American economic meeting, Mexico City, 10 November 1962, *FRUS, 1961–1963*, 12:113–15; Benjamin H. Read, Executive Secretary of NSC, to Bundy on inter-American economic meeting, São Paulo, 14 November 1962, ibid., 160–62; Rabe, *Road to OPEC*, 160–61.

48. Leoni, "View from Caracas," 643.

49. Speech by Michael Blumenthal, Deputy Assistant Secretary of State for Economic Affairs, *DSB* 47 (19 November 1962): 777–82; Rogers, *Twilight Struggle*, 157.

50. Rogers, *Twilight Struggle*, 195.

51. Dietz and Street, *Latin America's Economic Development*, 163; Stallings, *Banker to the Third World*, 86–93, 116.

52. Cobbs, *Rich Neighbor Policy*, 13–14; Collado, "Economic Development through Private Enterprise," 708–20; Rockefeller, "What Private Enterprise Means to Latin America," 403–16; summary of meeting of Interdepartmental Committee of Under Secretaries on Foreign Economic Policy, 20 March 1963, *FRUS, 1961–1963*, 12:137–42.

53. Memorandum of conversation between Kennedy and Presidents Kubitschek and Lleras Camargo, 13 December 1962, ibid., 117–25; Burrows OH, pp. 13–17, JFKL; Martin, *Kennedy and Latin America*, 127–29; Euraque, *Reinterpreting the Banana Republic*, 112–13.

54. Packenham, *Dependency Movement*, 14–31; Pérez, "Dependency," 99–110; Hughes and Mijeski, "Contemporary Paradigms," 24–25.

55. *DSB* 47 (23 July 1962): 137–38; Martin, *Kennedy and Latin America*, 108–9.

56. SCFR, *Survey of Alliance for Progress*, 163–98; OAS, *Latin America*, 230.

57. *DSB* 45 (6 November 1961): 739–45.

58. Levinson and de Onís, *Alliance That Lost Its Way*, 229, 247; OAS, *Latin America*, 232–33. See also Flores, *Land Reform*, 1–14.

59. SCFR, *Survey of Alliance for Progress*, 187–89; Smith, *America's Mission*, 225. See also Fitzgerald, "Exporting American Agriculture," 457–83.

60. Memorandum of conversation between Kennedy and Furtado, 14 July 1961, *FRUS, 1961–1963*, 12:439–41.

61. Gordon to State Department on conversation with Goulart, 21 October 1961, ibid., 448–49; Roett, *Politics of Foreign Aid*, 70, 92–93.

62. Special National Intelligence estimate, "The Character of the Goulart Regime in Brazil," 27 February 1963, *FRUS, 1961–1963*, 12:490–93, n. 1.

63. Fowler Hamilton, Administrator of Agency for International Development, to Kennedy, 9 February 1962, ibid., 455–56. See also summary record of 509th meeting of NSC, 13 March 1963, ibid., 132–33.

64. Roett, *Politics of Foreign Aid*, 112–38, 170. See also Kaplan and Bonsor, "Did United States Aid Really Help Brazilian Development," 25–46.

65. Draft memorandum by Martin on "Problems of Alliance," 1963, box 1, Alliance for Progress folder, Schlesinger papers, JFKL; Martin, *Kennedy and Latin America*, 72–77.

66. *PPP, 1963*, 458.

67. Bowles OH, pp. 30, 80, JFKL. See also Frei, "Alliance That Lost Its Way," 447.

68. Scheman, *Alliance for Progress*, 149–56; Levinson and de Onís, *Alliance That Lost Its Way*, 140.

Chapter Eight

1. Schlesinger, "Alliance for Progress," 57–92; Schlesinger, *Robert Kennedy*, 630–32; Schlesinger OH, pp. 21–22, LBJL; Scheman, *Alliance for Progress*, 67–72. See also Agudelo Villa, *La Alianza para el Progreso*, 71–72.

2. Guthman and Shulman, *Robert Kennedy*, 408. See also Agudelo Villa, *La revolución del desarrollo*, 381–86.

3. Kennedy, *To Seek a Newer World*, 60–121. See also interview with Kennedy in *New York Times*, 22 February 1967, 17.

4. Guthman and Shulman, *Robert Kennedy*, 298.

5. State Department to all posts in Latin America, 27 March 1963, *FRUS, 1961–1963*, 12:145.

6. Bundy to Johnson, 8 December 1963 and 9 December 1963, NSF: Memorandums, box 1, folder 1, LBJL.

7. Rusk, *As I Saw It*, 403. See also Beschloss, *Taking Charge*, 74, 87, 101.

8. LaFeber, "Thomas C. Mann," 166–203; Mann to Rusk on Bay of Pigs, 15 February 1961, NSFCO: Cuba, box 35, General, 1–4/61, folder, JFKL.

9. Berle, *Navigating the Rapids*, 785.

10. Mann OH, pp. 9–11, JFKL; Mann OH, pp. 4–13, LBJL; Mann speech in *DSB* 47 (19 November 1962): 772–77.

11. Gordon OH, pp. 31–32, JFKL; Gordon OH, pp. 1–31, LBJL.

12. Oliver OH, pp. 3–37, LBJL.

13. *New York Times*, 19 March 1964, 1–2.

14. Gordon Chase of NSC to Bundy, 19 March 1964, NSFCO: Latin America, box 1, folder 1, LBJL.

15. SCFR, *Executive Sessions, 1965*, 17:164; Mann to W. Marvin Watson of White House, 16 December 1965, NSFCO: Latin America, box 2, 7/65–8/66 folder, LBJL.

16. Bundy to Johnson, 25 March 1964, NSF: Memorandums, box 1, folder 2, LBJL; Bundy to Johnson, 16 June 1964, ibid., box 2, folder 5, LBJL.

17. *DSB* 50 (29 June 1964): 995–1000. See also Cochrane, "U.S. Policy toward Recognition of Governments," 275–91.

18. Martin, *Kennedy and Latin America*, 179, n. 41; Sorensen, *Kennedy*, 535–36; Rusk, *As I Saw It*, 370.

19. Parker, *Brazil and the Quiet Intervention*, 64–87; Kennedy, *To Seek a Newer World*, 106–7.

20. Schlesinger to Dungan, 15 October 1962, *FRUS, 1961–1963*, 12:107–10.

21. Morales-Carrión memorandum, 9 April 1962, ibid., 100–103.

22. Martin, *Kennedy and Latin America*, v–vi, 32–33; Goodwin, *Remembering America*, 214–17; Woodward OH, p. 14, LBJL.

23. Schlesinger, *Thousand Days*, 785. See also Slater, "Democracy versus Stability," 169–81.

24. Grace to Dungan, 19 December 1963, WHCF, box 11, CO-108 (South America), LBJL; John T. O'Connor of Merck & Co., 4 February 1964, ibid.; Humphrey to Johnson, 2 February 1966, WHCF, box 10, CO-108 (South America), LBJL.

25. Rusk (Mann) to U.S. Embassy in Buenos Aires, 20 June 1964, NSFCO: Argentina, box 6, Cables, 11/63–8/64, folder, LBJL.

26. Mann OH, pp. 34–36, LBJL; Levinson and de Onís, *Alliance That Lost Its Way*, 146–56; Sharp, *U.S. Foreign Policy and Peru*, 246–52.

27. Rusk, *As I Saw It*, 403.

28. Johnson, *Vantage Point*, 348–51.

29. Rogers, *Twilight Struggle*, 258.

30. Gordon OH, p. 112, LBJL.

31. Dungan OH, p. 23, LBJL; Rusk OH, Interview I, p. 34, LBJL.

32. Rostow to Johnson, 22 April 1968, NSFCO: Latin America, box 4, 3–5/68 folder, LBJL.

33. Sayre to Bundy, 11 February 1965, NSFCO: Latin America, box 2, 1/65–6/65 folder, LBJL; Gordon OH, p. 74, LBJL; Rockefeller to Johnson, 25 January 1966, WHCF: Name File, box 449, LBJL; Sayre memorandum of discussion with Foreign Secretary Carrillo Flores, 28 October 1967, NSFCO: Latin America, box 3, 10/67–4/68 folder, LBJL.

34. Bundy to Johnson, 12 March 1965, NSF: Memorandums, box 3, folder 9, LBJL. See also memorandum of conversation between Johnson and Mexican President Gustavo Díaz Ordaz, 15 April 1966, NSF: Memorandums, box 7, 4/66 folder, LBJL.

35. Linowitz OH, pp. 35–53, LBJL; Johnson, *Vantage Point*, 349–51; Rostow, *Diffusion of Power*, 430.

36. Minutes of 583rd meeting of NSC, 6 March 1968, NSF: Meetings, box 2, folder 5, tab 65, LBJL; Rusk, *As I Saw It*, 404.

37. Brands, *Wages of Globalism*, 31.

38. Rusk circular to all posts in Latin America, 18 January 1965, NSFCO: Latin America, box 2, folder 1, LBJL.

39. NSAM No. 297, 22 April 1964, NSFCO: Latin America, box 2, folder 2, LBJL.

40. General Andrew P. O'Meara to Robert Kennedy, 5 May 1964, NSF: Memorandums, box 1, folder 4, LBJL.

41. William Bowdler of NSC to Bundy, 20 August 1965, NSF: Memorandums, box 2, folder 4, LBJL.

42. Agee, *Inside the Company*, 325–494.

43. Notes on luncheon meeting, 18 July 1968, Tom Johnson Notes, box 1, LBJL; summary notes of 581st meeting of NSC, 7 February 1968, NSF: Meetings, box 2, folder 5, tab 63, LBJL.

44. Mann circular to U.S. ambassadors in Latin America, 2 January 1965, NSFCO: Latin America, box 2, folder 3, LBJL.

45. Chase to Bundy, 19 March 1964, NSFCO: Latin America, box 1, folder 1, LBJL; minutes of 90th meeting of Latin American Policy Committee, 9 July 1964, NSFCO: Latin America, box 2, folder 2, LBJL.

46. Bundy to Johnson, 20 September 1964, NSF: Memorandums, box 2, folder 6, LBJL.

47. Bundy to Johnson, 13 January 1966, NSF: Memorandums, box 6, folder 1, LBJL; Gaud of Agency for International Development to Johnson, 16 November 1966, NSFCO: Chile, box 13, Memorandums, 10/65–7/67, folder, LBJL.

48. Rusk to Ball, 17 November 1965, NSFCO: Argentina, box 6, Cables, 9/64–2/67, folder, LBJL.

49. CIA reports, 1 June 1966 and 6 June 1966, ibid.; Ball (Gordon) to U.S. Embassy in Buenos Aires, 6 June 1966, ibid.; Rusk (Gordon) to U.S. Embassy in Buenos Aires on meeting between Generals Yarborough of the United States and Shaw of Argentina, 15 June 1966, ibid.

50. Rostow to Johnson, 28 June 1966, ibid. See also Rostow, *Diffusion of Power*, 425.

51. Martin to State Department, 8 June 1965, NSFCO: Argentina, box 6, Cables, 9/64–2/67, folder, LBJL.

52. Ball to Johnson, 7 July 1966, ibid.

53. Martin OH, pp. 20–23, JFKL.

54. "Consultations with Congress on Panama Canal Policy and Relations with Panama," n.d. (but 1962), NSF: Meetings and Memoranda, box 336, NSAM No. 152 folder, JFKL; Martin, *Kennedy and Latin America*, 148.

55. Martin OH, pp. 17–19, JFKL; Rusk OH, Interview III, pp. 1–6, LBJL.

56. Memorandum of conversation between Ball and Chiari, 19 January 1962, *FRUS, 1961–1963*, 12:817–20; memorandum of conversation between Ball and Chiari, 12 October 1962, ibid., 839–42.

57. Major, *Prize Possession*, 333–35.

58. LaFeber, *Panama Canal*, 101-7; Mansfield to Johnson, 31 January 1964, NSF: Memorandums, box 1, folder 1, LBJL.

59. Ball to Kennedy, 27 April 1962, *FRUS, 1961–1963*, 12:822-24; NSAM No. 152, 30 April 1962, ibid., 824-26; Perloff, *Alliance for Progress*, 55.

60. Memorandum of conversation between Kennedy and Chiari, 12 June 1962, *FRUS, 1961–1963*, 12:831-38; NSAM No. 164, 15 June 1962, ibid., 838-39.

61. Memorandum of conversation between Martin and Panamanian Ambassador A. Guillermo Arango, 8 November 1962, ibid., 842-44; memorandum for record by Farland, 20 March 1963, ibid., 844-46; memorandum of conversation between Kennedy and Farland, 7 May 1963, ibid., 846-49; State Department to Embassy in Panama containing Kennedy letter to Chiari, 23 July 1963, ibid., 849-51.

62. Major, *Prize Possession*, 335.

63. Mann OH, p. 17, LBJL; Rusk OH, Interview III, pp. 1-6, LBJL.

64. Jorden, *Panama Odyssey*, 91-119; LaFeber, *Panama Canal*, 109-16; Major, *Prize Possession*, 336-38; Rostow to Johnson on Panama, 25 July 1966, NSF: Memorandums, box 9, folder 9, LBJL; Interagency Contingency Study on Panama, 16 September 1966, NSF: Memorandums, box 10, folder 13, LBJL.

65. Schlesinger OH, p. 21, LBJL; Kennedy, *To Seek a Newer World*, 103, 113-14; Schlesinger, *Robert Kennedy*, 691.

66. Gleijeses, *Dominican Crisis*; Lowenthal, *Dominican Intervention*.

67. Kennedy to McNamara, 4 October 1963, *FRUS, 1961–1963*, 12:739; Johnson, *Vantage Point*, 197.

68. Bundy to Johnson, 5 December 1963, NSF: Memorandums, box 1, folder 1, LBJL; Martin to Johnson, 5 October 1965, NSF: Memorandums, box 5, folder 15, LBJL; Berle to Johnson, 3 June 1965, WHCF, box 10, CO 108 (South America), LBJL.

69. Johnson, *Vantage Point*, 188-89; Rusk, Interview III, pp. 15-26, LBJL; Mann OH, pp. 18-24, LBJL; Gordon OH, pp. 47-49, LBJL.

70. Rockefeller, *Rockefeller Report on the Americas*, 21. See also OAS, *Final Report*, 9.

Conclusion

1. Schlesinger, "Alliance for Progress," 59; Slater, "Democracy versus Stability," 175.

2. Fursenko and Naftali, *"One Hell of a Gamble,"* 168-72.

3. Benjamin, "Framework of U.S. Relations," 91-112; Connell-Smith, "Latin America," 137-50; Gil, "Kennedy-Johnson Years," 3; Gilderhus, *Pan American Visions*, ix-xi; LaFeber, "Evolution of the Monroe Doctrine," 121-41; Pérez, "Intervention, Hegemony, and Dependency," 165-94; Schoultz, *National Security*, 11-33.

Bibliography

PRIMARY SOURCES

Private Papers

Ball, George W. Telephone Notes File. Lyndon Baines Johnson Library, Austin, Texas.

Berle, Adolf A., Jr. Franklin D. Roosevelt Library, Hyde Park, New York.

Eisenhower, Dwight D. Ann Whitman File. Dwight D. Eisenhower Library, Abilene, Kansas.

Fulbright, James William. University of Arkansas Library, Fayetteville, Arkansas.

Johnson, W. Thomas. Notes of Meetings File. Lyndon Baines Johnson Library, Austin, Texas.

Kennedy, John F. Pre-Presidential File. John F. Kennedy Library, Boston, Massachusetts.

Morse, Wayne L. University of Oregon Library, Eugene, Oregon.

Schlesinger, Arthur M., Jr. John F. Kennedy Library, Boston, Massachusetts.

Sorensen, Theodore C. John F. Kennedy Library, Boston, Massachusetts.

Unpublished Government Documents and Records

Administrative History File. Lyndon Baines Johnson Library, Austin, Texas.

National Security File. John F. Kennedy Library, Boston, Massachusetts.

———. Lyndon Baines Johnson Library, Austin, Texas.

President's Office File. John F. Kennedy Library, Boston, Massachusetts.

White House Central File. John F. Kennedy Library, Boston, Massachusetts.

———. Lyndon Baines Johnson Library, Austin, Texas.

White House Office of the Staff Secretary. Dwight D. Eisenhower Library, Abilene, Kansas.

Oral Histories

Bell, David E. Lyndon Baines Johnson Library, Austin, Texas.

Bernbaum, Maurice M. Lyndon Baines Johnson Library, Austin, Texas.

Bosch, Juan. John F. Kennedy Library, Boston, Massachusetts.

Bowles, Chester B. John F. Kennedy Library, Boston, Massachusetts.

Burrows, Charles R. John F. Kennedy Library, Boston, Massachusetts.

Cabot, John M. John F. Kennedy Library, Boston, Massachusetts.

———. Lyndon Baines Johnson Library, Austin, Texas.

Cole, Charles. John F. Kennedy Library, Boston, Massachusetts.

Dungan, Ralph A. Lyndon Baines Johnson Library, Austin, Texas.

Gaud, William S. John F. Kennedy Library, Boston, Massachusetts.

───. Lyndon Baines Johnson Library, Austin, Texas.

Gordon, Lincoln. John F. Kennedy Library, Boston, Massachusetts.

───. Lyndon Baines Johnson Library, Austin, Texas.

Linowitz, Sol. Lyndon Baines Johnson Library, Austin, Texas.

Mann, Thomas C. John F. Kennedy Library, Boston, Massachusetts.

───. Lyndon Baines Johnson Library, Austin, Texas.

Martin, Edwin McCammon. John F. Kennedy Library, Boston, Massachusetts.

Muccio, John J. John F. Kennedy Library, Boston, Massachusetts.

Oliver, Covey T. Lyndon Baines Johnson Library, Austin, Texas.

Rusk, Dean. Lyndon Baines Johnson Library, Austin, Texas.

Schlesinger, Arthur M., Jr. Lyndon Baines Johnson Library, Austin, Texas.

Smathers, George. John F. Kennedy Library, Boston, Massachusetts.

Telles, Raymond L., Jr. John F. Kennedy Library, Boston, Massachusetts.

Thurston, Raymond L. John F. Kennedy Library, Boston, Massachusetts.

Williams, Murat. John F. Kennedy Library, Boston, Massachusetts.

Woodward, Robert F. John F. Kennedy Library, Boston, Massachusetts.

───. Lyndon Baines Johnson Library, Austin, Texas.

Published Government and International Organization Documents and Records

Inter-American Development Bank. *Socio-Economic Progress in Latin America: Annual Report, 1966*. Washington: Inter-American Development Bank, 1967.

───. *Socio-Economic Progress in Latin America: Annual Report, 1971*. Washington: Inter-American Development Bank, 1972.

Organization of American States. *The Alliance for Progress and Latin American Development Prospects: A Five-Year Review, 1961–1965*. Baltimore: Johns Hopkins University Press, 1967.

───. *Alliance for Progress Newsletter, 1961–1962*. Nos. 1–14. Washington: Pan American Union, 1961–62.

───. *Alliance for Progress Weekly Newsletter, 1963–1973*. 11 vols. Washington: Pan American Union, 1963–73.

───. *Analysis of the Economic and Social Evolution of Latin America since the Inception of the Alliance for Progress*. 2 vols. Washington: Organization of American States, 1971.

───. *Final Report of the XXIII Meeting of the Inter-American Committee of the Alliance for Progress*. Washington: Organization of American States, 1971.

───. *Latin America: Problems and Perspectives of Economic Development, 1963–1964*. Baltimore: Johns Hopkins University Press, 1966.

U.N. Economic Commission for Latin America. *Development Problems in Latin America*. Austin: University of Texas Press, 1970.

U.S. Congress. House. Committee on Foreign Affairs. Subcommittee on Inter-American Affairs. *Castro-Communist Subversion in the Western Hemisphere*. 88th Cong., 1st sess. Washington: Government Printing Office, 1963.

———. *Hearings on "Communism in Latin America."* 89th Cong., 1st sess. Washington: Government Printing Office, 1965.

———. *Hearings on Communist Activities in Latin America, 1967.* 90th Cong., 1st sess. Washington: Government Printing Office, 1967.

———. *New Directions for the 1970s: Toward a Strategy of Inter-American Development.* 91st Cong., 1st sess. Washington: Government Printing Office, 1969.

U.S. Congress. House. Government Operations Committee. *U.S. AID Operations in Latin America under the Alliance for Progress.* 90th Cong., 2d sess. Washington: Government Printing Office, 1969.

U.S. Congress. Senate. Committee on Foreign Relations. *Executive Sessions of the Senate Foreign Relations Committee (Historical Series), 1959–1966.* Vols. 11–18. Washington: Government Printing Office, 1982–93.

———. *Foreign Assistance Act of 1962, Hearings.* 87th Cong., 2d sess. Washington: Government Printing Office, 1962.

———. *Foreign Assistance Act of 1963, Hearings.* 88th Cong., 1st sess. Washington: Government Printing Office, 1963.

———. *Survey of the Alliance for Progress: Compilation of Studies and Hearings.* Senate Document No. 91-17. 91st Cong., 1st sess. Washington: Government Printing Office, 1969.

U.S. Congress. Senate. Select Committee to Study Governmental Operations with Respect to Intelligence Activities. *Alleged Assassination Plots Involving Foreign Leaders.* Senate Report No. 465. 94th Cong., 1st sess. Washington: Government Printing Office, 1975.

———. *Covert Action in Chile, 1963–1973: Staff Report.* 94th Cong., 1st sess. Washington: Government Printing Office, 1975.

U.S. Department of Commerce. Office of Business Economics. *Business Statistics, 1961.* Washington: Government Printing Office, 1961.

U.S. Department of State. *Department of State Bulletin, 1961–1964.* Washington: Government Printing Office, 1961–64.

———. *Foreign Relations of the United States, 1958–1963.* Washington: Government Printing Office, 1991–97.

U.S. Department of State. Agency for International Development. *Overseas Loans and Grants, 1945–1975.* Washington: Government Printing Office, 1976.

———. *Seven Years of the Alliance for Progress.* Washington: Government Printing Office, 1968.

U.S. General Services Administration. *Public Papers of the President: John F. Kennedy, 1961–1963.* 3 vols. Washington: Government Printing Office, 1962–64.

Autobiographies, Memoirs, Published Papers

Agee, Philip. *Inside the Company: CIA Diary.* New York: Stonehill Publishing, 1975.

Balaguer, Joaquín. *Memorias de un cortesano de la era de Trujillo.* Santo Domingo: Editora Corripio, 1989.

Ball, George W. *The Past Has Another Pattern: Memoirs*. New York: W. W. Norton, 1982.

Berle, Adolf A., Jr. *Navigating the Rapids, 1918–1971: From the Papers of Adolf A. Berle*. Edited by Beatrice Bishop Berle and Travis Beal Jacobs. New York: Harcourt Brace Jovanovitch, 1973.

Beschloss, Michael R., ed. *Taking Charge: The Johnson White House Tapes, 1963–1964*. New York: Simon & Schuster, 1997.

Bissell, Richard M., Jr. *Reflections of a Cold Warrior: From Yalta to the Bay of Pigs*. With Jonathan E. Lewis and Frances T. Pudlo. New Haven: Yale University Press, 1996.

Goodwin, Richard N. *Remembering America: A Voice from the Sixties*. Boston: Little, Brown, 1988.

Gordon, Lincoln. *A New Deal for Latin America: The Alliance for Progress*. Cambridge: Harvard University Press, 1963.

Guthman, Edwin O., and Jeffrey Shulman, eds. *Robert Kennedy in His Own Words: The Unpublished Recollections of the Kennedy Years*. New York: Bantam Books, 1988.

Heinl, Robert Debs, Jr., and Nancy Gordon Heinl. *Written in Blood: The Story of the Haitian People, 1492–1971*. Boston: Houghton Mifflin, 1978.

Hilsman, Roger. *To Move a Nation: The Politics of Foreign Policy in the Administration of John F. Kennedy*. Garden City, N.Y.: Doubleday, 1967.

Jagan, Cheddi. *The West on Trial*. New York: International Publishers, 1972.

Johnson, Lyndon Baines. *The Vantage Point: Perspectives of the Presidency, 1963–1969*. New York: Holt, Rinehart, and Winston, 1971.

Jorden, William J. *Panama Odyssey*. Austin: University of Texas Press, 1984.

Kennedy, John F. *The Strategy of Peace*. Edited by Allan Nevins. New York: Harper & Bros., 1960.

Kennedy, Robert F. *Thirteen Days: A Memoir of the Cuban Missile Crisis*. New York: W. W. Norton, 1969.

——. *To Seek a Newer World*. New York: Bantam, 1968.

Martin, Edwin McCammon. *Kennedy and Latin America*. Lanham, Md.: University Press of America, 1994.

Martin, John Bartlow. *Overtaken by Events: The Dominican Crisis from the Fall of Trujillo to the Civil War*. Garden City, N.Y.: Doubleday, 1966.

May, Ernest R., and Zelikow, Philip D., eds. *The Kennedy Tapes: Inside the White House during the Cuban Missile Crisis*. Cambridge: The Belknap Press of Harvard University Press, 1997.

Morrison, Delesseps S. *Latin American Mission: An Adventure in Hemisphere Diplomacy*. New York: Simon & Schuster, 1965.

Perloff, Harvey S. *Alliance for Progress: A Social Invention in the Making*. Baltimore: Johns Hopkins University Press, 1969.

Rockefeller, Nelson A. *The Rockefeller Report on the Americas*. Chicago: Quadrangle Books, 1969.

Rogers, William D. *The Twilight Struggle: The Alliance for Progress and the Politics of Development in Latin America*. New York: Random House, 1967.

Romualdi, Serafino. *Presidents and Peons: Recollections of a Labor Ambassador in Latin America*. New York: Funk & Wagnalls, 1967.

Rostow, W. W. *The Diffusion of Power: An Essay in Recent History*. New York: Macmillan, 1972.

Rusk, Dean. *As I Saw It*. As told to Richard Rusk. New York: Norton, 1990.

Salinger, Pierre. *With Kennedy*. Garden City, N.Y.: Doubleday, 1966.

Schlesinger, Arthur M., Jr. *A Thousand Days: John F. Kennedy in the White House*. Boston: Houghton Mifflin, 1965.

Smith, Joseph Burkholder. *Portrait of a Cold Warrior*. New York: G. P. Putnam's Sons, 1976.

Sorensen, Theodore C. *Kennedy*. New York: Harper & Row, 1965.

Trujillo, Rafael L. *The Other Side of the Galíndez Case*. New York: Dominican Republic Cultural Society of New York, 1956.

Wofford, Harris. *Of Kennedys and Kings: Making Sense of the Sixties*. New York: Farrar, Straus, Giroux, 1980.

Newspapers

New York Times
Sunday Times (London)

SECONDARY SOURCES

Books

Anderson, Jon Lee. *Che Guevara: A Revolutionary Life*. New York: Grove Press, 1997.

Agudelo Villa, Hernando. *La Alianza para el Progreso: Esperanza y frustración*. Bogota: Ediciones Tercer Mundo, 1966.

―――. *La revolución del desarrollo: Origin y evolución de la Alianza para el Progreso*. Mexico City: Editorial Roble, 1966.

Aguilar, Alonso. *Pan Americanism from Monroe to the Present: A View from the Other Side*. Translated by Asa Zatz. New York: Monthly Review Press, 1966.

Alba, Víctor. *Alliance without Allies: The Mythology of Progress in Latin America*. New York: Frederick A. Praeger, 1965.

Almond, Gabriel A., and James S. Coleman, eds. *The Politics of the Developing Areas*. Princeton: Princeton University Press, 1960.

Ameringer, Charles D. *The Democratic Left in Exile: The Antidictatorial Struggles in the Caribbean, 1945–1959*. Coral Gables: University of Florida Press, 1974.

Balaguer, Joaquín. *El principio de la alternabilidad en la historia Dominicana*. Cuidad Trujillo: Impresora Dominicana, 1952.

―――. *Two Essays on Dominican History*. Cuidad Trujillo: Editora del Caribe, 1955.

Barber, Willard F., and C. Neale Ronning. *Internal Security and Military Power: Counterinsurgency and Civic Action in Latin America*. Columbus: Ohio State University Press, 1966.

Berle, Adolf A. *Latin America: Diplomacy and Reality*. New York: Harper & Row, 1962.

Beschloss, Michael R. *The Crisis Years: Kennedy and Khrushchev, 1960–1963*. New York: Edward Burlingame Books, 1991.

Black, Jan Knippers. *United States Penetration of Brazil*. Philadelphia: University of Pennsylvania Press, 1977.

Blasier, Cole. *The Giant's Rival: The USSR and Latin America*. Rev. ed. Pittsburgh: University of Pittsburgh Press, 1987.

Blaufarb, Douglas S. *The Counterinsurgency Era: U.S. Doctrine and Performance, 1950 to the Present*. New York: Free Press, 1977.

Blum, William. *The CIA: A Forgotten History: U.S. Global Interventions since World War 2*. London: Zed Books, 1986.

Brands, H. W. *The Wages of Globalism: Lyndon Johnson and the Limits of American Power*. New York: Oxford University Press, 1995.

Brogan, Hugh. *Kennedy*. London: Longman, 1996.

Calder, Bruce J. *The Impact of Intervention: The Dominican Republic during the U.S. Occupation of 1916–1924*. Austin: University of Texas Press, 1984.

Campos, Roberto de Oliveira. *Reflections on Latin American Development*. Austin: University of Texas Press, 1967.

Carey, James C. *Peru and the United States, 1900–1962*. Notre Dame: University of Notre Dame Press, 1964.

Chenery, Hollis B. *Toward a More Effective Alliance for Progress*. Washington: Agency for International Development, 1967.

Coatsworth, John H. *Central America and the United States*. New York: Twayne Publishers, 1994.

Cobbs, Elizabeth A. *The Rich Neighbor Policy: Rockefeller and Kaiser in Brazil*. New Haven: Yale University Press, 1992.

Corn, David. *Blond Ghost: Ted Shackley and the CIA's Crusades*. New York: Simon & Schuster, 1994.

David, Wilfred L. *The Economic Development of Guyana, 1953–1964*. London: Oxford University Press, 1969.

Despres, Leo A. *Cultural Pluralism and Nationalist Politics in British Guiana*. Chicago: Rand McNally, 1967.

Dietz, James L., and James H. Street, eds. *Latin America's Economic Development: Institutionalist and Structuralist Perspectives*. Boulder and London: Lynne Rienner Publishers, 1987.

Dreier, John C., ed. *The Alliance for Progress: Problems and Perspectives*. Baltimore: Johns Hopkins University Press, 1962.

Enríquez, Laura J. *Harvesting Change: Labor and Agrarian Reform in Nicaragua, 1979–1990*. Chapel Hill: University of North Carolina Press, 1991.

Euraque, Darío A. *Reinterpreting the Banana Republic: Region and State in Honduras, 1870–1972*. Chapel Hill: University of North Carolina Press, 1996.

Ewell, Judith. *Venezuela and the United States: From Monroe's Hemisphere to Petroleum's Empire*. Athens: University of Georgia Press, 1996.

Flores, Edmundo. *Land Reform and the Alliance for Progress*. Princeton: Woodrow Wilson School of Public and International Affairs, 1963.

Fursenko, Alexsandr, and Timothy Naftali. *"One Hell of a Gamble": Khrushchev, Castro, and Kennedy, 1958–1964*. New York: W. W. Norton, 1997.

Furtado, Celso. *Economic Development of Latin America: A Survey from Colonial Times to the Cuban Revolution*. Cambridge: Cambridge University Press, 1970.

Galíndez, Jesús de. *The Era of Trujillo: Dominican Dictator*. Edited by Russell H. Fitzgibbon. Tucson: University of Arizona Press, 1973.

Gardner, James A. *Legal Imperialism: American Lawyers and Foreign Aid in Latin America*. Madison: University of Wisconsin Press, 1980.

Giglio, James N. *The Presidency of John F. Kennedy*. Lawrence: University Press of Kansas, 1991.

Gilderhus, Mark T. *Pan American Visions: Woodrow Wilson in the Western Hemisphere, 1913–1921*. Tucson: University of Arizona Press, 1986.

Gleijeses, Piero. *The Dominican Crisis: The 1965 Constitutionalist Revolt and American Intervention*. Translated by Lawrence Lipson. Baltimore: Johns Hopkins University Press, 1978.

Gott, Richard. *Guerrilla Movements in Latin America*. Garden City, N.Y.: Doubleday, 1971.

Grimaldi, Víctor. *Los Estados Unidos en el derrocamiento de Trujillo*. Santo Domingo: Amigo del Hogar, 1985.

———. *Juan Bosch: El comienzo de la historia*. Santo Domingo: Editora Alfa y Omega, 1990.

Grose, Peter. *Gentleman Spy: The Life of Allen Dulles*. Boston: Houghton Mifflin, 1994.

Guerrero, Miguel. *El golpe de estado: Historia del derrocamiento de Juan Bosch*. Santo Domingo: Editora Corripio, 1993.

Gutiérrez Olivos, Sergio. *Subdesarrollo, integración, y alianza*. Buenos Aires: Emece Editores, 1963.

Halberstam, David. *The Best and the Brightest*. Greenwich, Conn.: Fawcett Publications, 1973.

Hanson, Simon G. *Five Years of the Alliance for Progress: An Appraisal*. Washington: Inter-American Affairs Press, 1967.

Hellmann, John. *The Kennedy Obsession: The American Myth of JFK*. New York: Columbia University Press, 1997.

Hersh, Seymour M. *The Dark Side of Camelot*. Boston: Little, Brown, 1997.

Hintzen, Percy C. *The Costs of Regime Survival: Racial Mobilization, Elite Domination, and Control of the State in Guyana and Trinidad*. Cambridge: Cambridge University Press, 1989.

Huntington, Samuel P. *The Soldier and the State: The Theory and Politics of Civil-Military Relations*. New York: Vintage Books, 1957.

Jackson, D. Bruce. *Castro, the Kremlin, and Communism in Latin America*. Baltimore: Johns Hopkins University Press, 1969.

Johnson, John J. *The Military and Society in Latin America*. Stanford: Stanford
University Press, 1964.

————. *Political Change in Latin America: The Growth of the Middle Sectors*.
Stanford: Stanford University Press, 1958.

Klare, Michael T. *War without End: American Planning for the Next Vietnams*.
New York: Vintage, 1972.

Klare, Michael T., and Cynthia Arnson. *Supplying Repression: U.S. Support for
Authoritarian Regimes Abroad*. Rev. ed. Washington: Institute for Policy
Studies, 1981.

Klarén, Peter F., and Thomas J. Bossert, eds. *Promise of Development: Theories
of Change in Latin America*. Boulder: Westview Press, 1986.

LaFeber, Walter. *The Panama Canal: The Crisis in Historical Perspective*. 2d ed.
New York: Oxford University Press, 1989.

Leacock, Ruth. *Requiem for Revolution: The United States and Brazil, 1961–1969*.
Kent and London: Kent State University Press, 1990.

Levinson, Jerome, and Juan de Onís. *The Alliance That Lost Its Way: A Critical
Report on the Alliance for Progress*. Chicago: Quadrangle, 1970.

Lieuwen, Edwin. *Generals vs. Presidents: Neo-Militarism in Latin America*. New
York: Praeger, 1964.

Lipset, Seymour Martin, and Aldo Solari, eds. *Elites in Latin America*. New
York: Oxford University Press, 1967.

Lowenthal, Abraham F. *The Dominican Intervention*. Cambridge: Harvard
University Press, 1972.

Maga, Timothy P. *John F. Kennedy and New Frontier Diplomacy, 1961–1963*.
Malabar, Fla.: Krieger Publishing, 1994.

Major, John. *Prize Possession: The United States and the Panama Canal,
1903–1979*. Cambridge: Cambridge University Press, 1993.

Manger, William, ed. *The Alliance for Progress: A Critical Appraisal*.
Washington: Public Affairs Press, 1963.

Meyer, Michael C., and William L. Sherman. *The Course of Mexican History*.
4th ed. New York: Oxford University Press, 1991.

Miller, Nicola. *Soviet Relations with Latin America, 1959–1987*. Cambridge:
Cambridge University Press, 1989.

Millikan, Max F., and W. W. Rostow. *A Proposal: Key to an Effective Foreign
Policy*. New York: Harper & Bros., 1957.

Millikan, Max F., and Donald L. M. Blackmer, eds. *The Emerging Nations:
Their Growth and United States Policy*. Boston: Little, Brown, 1961.

Morales Benítez, Otto. *Alianza para el Progreso y reforma agraria*. 2d ed.
Bogotá: Publicaciones Universidad Central, 1986.

Morris, George. *CIA and American Labor: The Subversion of the AFL-CIO's
Foreign Policy*. New York: International Publishers, 1967.

Ortega Aranda, Elena Luisa. *La Carta de Punta del Este y la Alianza para el
Progreso*. Santiago: Editorial Juridica de Chile, 1966.

Packenham, Robert A. *The Dependency Movement: Scholarship and Politics in
Development Studies*. Cambridge: Harvard University Press, 1992.

————. *Liberal America and the Third World: Political Development Ideas in Foreign Aid and Social Science*. Princeton: Princeton University Press, 1973.

Park, James William. *Latin American Underdevelopment: A History of the Perspectives in the United States, 1870–1965*. Baton Rouge: Louisiana State University Press, 1995.

Parker, Phyllis R. *Brazil and the Quiet Intervention, 1964*. Austin: University of Texas Press, 1979.

Parmet, Herbert S. *JFK: The Presidency of John F. Kennedy*. New York: Dial Press, 1983.

Paterson, Thomas G., ed. *Kennedy's Quest for Victory: American Foreign Policy, 1961–1963*. New York: Oxford University Press, 1989.

Pike, Frederick B. *The United States and the Andean Republics: Peru, Bolivia, and Ecuador*. Cambridge: Harvard University Press, 1977.

Plummer, Brenda Gayle. *Haiti and the United States: The Psychological Moment*. Athens: University of Georgia Press, 1992.

Potash, Robert A. *The Army and Politics in Argentina, 1945–1962: Perón to Frondizi*. Stanford: Stanford University Press, 1980.

————. *The Army and Politics in Argentina, 1962–1973: From Frondizi's Fall to the Peronist Restoration*. Stanford: Stanford University Press, 1996.

Rabe, Stephen G. *Eisenhower and Latin America: The Foreign Policy of Anticommunism*. Chapel Hill: University of North Carolina Press, 1988.

————. *The Road to OPEC: United States Relations with Venezuela, 1919–1976*. Austin: University of Texas Press, 1982.

Radosh, Ronald. *American Labor and United States Foreign Policy*. New York: Random House, 1969.

Randall, Stephen J. *Colombia and the United States: Hegemony and Interdependence*. Athens: University of Georgia Press, 1992.

Reeves, Richard. *President Kennedy: Profile of Power*. New York: Simon & Schuster, 1993.

Reeves, Thomas C. *A Question of Character: A Life of John F. Kennedy*. New York: Free Press, 1991.

Roett, Riordan. *The Politics of Foreign Aid in the Brazilian Northeast*. Nashville: Vanderbilt University Press, 1972.

Rostow, W. W. *Eisenhower, Kennedy, and Foreign Aid*. Austin: University of Texas Press, 1985.

————. *The Stages of Economic Growth: A Non-Communist Manifesto*. London: Cambridge University Press, 1960.

Ruelas Crespo, Alejandro. *Alianza para el Progreso*. Mexico City: Universidad Nacional Autonoma de México, 1963.

Ruíz, Ramón Eduardo. *Cuba: The Making of a Revolution*. New York: W. W. Norton, 1970.

Sater, William F. *Chile and the United States: Empires in Conflict*. Athens: University of Georgia Press, 1990.

Schaffer, Howard B. *Chester Bowles: New Dealer in the Cold War*. Cambridge: Harvard University Press, 1993.

Scheman, L. Ronald, ed. *The Alliance for Progress: A Retrospective*. New York: Praeger, 1988.

Schlesinger, Arthur M., Jr. *Robert Kennedy and His Times*. Boston: Houghton Mifflin, 1978.

Schoultz, Lars. *Human Rights and United States Policy toward Latin America*. Princeton: Princeton University Press, 1981.

————. *National Security and United States Policy toward Latin America*. Princeton: Princeton University Press, 1987.

Shafer, D. Michael. *Deadly Paradigms: The Failure of U.S. Counterinsurgency Policy*. Princeton: Princeton University Press, 1988.

Sharp, Daniel A., ed. *U.S. Foreign Policy and Peru*. Austin: University of Texas Press, 1972.

Sigmund, Paul E. *The United States and Democracy in Chile*. Baltimore: Johns Hopkins University Press, 1993.

Singh, Chaitram. *Guyana: Politics in a Plantation Society*. New York: Praeger, 1988.

Skidmore, Thomas F. *Politics in Brazil, 1930–1964: An Experiment in Democracy*. New York: Oxford University Press, 1967.

Slater, Jerome. *Intervention and Negotiation: The United States and the Dominican Intervention*. New York: Harper & Row, 1970.

————. *The OAS and United States Foreign Policy*. Columbus: Ohio State University Press, 1967.

Smith, Peter H. *Talons of the Eagle: Dynamics of U.S.–Latin American Relations*. New York: Oxford University Press, 1996.

Smith, Tony. *America's Mission: The United States and the Worldwide Struggle for Democracy in the Twentieth Century*. Princeton: Princeton University Press, 1994.

Stallings, Barbara. *Banker to the Third World: U.S. Portfolio Investment in Latin America, 1900–1986*. Berkeley: University of California Press, 1987.

Stebbins, Richard P. *The United States in World Affairs, 1961*. New York: Harper & Bros., 1962.

Stepan, Alfred. *The Military in Politics: Changing Patterns in Brazil*. Princeton: Princeton University Press, 1971.

Szulc, Tad. *Twilight of the Tyrants*. New York: Henry Holt, 1959.

Thomas, Evan. *The Very Best Men: Four Who Dared, the Early Years of the CIA*. New York: Simon & Schuster, 1995.

Thompson, Kenneth W., ed. *The Kennedy Presidency*. New York: University Press of America, 1985.

Tulchin, Joseph S. *Argentina and the United States: A Conflicted Relationship*. Boston: Twayne Publishers, 1990.

Vandenbroucke, Lucien S. *Perilous Options: Special Operations as an Instrument of U.S. Foreign Policy*. New York: Oxford University Press, 1993.

Vega, Bernardo. *Kennedy y los Trujillo*. Santo Domingo: Fundación Cultural Dominicana, 1991.

Walton, Richard J. *Cold War and Counterrevolution: The Foreign Policy of John F. Kennedy*. New York: Viking Press, 1972.

Weis, W. Michael. *Cold Warriors and Coups d'Etat: Brazilian-American Relations, 1945–1964*. Albuquerque: University of New Mexico Press, 1993.

Whitaker, Arthur P. *The Western Hemisphere Idea: Its Rise and Decline*. Ithaca: Cornell University Press, 1954.

Woods, Randall Bennett. *Fulbright: A Biography*. Cambridge: Cambridge University Press, 1995.

Zeiler, Thomas W. *American Trade and Power in the 1960s*. New York: Columbia University Press, 1992.

Articles

Adams, Richard N. "Development of the Guatemalan Military." *Studies in Comparative International Development* 4 (1968–69): 91–110.

Baer, Werner. "The Economics of Prebisch and ECLA." In *Latin America: Problems of Economic Development*, edited by Charles T. Nisbet, pp. 203–18. New York: Free Press, 1969.

Beck, Kent M. "Necessary Lies, Hidden Truths: Cuba in the 1960 Campaign." *Diplomatic History* 8 (Winter 1984): 37–59.

Benjamin, Jules R. "The Framework of U.S. Relations with Latin America in the Twentieth Century: An Interpretive Essay." *Diplomatic History* 11 (Spring 1987): 91–112.

Berle, Adolf A., Jr. "The Cuban Crisis." *Foreign Affairs* 39 (October 1960): 40–55.

Booth, John A. "Socioeconomic and Political Roots of National Revolts in Central America." *Latin American Research Review* 26, no. 1 (1991): 33–73.

Cobbs, Elizabeth A. "Decolonization, the Cold War, and the Foreign Policy of the Peace Corps." *Diplomatic History* 20 (Winter 1996): 79–105.

Cochrane, James D. "U.S. Policy toward Recognition of Governments and Promotion of Democracy in Latin America since 1963." *Journal of Latin American Studies* 4 (November 1972): 275–91.

Collado, Emilio. "Economic Development through Private Enterprise." *Foreign Affairs* 41 (July 1963): 708–20.

Collins, Robert M. "The Economic Crisis of 1968 and the Waning of the 'American Century.'" *American Historical Review* 101 (April 1996): 396–422.

Connell-Smith, Gordon. "Latin America in the Foreign Relations of the United States." *Journal of Latin American Studies* 8 (May 1976): 137–50.

Dean, Robert D. "Masculinity as Ideology: John F. Kennedy and the Domestic Politics of Foreign Policy." *Diplomatic History* 22 (Winter 1998): 29–62.

Desch, Michael C. "'That Deep Mud in Cuba': The Strategic Threat and U.S. Planning for a Conventional Response during the Missile Crisis." *Security Studies* 1 (Winter 1991): 317–51.

Divine, Robert A. "The Education of John F. Kennedy." In *Makers of American Diplomacy*, edited by Frank J. Merli and Theodore A. Wilson, pp. 317–43. New York: Charles Scribner's Sons, 1974.

Dosal, Paul J. "Accelerating Dependent Development and Revolution:

Nicaragua and the Alliance for Progress." *Inter-American Economic Affairs* 38 (Spring 1985): 75–96.

Fitzgerald, Deborah. "Exporting American Agriculture: The Rockefeller Foundation in Mexico, 1943–53." *Social Studies of Science* 16 (1986): 457–83.

Francis, Michael J. "Military Aid to Latin America in the U.S. Congress." *Journal of Inter-American Studies* 6 (July 1964): 389–404.

Frei Montalva, Eduardo. "The Alliance That Lost Its Way." *Foreign Affairs* 45 (April 1967): 437–48.

Galtung, Johan. "A Structural Theory of Imperialism." *Journal of Peace Research* 8, no. 2 (1971): 81–117.

Gil, Federico. "The Kennedy-Johnson Years." In *United States Policy in Latin America: A Quarter Century of Crisis and Challenge, 1961–1986*, edited by John D. Martz, pp. 3–27. Lincoln: University of Nebraska Press, 1988.

Gonzalez, Helidoro [pseud.]. "The Failure of the Alliance for Progress in Columbia." *Inter-American Economic Affairs* 23 (Summer 1969): 87–96.

Gordon, Lincoln. "US-Brazilian Reprise." *Journal of Inter-American Studies and World Affairs* 32 (Summer 1990): 165–78.

Guevara, Ernesto Ché. "Cuba and the 'Kennedy Plan.'" *World Marxist Review* 5 (February 1962): 33–39.

Herring, George C. "My Years with the CIA." *Organization of American Historians Newsletter* 25 (May 1997): 5–6.

Hildebrand, John R. "Latin-American Economic Development, Land Reform, and U.S. Aid with Special Reference to Guatemala." *Journal of Inter-American Studies* 4 (July 1962): 351–61.

Holden, Robert H. "The Real Diplomacy of Violence: United States Military Power in Central America, 1950–1990." *The International History Review* 15 (May 1993): 283–322.

Hughes, Steven W., and Kenneth J. Mijeski. "Contemporary Paradigms in the Study of Inter-American Relations." In *Latin America, the United States, and the Inter-American System*, edited by John D. Martz and Lars Schoultz, pp. 19–43. Boulder: Westview Press, 1980.

Kaplan, Stephen S., and Norman C. Bonsor. "Did United States Aid Really Help Brazilian Development? The Perspective of a Quarter-Century." *Inter-American Economic Affairs* 27 (Winter 1973): 25–46.

Kaufman, Burton I. "John F. Kennedy as World Leader: A Perspective on the Literature." *Diplomatic History* 17 (Summer 1993): 447–69.

LaFeber, Walter. "The Evolution of the Monroe Doctrine from Monroe to Reagan." In *Redefining the Past: Essays in Diplomatic History in Honor of William Appleman Williams*, edited by Lloyd C. Gardner, pp. 121–41. Corvallis: Oregon State University Press, 1986.

———. "Latin American Policy." In *Exploring the Johnson Years*, edited by Robert A. Divine, pp. 63–90. Austin: University of Texas Press, 1981.

———. "Thomas C. Mann and the Devolution of American Policy: From the Good Neighbor to Military Intervention." In *Behind the Throne: Servants of Power to Imperial Presidents, 1898–1968*, edited by Thomas J. McCormick and Walter LaFeber, pp. 166–203. Madison: University of Wisconsin Press, 1993.

Leoni, Raúl. "View from Caracas." *Foreign Affairs* 43 (July 1965): 639–46.

Lleras Camargo, Alberto. "The Alliance for Progress: Aims, Distortions, Obstacles." *Foreign Affairs* 42 (October 1963): 25–37.

Love, Joseph L. "Raúl Prebisch and the Origins of Unequal Exchange." *Latin American Research Review* 15, no. 3 (1980): 45–72.

Lowenthal, Abraham F. "United States Policy toward Latin America: 'Liberal,' 'Radical,' and 'Bureaucratic' Perspectives." *Latin American Research Review* 8, no. 3 (1974): 3–25.

McCann, Frank D. "Brazil, the United States, and World War II." *Diplomatic History* 3 (Winter 1979): 59–76.

Michaels, Albert L. "The Alliance for Progress and Chile's 'Revolution in Liberty,' 1964–1970." *Journal of Inter-American Studies and World Affairs* 18 (February 1976): 74–99.

Murrary, Robert K., and Tim H. Blessing. "The Presidential Performance Study: A Progress Report." *Journal of American History* 70 (December 1983): 535–55.

Nye, Joseph S. "The Changing Nature of World Power." *Political Science Quarterly* 105 (Summer 1990): 177–92.

Painter, David S. "Explaining U.S. Relations with the Third World." *Diplomatic History* 19 (Summer 1995): 525–48.

Pérez, Louis A., Jr. "Dependency." In *Explaining the History of American Foreign Relations*, edited by Michael J. Hogan and Thomas G. Paterson, pp. 99–110. New York: Cambridge University Press, 1991.

———. "Intervention, Hegemony, and Dependency: The United States in the Circum-Caribbean, 1898–1980." *Pacific Historical Review* 51 (May 1982): 165–94.

Prendas, Ralph D. "Guyana: Socialist Reconstruction or Political Opportunism?" *Journal of Inter-American Studies* 20 (May 1978): 133–84.

Pye, Lucian W. "Armies in the Process of Political Modernization." In *The Role of the Military in Underdeveloped Countries*, edited by John J. Johnson, pp. 69–89. Princeton: Princeton University Press, 1962.

Quadros, Jânio. "Brazil's New Foreign Policy." *Foreign Affairs* 40 (October 1961): 19–27.

Rabe, Stephen G. "The Caribbean Triangle: Betancourt, Castro, and Trujillo and U.S. Foreign Policy, 1958–1963." *Diplomatic History* 20 (Winter 1996): 55–78.

———. "Controlling Revolutions: Latin America, the Alliance for Progress, and Cold War Anti-Communism." In *Kennedy's Quest for Victory: American Foreign Policy, 1961–1963*, edited by Thomas G. Paterson, pp. 105–22. New York: Oxford University Press, 1989.

———. "John F. Kennedy and Constitutionalism, Democracy, and Human Rights in Latin America: Promise and Performance." *The New England Journal of History* 52 (Fall 1995): 38–57.

————. "The Johnson (Eisenhower?) Doctrine for Latin America." *Diplomatic History* 9 (Winter 1985): 94–100.

Rockefeller, David. "What Private Enterprise Means to Latin America." *Foreign Affairs* 44 (April 1966): 403–16.

Roorda, Eric Paul. "Genocide Next Door: The Good Neighbor Policy, the Trujillo Regime, and the Haitian Massacre of 1937." *Diplomatic History* 20 (Summer 1996): 301–19.

Rostow, W. W. "Guerrilla Warfare in Underdeveloped Areas." In *The Viet-Nam Reader*, edited by Marcus G. Raskin and Bernard Fall, pp. 108–16. Rev. ed. New York: Vintage, 1967.

Schlesinger, Arthur M., Jr. "The Alliance for Progress: A Retrospective." In *Latin America: The Search for a New International Role*, edited by Ronald G. Hellman and H. Jon Rosenbaum, pp. 57–92. New York: Halsted Press, 1975.

————. "The Ultimate Approval Rating." *New York Times Magazine*, 15 December 1996, 46–51.

Silvert, Kalman. "The Politics of Social and Economic Change in Latin America." In *Promise of Development: Theories of Change in Latin America*, edited by Peter F. Klarén and Thomas J. Bossert, pp. 76–87. Boulder: Westview Press, 1986.

Slater, Jerome. "Democracy versus Stability: The Recent Latin American Policy of the United States." *Yale Review* 55 (December 1965): 169–81.

Smetherman, Robert M., and Bobbie B. Smetherman. "The Alliance for Progress: Promises Unfulfilled." *American Journal of Economics and Sociology* 31 (January 1972): 79–86.

Spalding, Hobart A. "The Two Latin American Foreign Policies of the U.S. Labor Movement: The AFL-CIO Top Brass vs. Rank-and-File." *Science and Society* 56 (Winter 1992–93): 421–39.

————. "U.S. Labour Intervention in Latin America: The Case of the American Institute of Free Labor Development." In *Trade Unions and the New Industrialisation of the Third World*, edited by Roger Southall, pp. 259–86. Pittsburgh: Pittsburgh University Press, 1988.

"Tale of Two Books." *Nation* 250 (4 June 1990): 763–64.

Tulchin, Joseph S. "The Promise of Progress: U.S. Relations with Latin America during the Administration of Lyndon B. Johnson." In *Lyndon Johnson Confronts the World: American Foreign Policy, 1963–1968*, edited by Warren I. Cohen and Nancy Bernkopf Tucker, pp. 211–43. New York: Cambridge University Press, 1994.

————. "The United States and Latin America in the 1960s." *Journal of Inter-American Studies and World Affairs* 30 (Spring 1988): 1–36.

Van Cleve, Jonathan V. "The Latin American Policy of President Kennedy: A Reexamination Case: Peru." *Inter-American Economic Affairs* 30 (Spring 1977): 29–44.

Walker, William O., III. "Mixing the Sweet with the Sour: Kennedy, Johnson, and Latin America." In *The Diplomacy of the Crucial Decade: American Foreign Relations during the 1960s*, edited by Diane B. Kunz, pp. 42–79. New York: Columbia University Press, 1994.

Index

62–63; and Soviet Union, 138; under military rule, 141; and Alliance for Progress, 157, 165–66; and oil, 180
Arosemena Monroy, Carlos Julio, 62, 124

Balaguer, Joaquín, 38, 41–43, 193
Ball, George, 15, 23, 29, 45, 53, 87, 151, 180, 187; and Brazil, 70, 179; and Panama, 188–89
Baran, Paul, 86
Barrientos, René, 142
Batista, Fulgencio, 11, 38, 134
Bay of Pigs, 8, 15, 16, 20, 30, 65, 83, 104, 111, 117, 127, 158, 176, 179; and Dominican Republic, 38–40; and Guatemala, 72–73
Belaúnde Terry, Fernando, 116, 118, 121, 181
Belgian Congo, 5
Belgium, 11, 29
Belize, 72
Bell, David E., 154
Bell, John O., 75–77
Bello, Andrés, 96
Beltrán, Pedro, 116–17
Berle, Adolf A., Jr., 2, 14, 40, 50, 65, 157, 170, 177, 193; on appointing under secretary of state for Latin American affairs, 16, 151; and origins of Alliance for Progress, 22, 24–25, 28; and Venezuela, 100, 103
Berlin, 4, 60
Betancourt, Rómulo, 5, 8, 11, 14, 24, 28, 74, 112, 123, 157, 218 (n. 15); and Kennedy, 17, 99–101, 198; and Dominican Republic, 36, 44; background of, 99–100; policies of, 101–8; and Peru, 118, 120
Betancourt Doctrine, 101, 122
Bolivia, 10, 17, 22, 142–43, 178; and Cuba, 59–60; and Guevara, 137–38, 141
Bosch, Juan, 53–54, 100–101; leader-

ship of, 44–47; overthrow of, 122, 192–93
Bowles, Chester, 15, 20, 40, 133, 180; on Alliance for Progress, 155–56, 169, 171
Boxer, USS, 53
Brazil, 23, 26–28, 32, 63, 71, 108, 124, 132, 143, 148, 183, 193, 197, 199; and Dominican Republic, 43, 192; and Cuba, 58–60, 64–67, 70; and Soviet Union, 64–65, 71; under Quadros, 64–67; under Goulart, 66–70; under Castello Branco, 70–71; under military rule, 71, 141–42; and Alliance for Progress, 149, 157, 161–62, 165–66, 170–71; and Mann Doctrine, 178–79
Briceño Linares, Antonio, 104
British Guiana, 7, 19, 78, 148, 193, 197, 199; history of, 79–81; under Jagan, 81–93, 95; under Burnham, 93–95; and Kennedy Doctrine, 97–98. *See also* Guyana
British Honduras, 72
Bruce, David, 86
Bundy, McGeorge, 16, 84, 90, 100, 147, 185; and Dominican Republic, 38–39; and Brazil, 70, 179; and Kennedy Doctrine, 97–98; and Cuba, 107–8; and post-1963 Alliance for Progress, 176, 178, 192–93
Bureau of the Budget, 134
Burnham, Forbes: background of, 80–81; and opposition to Jagan, 82–92 passim; U.S. support of, 89–90, 94, 98; rule of, 93–95
Burrows, Charles R., 122, 134, 143
Bush, George W., 7
Business Advisory Group on Latin America, 180
Byroade, Henry, 106

Cabot, John Moors, 65
Caldera, Rafael, 28, 104

Calvo, Carlos, 96
Campallas, 110
Canada, 80
Canal Zone. *See* Panama Canal Zone
Cárdenas, Lázaro, 169
Cardoso, Fernando Henrique, 167
Carrillo Flores, Antonio, 182
Carter, Jimmy, 195
Cassini, Igor, 38, 206 (n. 14)
Cassini, Oleg, 38
Castello Branco, Humberto de Alencar, 70–71, 186
Castro, Fidel, 8, 16, 28, 51, 73, 111, 117, 124, 193, 199; and Cuban Revolution, 11–12, 29–30, 137–39; and Dominican Republic, 35–37, 41, 45, 47–48; and Brazil, 65–66, 71; war against, 70, 218 (n. 15); and Jagan, 82–83, 86, 89; and Venezuela, 103–4, 106–7, 109; and counterinsurgency, 127, 134–35
CBS News, 3
Central American Common Market, 158, 162
Central Intelligence Agency, 7, 12, 25, 62, 175, 184–86; and Castro, 20, 137, 139; and Guatemala, 34, 72, 74–75, 96, and Dominican Republic, 36–39, 41, 46; and Haiti, 51–54; and Brazil, 67–69, 170; and British Guiana, 84, 88–90; and Venezuela, 103, 106–8; and Chile, 114–15, 185; and counterinsurgency, 129–30, 145
Chalmers, René, 51
Chamizal, 176–77
Chase, Gordon, 185
Chase Manhattan Bank, 166, 180
Chiari, Roberto Francisco, 17, 18, 187–91
Chicken of the Sea, 121
Chile, 10, 18, 23, 26, 108, 141, 145, 148, 157, 164, 165, 169, 184, 185, 195, 199; and Cuba, 58–60, 111; background of, 109–11; under

Alessandri, 111–13; under Frei, 113–16; under Pinochet, 116
China. *See* People's Republic of China
Christian Anti-Communist Crusade, 84
Christian Democratic Party of Chile, 110–15
Christian Democratic Party of Venezuela, 28, 104
Churchill, Winston, 81
CIA. *See* Central Intelligence Agency
Civic action programs, 132, 144, 146
Cleveland, Grover, 92
Clinton, William Jefferson, 7, 95
Coerr, Wimberley De R., 15
Coffee, 10, 29, 165
Cole, Charles, 112, 114, 195
Colombia, 1, 11, 19, 23, 27, 137, 190; turmoil in, 135, 139, 146; and counterinsurgency, 140–41; and Alliance for Progress, 159–60, 162
Colorado River, 183
Columbus, Christopher, 79
Communist parties, Latin American, 66, 81, 103, 106, 108, 116, 118, 136–39
Congo, 42
Conservative Party of Colombia, 141
Conservative Party of United Kingdom, 91
Costa e Silva, Artur da, 182
Costa Rica, 1, 17, 99–100, 120, 157, 162, 195
Counterinsurgency, 5, 12, 16, 48, 76, 197; and Venezuela, 103, 106, 108; background of, 126–27; doctrine of, 127–34; and Communist threat, 135–41; impact of, 141–47; under Johnson, 184–85. *See also* Special Group on Counterinsurgency
Cox, Archibald, 14
Cripps, Richard Stafford, 88
Cuba, 4, 8, 12, 32, 73, 132, 167, 174, 184, 185, 187, 197; and Soviet Union, 13–14; fear of, 19–22; and

U.S. Army Special Forces, 76, 128, 145
U.S. Information Agency, 108, 119
U.S. Information Services, 83
U.S. Marine Corps, 49
U.S. Senate Foreign Relations Committee, 144, 159, 170
Uruguay, 58–60, 108, 138, 183

Valencia, Guillermo León, 160
Vargas, Getulio, 71
Venezuela, 1, 11, 19, 27, 120, 135, 140, 157, 169, 192, 195, 197; background of, 99–100; under Betancourt, 100–108; under Leoni, 108–9; and Castro, 137, 139; and oil, 165–66, 181
Venezuela: política y petroleo, 100
Vietnam, 4, 103, 106, 148, 153, 174, 182–83
Villeda Morales, José Ramón, 18, 83, 122, 167
Violencia, La, 141
Voice of America, 9

Walker, Patrick Gordon, 94
Walker, William O., III, 6
Walter Reed Army Hospital, 95
Walters, Vernon, 70
Walton, Richard J., 4
Wars of national liberation, 20–22, 127, 139
Washington, George, 3
Washington Post, 178
Wessin y Wessin, Elías, 48
West Germany. *See* Germany
Whitaker, Arthur P., 26
Williams, Murat, 145
Wilson, Harold, 94
Wilson, Woodrow, 7, 34, 199
Woodward, Robert F., 15–16, 118
World Bank, 105, 154
World Court, 183
World War II, 111, 117

Ydígoras Fuentes, Miguel, 8, 72–76
Yon Sosa, Marco Antonio, 73
Yugoslavia, 11, 87